SHACKLETON'S
CAPTAIN

SHACKLETON'S
CAPTAIN

A biography of
Frank Worsley

JOHN THOMSON

Mosaic Press
TORONTO PARIS NEW YORK

Canadian Cataloguing in Publication Data

Thomson, John, 1931-
    Shackleton's captain: a biography of Frank Worsley

ISBN 0-88962-678-2

1. Worsley, Frank Arthur, 1872-1943. 2. Shackleton, Ernest Henry, Sir, 1874-1922. 3. Antarctica – Discovery and exploration. 4. Explorers – New Zealand – Biography. 5. Seamen – New Zealand – Biography.
I. Title.

G875.W67T46 1999 919.8'904   C99-931547-9

Published by MOSAIC PRESS, P.O. Box 1032, Oakville, Ontario, L6J 5E9, Canada. Offices and warehouse at 1252 Speers Road, Units #1&2, Oakville, Ontario, L6L 5N9, Canada and Mosaic Press, 85 River Rock Drive, Suite 202, Buffalo, N.Y., 14207, USA.

Mosaic Press acknowledges the assistance of the Canada Council and the Dept. of Canadian Heritage, Government of Canada, for their support of our publishing programme.

Copyright © 1999 John Bell Thomson
ISBN 0-88962-678-2
The Author asserts his moral rights in the work.
Printed and bound in Canada

Production and design by Orca Publishing Services Ltd.
Cover Painting by Arther Shilstone
Cover design by John Burt

First published by Hazard Press, Christchurch, New Zealand
Printed in North America by:

MOSAIC PRESS, in Canada:
1252 Speers Road, Units #1&2, Oakville, Ontario, L6L 5N9
Phone / Fax: (905) 825-2130
E-mail: cp507@freenet.toronto.on.ca

MOSAIC PRESS, in the USA:
85 River Rock Drive, Suite 202, Buffalo, N.Y., 14207
Phone / Fax: 1-800-387-8992
E-mail: cp507@freenet.toronto.on.ca

Frontispiece:
Frank Worsley in uniform as a captain in the
New Zealand Government steamer service, taken in 1903.
H.J. Schmidt Collection,
Alexander Turnbull Library,
Wellington, NZ, No. G-4931-1/2

Contents

Acknowledgments

Researching Frank Worsley took me to the wonderful world of polar experience and into contact with men and women who know and love it. I had hoped for co-operation as I groped to fill huge gaps that appeared in the Worsley story; I was rewarded beyond expectation by their generosity.

Individuals and institutions alike opened memories and records – all, it seemed, eager for the story of this most likeable mariner with a strong larrikin streak to be told in the fullest possible detail for the first time. The man who helped more than any other was Pat Bamford of Claygate, Surrey. Worsley and his wife, Jean, lived at the Bamford family home through hard times between the world wars, and both died there, leaving with Pat Bamford a trove of letters, photos and other records, which were made freely available to me.

Harding McGregor Dunnett and Jan Piggott of the James Caird Society and Dulwich College, London, were also most generous with time and assistance, and Dev Barot, Jnr, of London, earns much thanks for his work preparing photographs.

Some of the people who helped I still have not met. Angus Erskine of Edinburgh is one. But he regularly steered me in the right direction. Robert Burton of the South Georgia Whaling Museum, and Caroline Alexander of New York are others. Alfred Stephenson, Duncan Carse, Geoffrey Hattersley-Smith, Ann Shirley, David Yelverton, Patricia Mantell, A.G.E. Jones and Maureen Mahood also responded with detail and encouragement to calls from a stranger.

The Alexander Turnbull Library in Wellington, New Zealand, and the Scott Polar Research Institute at Cambridge, UK, held many of the records I needed for the research. My grateful thanks go to the devoted staffs of these great institutions for their professionalism. Robert Headland at SPRI was of particular assistance during my several visits. The British Film Institute, the British Public Records Office, the Marine Safety Agency, the British Red Cross and the Ministry of Defence all responded to requests for Worsley detail.

In New Zealand, Arthur Helm started the project by introducing me to Worsley and to the challenge of writing a biography of a too-long-ignored local hero more than 50 years after his death. Canterbury Museum, Akaroa Museum and the National Archives were generous with information, and members of the Wellington branch of the New Zealand Antarctic Society were consistently encouraging. Colin Monteath, F. H. (Mac) McClusky and Jocelyn Chisholm read and approved the first effort. The Cass family, the Parkinson family, William Chisholm, Wendy Dunlop, the late Gwenda Burt, Phillip O'Shea and John Best also deserve thanks, as do my immediate family for outstanding patience and encouragement. If I have ignored any who also helped, please accept my apologies.

Finally I am most grateful to Frank and Jean Worsley, whose books and records shaped this biography and whose blatant lust for life inspired the challenge of filling the gaps, and to all those Antarctic old-hands who still swear to me that they had planned to do just such a work when time presented, and who did not do so.

JOHN BELL THOMSON, WELLINGTON, NEW ZEALAND

Prologue

It is popularly known as 'Shackleton's Boat Journey'. This is also the title of one of the books by Frank Worsley who shared the incredible journey, one of the many books written about the 1914–16 expedition to Antarctica led by Sir Ernest Shackleton.

The boat journey is perhaps the most enduring feat of the expedition, which failed in almost all of its planned endeavours yet is remembered for achievements that enhanced the vision of the strength, faith and perseverence of mankind itself. Only the exploration of the universe, which occupies the popular imagination today, comes close to the public enthusiasm for polar exploration in the early part of the 20th century.

And Shackleton had every right to claim it as his own. After all, he dreamed up, planned, and brought himself to near bankruptcy and death to try to make his Imperial Trans-Antarctic Expedition of 1914 the final British south polar achievement, perhaps the greatest. He alone would be judged on the result.

The race for the South Pole had already been won by another. Shackleton had run that race before, in his own 1907–09 expedition, showing his leadership and sanity by stopping a mere 97 miles short of the mark when it became obvious that he could not both reach the pole and return with his party alive. He chose to live to explore again.

The Imperial Trans-Antarctic Expedition, the first crossing of the continent via the South Pole from the Weddell Sea to the Ross Sea, was to be, in his own words, 'an achievement of historic value and a journey of great scientific importance'.

The expedition, in those terms, failed totally: the explorers approaching through the Weddell Sea did not even reach the continent, their ship, the aptly named *Endurance*, being trapped in heavy ice (19 January 1915) before reaching the scheduled landing place. The *Endurance* then drifted around the Weddell Sea, beset in the ice, until she was crushed and sank (15 November 1915), stranding the 28-strong party on ice-floes for months until the men were forced to take to the three small lifeboats saved from the *Endurance* for just that contingency.

They reached firm land on a desolate rock called Elephant Island (12 April 1916) after a terrifying passage, then had to face the awful truth that while being free at last from the ice, they were still in immense danger.

Shackleton and his men had simply disappeared; nobody knew whether they were still alive, and nobody was looking for them. The world they left behind was in turmoil in what became known as the Great War (1914–18). At the very least, they faced slow death by starvation. There were signs of madness in some of the men; there was also talk of suicide.

That was when Shackleton's boat journey was conceived. It was to be the desperate endeavour of a leader whose inspiring personality had brought his shipwrecked seamen and scientists safely to this point, only to find that even more terrible demands were to be made of him, and them.

Shackleton had to get one of his battered small boats 800 miles across the worst ocean in the world to another dot on the map, South Georgia.

There were to be six men in the rescue mission, led by Shackleton. The first man he chose for the journey was the New Zealander Frank Worsley, on whose shoulders rested the task of navigating the lifeboat called the *James Caird* to South Georgia.

Worsley had been the captain of the *Endurance*, and he had shown himself to be a brilliant navigator, as well as a superb small-boat sailor.

They left Elephant Island on 25 April 1916. Shackleton and Worsley sailed, and Worsley navigated, the *James Caird* in conditions that almost defy imagination, to South Georgia in 16 days. They should have been overwhelmed by the savage elements of the region a dozen times; that the navigation was accurate was another miracle.

Badly weakened, a little mad with thirst and with one of their number having simply given up trying to save himself, the crew of the *James Caird* immediately had to fight their way back to sea to avoid being swept into cliffs and crushed in a hurricane. Worsley alone had the skills to keep the *James Caird* offshore until the hurricane passed, to save not only the boat's exhausted crew but also the lives of the 22 men left behind on Elephant Island.

Yet there was another ordeal to be faced: they had landed by necessity on the uninhabited side of South Georgia, and neither the battered boat nor the shattered crew were capable of sailing to the other coast and the safety of a whaling station.

South Georgia, a narrow snow-capped mountainous island laced with glaciers, was first sighted by Antoine de la Roche in 1657 and rediscovered by Gregorio

Route taken by the *Endurance* from South Georgia into the Weddell Sea and the site of its destruction off the Antarctic Peninsula. The map also traces the path of the survivors, the small boat journey from Elephant Island to South Georgia in the *James Caird*, and the four rescue attempts. It shows in insets Elephant Island (first landing and the camp site) and South Georgia, featuring the last hair-raising track of the *James Caird* as Frank Worsley fought to keep the boat from being swept on to rocks in a hurricane, and the crossing of the island from King Haakon Bay to Stromness Bay by Shackleton, Worsley and Crean.

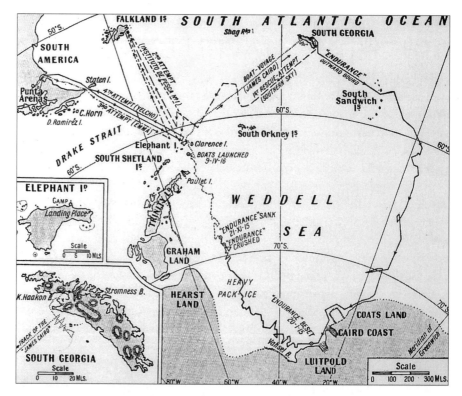

Jerez of Spain in 1756. Captain James Cook, the great English navigator and explorer, named the island South Georgia after King George III. He surveyed the northern coast and landed at Possession Bay during his second voyage in HMS *Resolution* in 1775. Cook found it ice- and snow-bound, bleak and barren.

Cook recorded that the interior was 'not less savage and horrible' than its shores, though none of his party dared venture far inland. Before Shackleton, more than 140 years later, nobody had ever faced the necessity of climbing across its wind-whipped, icy mountains and glaciers.

But that is what Shackleton, Worsley and a tough sailor and polar veteran called Tom Crean – three sailors, none of them with any claim to be a mountaineer, weak from their awful ordeals, pathetically dressed in tattered and unsuitable clothing and with wholly inadequate footwear – did in an incredible 36-hour journey that brought all of them to a point where death was so close that each man, independent of the others, imagined that there was a fourth person in their small party.

In extremis, they believed they were guided by providence through the terrible night on the mission that ended at a South Georgia whaling station.

It was to take Shackleton another four months before he could finally rescue the 22 men left on Elephant Island. Worsley was with him at every step of four attempts to return to the desolate rock.

When that glorious day arrived, it was just two months short of two years since the expedition first set out on what was to have been the last great journey in Antarctica, a trans-continental crossing that was finally achieved 40 years later in the Fuchs–Hillary expedition of 1955–58. It was also 40 years before anyone successfully re-crossed South Georgia, roughly tracing the route taken by Shackleton, Worsley and Crean, and even longer – 77 years – before anyone duplicated the small-boat journey in a facsimile craft between Elephant Island and South Georgia.

Frank Worsley literally dreamed his way into the company of Sir Ernest Shackleton. He was already a vastly experienced sailor, aged 42, a man who had learned his calling under sail while making his first voyage as a teenager on a wool clipper from New Zealand to London.

In 1914 Worsley was employed as second officer on a ship trading across the Atlantic. He was in London when, in his own words, 'I dreamed that Burlington Street was full of ice blocks and that I was navigating a ship along it – an absurd dream.' Next day he walked down Burlington Street and while reflecting on his dream, he saw the sign 'Imperial Trans-Antarctic Expedition'. It was Shackleton's recruiting office.

'I turned into the building with the conviction that it had some special significance for me,' wrote Worsley in his book, *Endurance*. He met Shackleton, spent only a few minutes with him, and was hired to be captain of the expedition's Weddell Sea vessel, the *Endurance*.

Shackleton had a set task for the *Endurance* and her crew, under Worsley. Fourteen men of the party of 28 were to be landed on the continent, six of them making up the trans-continental party led by Shackleton; the other eight were to construct a base and make various marches for geological and other observations.

On the other side of the continent another party, from the ship *Aurora*, which had sailed from Tasmania, would send men ashore to lay down depots on the route of the trans-continental party, march south to assist the party, and also make scientific observations.

Worsley, as captain of the *Endurance*, was to have no part in the land adventures. His task, after dropping the party on the continent, was to explore the unknown coastline of Graham Land, the ship having been equipped for dredging, sounding and other hydrological work. Scientists working from both ships were to carry out geographical and scientific work 'on a scale and over an area never before attempted by any one polar expedition,' said Shackleton in his book, *South*. While Shackleton was crossing the continent to the Ross Sea, Worsley would then pick up the scientists from the Weddell Sea base and proceed to England to await the return of the triumphant leader.

It was a good plan. But 1914 was a bad year for ice in the Weddell Sea: it spread much farther north than usual. Shackleton ignored one possible landing place for his trans-continental party in an effort to get to his preferred site at Vahsel Bay, which would make the land journey shorter. Soon after, the *Endurance* was beset in the ice, never to be released. On the other side of Antarctica, the *Aurora* party was also in trouble, with neither group knowing of the other's misfortune.

Worsley became a master without a ship. But the circumstances offered the chance of unimagined adventure with a man to whose fortunes he was by then firmly committed. And for his part, Shackleton in the years left to him had no reason to regret the day in Burlington Street that brought into his life a dreamer from New Zealand called Frank Worsley.

Shackleton, his second-in-command Frank Wild, and Frank Worsley had the responsibility of preserving, guiding and ultimately saving the entire party of 28. While the expedition was a failure, the rescue was brilliantly achieved.

The segment known as Shackleton's boat journey, to many, in retrospect, was equally one of Worsley's finest moments. But it was only one of the many adventures of Frank Worsley, who outlived his friend by more than 20 years. The New Zealander was to win medals for gallantry at sea and on land in the Great War; he was to command another Shackleton expedition vessel and help bury the great explorer on South Georgia in 1922; he was to be co-leader of an Arctic expedition in the mid-1920s; and when past 60 years of age, he was to spend two years treasure-hunting for Inca gold on an island in the Pacific Ocean.

Early in World War 2, he was associated with the British Red Cross. Worsley, aged 69, then lied about his age to secure active service in wreck-disposal work in the English Channel before the Admiralty found him out and diverted him to land jobs. He was on the administrative staff at the Royal Naval College at Greenwich when he died in 1943.

Acclaim for the man

Excerpt from a letter from Albert Armitage, who was second-in-command of the National Antarctic Expedition 1900–04, under Robert Falcon Scott in the ship *Discovery*, to Commander Frank Worsley, dated 7 March 7 1933:

> Dear Worsley,
> …you are too modest in regard to yourself.
> I had a great personal affection for Shackleton, and much admired his qualities. I knew him well: it was due to my report about him that he joined the *Discovery* in 1901. At the same time I cannot help knowing that he had neither the experience nor the practice nor, indeed, that love of the sea which one must have to become a great seaman.
> I say that you were too modest for I know that Worsley was the seaman, the sailor-man, who made that boat journey from Elephant Island possible.
> Anyhow, I salute you!

From the foreword by Duncan Carse to the Folio Society 1974 edition of the book *Shackleton's Boat Journey* by Commander Frank Worsley. Carse in 1956 tracked the journey by Shackleton, Worsley and Crean across South Georgia Island 40 years earlier.

> Without Shackleton's extraordinary nursing of his companions, not all would have lived to see the land… without Worsley's equally extraordinary navigation there would have been no land to see.
> I think Frank Worsley's share in the saga has been undervalued, never on purpose, but because fewer and fewer seafarers have the knowledge and experience to appreciate how great his contribution must have been…

From *Shackleton*, by Roland Huntford, on the battle to keep the small boat, the *James Caird*, afloat in a hurricane approaching South Georgia in 1916:

> In the crisis, Worsley showed his true stature. It was not only that he displayed no fear. He became possessed of a fierce detachment out of which he was able to apply his knowledge of boats and experience of the sea. A sense of being above the battle was the quality he concealed under the adolescent wildness of himself ashore or on bigger boats.

From the preface written by Grettir Algarsson to *Under Sail in the Frozen North*, by Commander Frank Worsley:

> So obviously written by a sailor in love with his ship… the contempt in which he holds mere steamboat sailors, and his secret joy when the propellor went, all show where lies the wind. The Skipper is really out of place in this century. He would be in his element in a frigate duel of the old days, or sailing some high-pooped galleon with Morgan or Dampier…

From *Seventh Continent*, by Arthur Scholes:

> Whenever he came into a room, they said it was like a gust off the Seven Seas! It was impossible not to associate him with ships and the sea, and those who were lucky enough to know him admired his rolling gait and cheerful stentorian voice. He seemed to have been born on the crest of an ocean wave, cradled in the sailing ships and always retaining that gay, romantic, tough quality which novelists associate most with the Eliza-bethans…those who knew Worsley say he was fearless…

CHAPTER 1

The Family

The Worsley family arrived in New Zealand a year later than the Canterbury Pilgrims, those settlers who landed from the first four ships late in 1850 to become part of the colonial aristocracy of Canterbury province. Henry Francis Worsley, a gentleman described by his grandson Frank Worsley as having 'the air of a prince but no business instincts', sold his property in Rugby, England, and sailed for New Zealand in the bark *Cornwall*, arriving at Port Cooper – now Lyttelton – in December 1851, after a journey of 116 days.

There were many Worsleys in the party: Henry Francis took with him his second wife and a total of 11 children, said by Frank Worsley to be of three families, 'three brands of step-sisters and step-brothers'.

Henry Francis also brought with him furniture and two thoroughbred racing horses, and he appears to have lived up to Frank Worsley's assessment of him by being not very successful in business and by being remembered mainly as 'a racing man and an early committee member of the Canterbury Jockey Club'. He was a judge at early meetings in Hagley Park from Anniversary Day, 1853, and was on the sub-committee that drew up the original rules of the CJC.

Canterbury Province was to be the English (i.e. Church of England) settlement as Otago to the south had been the Presbyterian. Development of land outside the main centre, Christchurch, was to be carefully organised, leading to establishment of what was deemed to be the best of English society, from church hierarchy and gentry to artisans and labourers. Colonists were encouraged to buy land and become freeholders, those with the financial means to have large estates while the yeomen would have small freehold farms. The high price of land was meant to ensure that those of small means did not become landowners too soon, and would provide an adequate pool of farm labour.

The orderly approach was thwarted when the land sold slowly, and there was pressure for money for development. About the same time (1850) there was drought in Australia, and this sent a number of squatters to New Zealand. They encouraged the provincial government to relax its regulations, and to accommodate the 'new' money, what were deemed to be waste lands were opened in runs of from five to 50,000 acres.

In the scramble that followed, most of the best land was leased cheaply in large blocks by the end of 1855. To claim a run, a man had only to apply at a land office, binding himself to stock the run within six months, with one sheep for every 20 acres or one head of cattle for each 120 acres.

H.F. Worsley applied to the Canterbury Association for a land allocation and according to Canterbury Museum records, he got 50 acres in the main loop of the Avon River at Fendalton, with a river boundary on three sides. Frank Worsley spoke of a one-acre block, adding that it was on what grew to be Cathedral Square in the city centre; writing in 1938, he regretted that he did not own it, the land having been sold 70 years earlier, and he by then having recognised that he too had neither a sense of business nor the ability to accumulate wealth.

H. F. Worsley bought Run 134, of 5000 acres, situated over the Rakaia River, in 1854. A neighbour was William Browning Tosswill (run 134a), and they formed a partnership and worked their runs together as a dairy farm which they called Waihora.

Local records note that H. F. Worsley was prosecuted several times for allowing his cattle to stray, and that he and Tosswill dissolved their partnership after a year. Both runs were sold or were abandoned in 1862 and became part of Broadlands station.

H.F. Worsley also owned land on the Lyttelton side of Marleys Hill, which he bought in 1856, and some property in suburban Hoon Hay, and constructed an access road that linked Hoon Hay with the hills behind. Worsley's Road started at Cracroft Wilson's, climbed the eastern ridge of Hoon Hay Valley to Marleys Hill, then curved around the Summit Ridge to Dyer's Pass. It was also known as the Gorse Track.

These were exciting days for young colonials, and H. F. Worsley's eldest boy Henry Theophilus, aged 17 when the family migrated, revelled in the adventurous environment.

Some of the earliest settlers who stocked land with cattle later abandoned the properties and the stock. The cattle turned wild, and offered the chance for bold young men to make quick money by rounding them up for sale in Christchurch. In 1854 Henry Worsley, at 21, led a party of five youths, two of them younger brothers, in expeditions into the high country to the foothills of the Southern Alps to find cattle.

Frank Worsley recorded that the five partners camped at the junction of three rivers and called the area Mesopotamia, after the ancient region of Asia between the rivers Tigris and Euphrates. Some years later, in 1860, Samuel Butler, the English novelist and philosopher, whose mother was Fanny Worsley from Bristol, migrated to New Zealand and settled in the same Canterbury high country, successfully applying for thousands of acres of the unclaimed land where the Worsley boys five years earlier had camped on their cattle round-ups.

Butler and the New Zealand Worsleys appear to have been related by marriage, though this is not acknowledged in any Butler manuscript, or by Frank Worsley. However, Henry Francis Worsley had a cousin, Philip Worsley, whose wife may have been Butler's aunt; in September 1861, Butler reflected on his good life in New Zealand in a letter to his aunt, Mrs Philip Worsley. The possibility of a link between Butler and the New Zealand Worsleys is tantalising. The name Meso-potamia being given to the leasehold is generally credited to Butler; perhaps he simply adopted the title already given the area by his kin, the Worsley cowboys.

Frank Arthur Worsley photographed at Akaroa, New Zealand, about 1880. He was born there in February 1872, the third child and second son of Henry Theophilus and Georgina Worsley.
Bamford family

Before the Butler tenure, the wild colonial boys made several trips into the area. It was a dangerous but rewarding life; after one round-up each of the partners received 400 pounds. On one search for more cattle, Henry Worsley discovered a pass in the Southern Alps mountain chain that still carries his name.

The last venture of the partners ended in tragedy for Arthur Worsley, the youngest in the family. The round-up went well to the point where the wild cattle were being driven off the hills and on to the plain. A large bull broke back and Arthur rode after it. The bull turned and charged. Arthur's horse stopped in fright and the bull tossed horse and rider. Arthur was killed outright.

Henry Worsley and his brother Charles settled down to a saner life and in the same church on the same day, they married the Fulton sisters, Georgina and Fanny. Henry and Georgina took over a run on hills high above Akaroa township on the edge of the harbour, where the land had to be cleared of native bush before it could be made productive. Frank Worsley was born at Akaroa on 22 February 1872. He was the third and last child and the second son of the family, coming four years after his brother Harry, and two years after his sister Helen.

The hardships of bush colonial life took a big toll on Georgina Worsley, and after 10 years of marriage she died. Henry boarded Frank and Helen at what Frank Worsley later called 'an old maid's school'. But this did not last long, as the 'old maid' set her cap at the widower, who took fright and removed the children from her care. Frank was then sent to Harry's boarding school, known as Harlock's Academy, in Akaroa.

It was a place of study in name only, according to the reminiscences of Pat Keegan, who attended the school with his brother Fred at the time Harry and Frank Worsley were there. Keegan said he was 'packed off' to the private school for boys run by A.K. Harlock, BA, when he was aged five. The Keegan boys were among the smallest boys at the school: 'Frank Worsley came next.'

The schooling at Harlock's had to be paid for. It was considered *infra dig* to go to the government school, which was free. Another difference was that at Harlock's the boys had to wear boots. To go to school bare-footed was 'just not done'. For all its pretensions, Harlock's was a poor establishment. Keegan said the master was one of the old school who believed in flogging. Harlock was often half drunk and used the cane freely. 'No doubt it was often deserved, but when he had been drinking he was extra severe.' After the master thrashed a boy particularly badly, one of the bigger pupils attacked him and knocked him down. 'After that, there was not much discipline.' A year later the school closed.

Keegan said he didn't learn much at the school that was of any use: 'I didn't even learn to swear.' Like the other boys in Akaroa and the surrounding farms, even at his tender age, he knew all the words from listening to the bullock-drivers bringing loads of timber from the hills to the port.

Searching for adventure was a major part of growing up in the colony, and Harry and Frank were keen players. One day, at the ages of twelve and eight, they took a day off school to visit their father at his run high in the hills. After tramping around the coast, they climbed part of the crater rim of Banks Peninsula, into thick mist and finally to their father's run above the town. The boys were taken back to the school, Frank riding with his father on a horse, Harry hanging on by the stirrup leather. The tough little boys had walked about 23 miles, and got a caning for their trouble.

The boys spent all their holidays with their father, who was clearing his land and selling the timber for firewood. It was a hard, exciting life in the open, inculcating the pleasure of adventure into young minds. Every opportunity to experience something new was taken. Harry on one occasion was given half a crown to take a horse nine miles to a farm at the head of the bay. Frank went with him, and later instead of walking back they went along the other side of the harbour to Wainui, opposite Akaroa, to cross the three-mile-wide harbour in a raft they made from flax stems. They used their jackets as sails, made a couple of rough paddles, and set off as the sun was setting.

It was their first taste of sailing; the sea had obviously got into their blood.

Half-way across the harbour the wind came up and the sea was washing through the raft. Spray began to break over them. 'Wet through, we paddled hard to keep warm,' Frank Worsley wrote. When it became dark, they steered by the lights of Akaroa, finally landing on the rocks of St John's Peninsula. As they made their way up the hill to the run, a horseman appeared through the dark: their father. Harry got a brief, sharp hiding, Frank was shaken and he was put back in the saddle with his father while Harry was forced to cling to the stirrup all the way home.

When Henry took up a bush-felling contract on another run, at Peraki, it was found the nearest school was eight miles away, over hills sometimes deep in snow during winter. So Henry taught the boys himself, and Frank Worsley records that they learned from him the Greek alphabet, Latin roots and verses of dog-Latin. Henry also sternly checked any tendency to speak with a colonial twang, and infused in the boys his own love of fair play and distaste for lies.

Frank was small-built but the hard physical life he was leading toughened his wiry frame and helped him develop a hardy constitution. His toughness was to become legendary.

At the age of 10 he had his own small axe and worked beside his father and the hired tree-fellers – the bush-whackers. Years later, when writing *First Voyage*, he regretted the deforestation: 'It was a mad waste: the colonists in their greed for more grass seed and sheep pasture burned millions of pounds worth of timber, recklessly destroying the wonderful beauty of the bush, bared the soil till it was carried away by landslides, lowered the rainfall and laid waste the homes of countless sweet songsters.'

But at the time, 'I loved the axe-work and the sweet scent of wood-chips…I shouted with joy and pride in my puny strength as the chips flew outward at the axe's ringing blows and the swishing branches overhead swept to destruction, carrying away another feathered songster's home and family, adding another space to the blue sky where formerly all had been green and leafy loveliness. Poor young vandal! I knew no better.'

He recalled those early days in poetic and sensitive words that paint a glorious picture of a young settler's life, and a portrait of the beautiful land that existed before settlers cleared the native forests to grow crops to feed sheep.

When the weather was bad the two boys – 'in rags, between poverty and tree-climbing'– sat with the men as they yarned and smoked, listening to tales of earlier colonial times; of old England 'our home that we had never seen'; of old Rugby School days, where Henry had learned under the famed Dr Arnold, school fights, fox-hunting, London theatres and 'gals'. Anglomania was impressed on these colonial boys from an early age; it stayed with Frank Worsley all his life.

Brother Harry's lust for adventure beyond the colony turned him towards the sea, and he persuaded his father to apprentice him to the New Zealand Shipping Company. He was 15 years old. Harry sailed in the wool clipper ship *Waitara* (833 tons) for England, where he enthusiastically reported meetings with 'new' cousins and other relatives. But five days out when sailing back to New Zealand, the *Waitara* sank in a collision with another New Zealand Shipping Company clipper, the 1012-ton *Hurunui*.

The two ships had left London on the same day in 1883 and were beating down

Henry Theophilus Worsley at Akaroa, New Zealand, 1880s. He often had to ride over the hills of Banks Peninsula above Akaroa in search of his two sons, Harry and Frank, who, at an early age, were prone to wandering from home in search of adventure.
Bamford family

16

the English Channel when they collided because of an error by the *Waitara*'s second mate who, when on a port tack, failed to keep his ship clear. Harry was one of 16 survivors; 20 others, including the second mate, drowned.

About this time Henry decided to remarry, and the family moved from Peraki to Fendalton, Christchurch, for a more civilised life. Frank, the wild bush boy, was sent to Fendalton School to have his rough edges honed under the guidance of the headmaster, Samuel Bullock. Frank recorded that he found civilised life 'very irksome, and I consistently raised hell to vary the monotony, which must have been a sore trial…' His previous experience of public schooling, at Harlock's Academy, must have made his edges particularly rough.

Bullock, who 'lightheartedly undertook the task of educating me', found himself caning Worsley 'every day of my life – Saturdays, Sunday and holidays excepted' as he tried to tame the youngster. But there seemed to be no malice: Bullock was a good and caring man and a dedicated teacher. Frank later estimated that in four years between the ages of 11 and 15, Bullock administered about 3000 'cuts' of his cane to the palms of Frank Worsley's hands. And in later years, Bullock would boast that Frank Worsley never cried, whimpered, tried to evade punishment or told him a lie.

Harry Worsley returned to New Zealand after the drama of the channel collision, but his experience and his swim for life affected his health and he gave up the sea. He became a wanderer, working for some time in Australia, the East Indies and the South Pacific before joining the New Zealand Army's 2nd Contingent for the Boer War.

Helen Worsley, now nearly grown up, was sent Home, to England, to meet relatives and to finish her education, while Frank suddenly settled down at school to the delight and amazement of Samuel Bullock, working hard and coming out near the top of each class until finally, at 15, he won 12 prizes and the Dux Medal by becoming the head boy of Fendalton School.

When Frank boldly stated that he too was going to sea, the family raised no objections; the young man was clearly not destined for a desk job, and he had an appetite for adventure best catered for in a disciplined environment. But when his father took Frank to the Christchurch office of the New Zealand Shipping Company, the manager shook his head and said, 'Too small; give him six months to grow.' Six months later, still diminutive, Frank was presented again and this time he was accepted. Indentures were arranged and signed before Mr Rose, the Collector of Customs. Henry Worsley paid 50 pounds as a premium and Frank Worsley became a 'brass-bounder', a junior midshipman or apprentice, on the 1057-ton *Wairoa*, bound for London via Cape Horn with a cargo of wool. The year was 1888.

Two years later, on the other side of the world, another young man started his sea-going career, also in a sailing ship, the *Hoghton Tower*. His name was Ernest Shackleton.

Frank Worsley in the Fendalton School uniform, about 1887. The unruly youngster presented a challenge to the headmaster, Samuel Bullock, who had to cane him 'every day of my life – Saturdays, Sunday and holidays excepted'.
Bamford family

Samuel Bullock's letter of recommendation on the departure of Frank Worsley from Fendalton School. Worsley was by then a model student, becoming head boy and dux for the year 1887. He went to sea the following year.
Bamford family

CHAPTER 2

First Voyage

The *Wairoa* was to sail on her voyage of 13,500 miles on Christmas Eve, 1888. Little Frank Worsley was one of two junior apprentices, each of whom was attached to a senior apprentice. The other junior was Ted Tosswill, also from Akaroa and known to the Worsley boys.

The apprentices were contracted to the company for four or five years, according to their age. Worsley was to receive 10 shillings a month and found. As well as teaching the apprentices seamanship, the masters under whom they served were supposed to teach the youngsters navigation. Not all the masters bothered.

At the end of the four years the apprentices were entitled to be examined for navigation and seamanship by the Board of Trade; if competent they were granted a second mate's certificate to serve at that grade in any British merchant ship. Those who achieved this level under sail were proud to call their qualification a 'square-rigged ticket'. The New Zealand Shipping Company tried to place its newly qualified apprentices in company vessels; failing that, the company would seek places with other shipping concerns.

Worsley's senior was Stringer, 'a big fair-headed youngster' four years older, whose first remark when Worsley stood up in their cabin was, 'Holy smoke…do they think I'm a baby-farmer?' But he was pleasant, and promised to be 'mother, father and all' to his small charge. Worsley wrote: 'I felt that I was lucky to start sea life with such a big good-natured fellow who had already constituted himself protector of the small child, as he considered me, thrust into his care.'

The story of the *Wairoa*'s journey to London is told in loving detail in Worsley's book *First Voyage in a Square-Rigged Ship*, the last of Worsley's four books and the only one that deals with his life in New Zealand.

By the time it was published, in 1938, Worsley was aged 67 and in its crafting he applied what was close to his lifetime's accumulation of sea lore. But it was more than simply a sailor's account of his first ocean-going experience: in his adventurous life Worsley became a sharp observer of nature, of sea and bird life; of the making and breaking of phenomenon such as icebergs; of the mysteries of the wind and the ocean currents. And he was by then a confident writer, fully capable of expressing feelings and describing events, what Roland Huntford called, in a reference to his *Endurance* diaries, 'a surprising sensitivity and capacity for observation'. He brought all these qualities together in *First Voyage*.

In fact, Worsley was well grounded in the basics of a classical education by his father, and could read before going to school at the age of five. By the time he left school, he had had as good a formal education as was possible in the colony. This was rounded off in later life through the discipline of keeping a log at sea, and was maintained in personal diaries which he chose to write during some voyages.

He also had a talent for pencil drawings, starting the practice of sketching passing ships during the return to New Zealand on that first voyage. He kept his sketch-books handy, which meant that they went down with the *Endurance* and lie under the Antarctic ice, 'so those rough records of a vanished beauty, for what they were worth, are lost'.

Worsley's books on the Shackleton adventures and the British Arctic Expedition in 1925 sold well over a long period and were well received, as was his *First Voyage*, described by his publisher as showing 'an unusual talent for recalling the day-by-day details of life in a windjammer. His description of a passage in sail takes a place high in the literature of the sea'. The critics agreed.

He recorded the mood of the time in the colony in his account of the sailing of the *Wairoa* from Lyttelton:

> As the last rope holding her to New Zealand fell in the water, the watchers on the jetty raised three cheers – a little thin, but charged with feeling. The arrival or departure of a ship had in the latter half of the last century a far greater significance in New Zealand, where every white man, woman and child, or their parents, had left Home and emigrated in such ships, than can be realized in England where hundreds of vessels come and go unnoticed every day.

And on being towed by a tug to the harbour entrance:

> Even with her sails fast the beautiful little New Zealand clipper, like all the company's ships, made a perfect picture of grace and symmetry. Her clean black hull moved easily through the water, the broad white band with 12 painted ports revealing her graceful sheer.

The *Wairoa* under the New Zealand Shipping Company flag. In *First Voyage*, Frank Worsley said that even with her sails fast, 'the beautiful little New Zealand clipper… made a perfect picture of grace and symmetry. Her clean black hull moved easily through the water, the broad white band with 12 painted ports revealing her graceful sheer.'

D.A. De Maus Collection, Alexander Turnbull Library, Wellington, NZ, No. G-2535-1/1

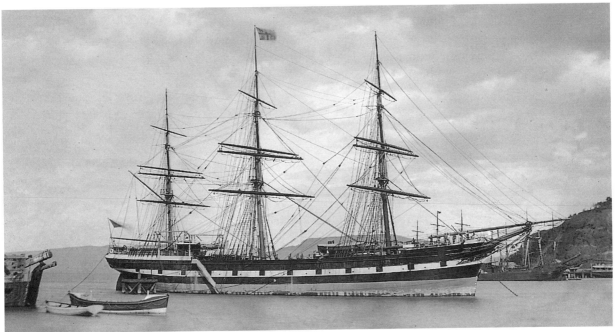

Below the black paint the pink boot-topping picked out her elegant lines with a saucy triangle along the waterline at her cutwater and another at her stern. A snow-white figurehead surmounted the beautiful curve of her clipper stem and set off her out-flared bows with the anchor hanging ready at the cathead.

The poop and dazzling white half-round gave a finish to her clean run aft, terminating in the rudder, now gently swinging to port as the helm was starboarded for the harbour mouth. As she met the Pacific swell her forefoot lifted; she curtsied daintily and her lofty spars swung their tracery in easy arcs across the clouds.

Freed from the tug, the *Wairoa* met a nor'westerly blowing half a gale and promising more. Worsley followed his senior apprentice into the rigging and learned first lessons about setting sails, as well as the seaman's creed when aloft: 'One hand for yourself, and one for the ship.' He wrote: 'I was not afraid, being so used to being up trees, but the height of the lowermast magnified the movement of the ship so much that my stomach felt uneasy.'

Worsley described the setting of the sails and the incident that gave him a cognomen for the journey: 'A yell from the foremast of "sheet home!" incited me to a frantic squeak of "Hoist away main topsail!" to Stringer's glee and answering shouts of laughter from below. Thereafter I was known as Tommy the Squeaker!'

The small apprentice 'laboured dizzily, my bowels straining as we sheeted home, the *Wairoa*'s lee rail hissing through the seas and her maindeck awash. Enviously I watched Tosswill as we hoisted the topgallantsails – he was only yellow; I was green.' Worsley made a rush to the lee rail 'and offered oblation to Neptune, cheered by the crew and encouraged by Stringer.' The *Wairoa* had set the mainsail and she went over in the gale until the lee rail was buried and the bosun reported a speed of 12 knots.

'To stave off nausea I gazed aloft at the three great towers of wildly straining canvas that seemed every moment to burst from the bolt ropes and fly off in one huge pearl-grey cloud towards my native land to leeward.' But the youngster soon lost interest in life: 'My head was swimming and my stomach heaving painfully at the wretched vacuum that it had formed. I fell against the lee rail and hoped that I would go overboard.'

'Take that boy below,' said the mate. A sailor tucked Worsley under one arm, slid down a ladder and ploughed through the water in the ship's waist to the abode of the apprentices on the halfdeck.

'He removed my shoes and jersey and having covered me with a blanket, placed a tin handy and returned on deck. As he went I heard: "Poor little booger", from the great soft-hearted sailor.'

After four days of heavy gale the *Wairoa* had covered more than 1000 miles, or one-quarter of the way to Cape Horn, and Worsley was weak and pale but with sea legs 'of a sort' and the appetite of a wolf.

On the fifth day the boatswain took him around the ship and enumerated the ropes and other rigging paraphernalia, telling him to remember all 240. Next day he was tested and discovered that when making a mistake, 'the sharp swish of a rope's end fell painfully on my stern to emphasise the boatswain's correction…this brightened up my memory wonderfully, but even so I was not yearning to sit down when we finished our round.'

The greatest hardship the apprentices faced on a first voyage was the four-hours-on, four-hours-off watch system, to be followed every day for the duration of the voyage except in bad weather when they might be called out at any time for any number of hours. Like any other youngster, Worsley found it almost impossible to wake in the middle of the night. He hated anyone who called him out – the captain, officers, ship, routine and even the sea. 'Once when they had succeeded in bringing me to life six minutes before midnight I lay in my bunk and prayed that a sea would sweep all hands overboard and leave me to slumber peacefully until the ship foundered.'

Each night before sleep, he wrote, he still wetted his pillow 'with tears for home and loved ones. I was desperately ashamed of this and it was not till years after that I found that many of our youngsters had been affected in the same way.'

Eighteen days out and into the great unceasing westerly swell and the *Wairoa* was within 1000 miles of the Horn; 18 days of 'gales, hail and snow squalls, thunder and lightning'. In yet another howling gale the *Wairoa*

sweeps triumphantly, lurching, rolling and plunging at dizzy speed down the steep fronts of the walls of water. As she lags on the back of each comber the onrushing gale emits booming howls from ten thousand devils through her vibrating rigging. She sinks in the trough, decks full from rail to rail, and shudders fore and aft to one thunderous flap of the decalmed foresail…

The terrific grandeur of the scene and the danger of the toppling seas rolling on,

The New Zealand wool clipper, the *Wairoa*, in which Frank Worsley made his first voyage in 1888. The artist, 'W.E.H.', was Walter How, an able seaman on the *Endurance*.
Bamford family

ridge behind ridge, are evident even to a greenhorn like me. It is too late to heave-to; the ship might founder in the attempt. It is necessary to drive her to prevent her from pooping or broaching-to, and so the captain cracks on with four full sails and reefed mainsail and defying the gale, refuses to lower the topsail.

This was Worsley's entry to the great ocean where 25 years later he would sail again, navigating through equally wild conditions a lifeboat barely 22 feet long, on a mission to save 28 men of Shackleton's Trans-Antarctic Expedition.

The *Wairoa* was running well to the south, seeking the landmark of the Diego Ramirez Islands – the most southerly land of America – 60 miles south-west of Cape Horn. The group was sighted five miles north of the ship, and 24 days out from Lyttelton the *Wairoa* was in Drake Strait, the passage that separates South America from Antarctica, and rounded Cape Horn.

The tropics beckoned, but first the ship had to negotiate the Burdwood Bank, the submarine plateau south of the Falklands that rises within 60 metres of the surface and topples the crests of the huge south-westerly swells as the bases of the swells drag on the submerged island. Worsley wrote with great clarity of the danger from the mad rolls of the *Wairoa* as the swells became steeper and more violent. 'I knew there must be grave danger, but revelled in it. "The joy of ignorance," Stringer called it.'

All night the ship stormed into the South Atlantic, passed the Falklands and made north 'into flying-fish weather. The air was milder and a different atmosphere was evident among the crew as we left the Falklands astern.' All they saw of the islands was a faint blue line on the horizon as another gale howled in from the south-west and all crew were called out to reef the fore and main topsails.

Aloft and 'lost in a fog of streaming snow,' the topsail was reefed and little Worsley was coming in towards the rigging.

Collins growled in my ear: 'One hand for the queen and one for yerself, Squeaker'. The next second the sail, in the eddy of the main topsail, gave one thunderous slat against us.

My hold on the becket was broken, my arms flung up and out, and I felt myself falling backward to death.

A long lean arm shot out, steel-like claws seemed to grip my ribs and I found myself seated on the footrope clutching the stirrup and Collins' leg. When he pulled me up alongside of him I noticed that his red mahogany face seemed pale.

I had so little sea sense that I grinned nervously as I spluttered 'thanks'. My reward was a well-deserved clout on the head. 'Don't you grin at me,' he rumbled 'And don't you split,' he growled a few minutes later. It seemed that life-saving was a crime to be ashamed of by an honest old seaman.

The snow-squall thinned out and on the starboard bow was 'a lovely silver, blue and crystal castle' of an iceberg with a great cliff higher than the *Wairoa*'s masts, topped by a peak reaching 300 feet (90 metres) above sea-level. It was another introduction for Worsley to an element of nature that would cause him many more nervous moments in his life at sea.

Icebergs posed a particular menace to sailing ships. Apart from the danger of simply being driven into one by the wind and the swell, there was the chance of meeting one that had a hook, with a bay between the shanks. Oncoming ships running before a gale could be swept into the bay and be unable to sail out against the elements.

In 1854 a migrant ship, the *Guiding Star*, bound for Australia with 160 passengers, had been so trapped. Her captain tacked across the bay trying to work to windward, but finally struck the ice-cliffs. Her masts fell, she turned turtle and foundered and 200 people perished. The drama was observed from two other ships similarly trapped, but which had more room to manoeuvre and escaped.

Worsley admired the beauty of the iceberg and recorded: 'We fled northward past it, northward from the gales, the snow-squalls, the dreaded bergs and the bitter cold. Northward to the welcome tropics. Seamanship be damned! Let's get warm.'

For two days the *Wairoa* 'roared northward', twice reaching speeds of 14 knots, and at the end of January 1889 she was rolling on long, lazy swells and 'we seemed to be in a new world of summer, where gales never blew, where the sun shone and the sea smiled.'

There was more time now to learn detail of seamanship and navigation, and to exercise eager young muscles in the rigging, 'happy days of hard work, open air, sunshine and shower, swinging high aloft on the mizen, learning to do a seaman's work'. Tosswill, a year older 'and some years more sensible' was by now ahead of his smaller fellow-apprentice, and in competition Worsley said he 'felt the demon of jealousy'. One day while skylarking the two had a wrestle, won by Tosswill, whereupon Worsley challenged him to a fist-fight. Tosswill won that too, and Worsley learned his place as 'the smallest and cheekiest kid in the *Wairoa*'.

Worsley loved to watch the dawn from high in the rigging and once when ordered back to the deck by the mate, he said,

> Barely was the order out of his mouth before I was sliding down at high speed, the soles of my shoes pressed hard against the skysail backstay to prevent burning myself. Half-way, the crosstrees checked me. I swung lightly over them, renewed my descent with my shoes smoking from friction and landed on deck three seconds from the skysail yard 140 feet above.
>
> I was in high favour with myself, but the commendation I got from the mate was 'Don't play the fool aloft. Go to the main skysail again and come down properly'.

Stringer later warned him about circus-tricks aloft: 'The mate doesn't give a damn if you break your ruddy little neck, but he doesn't want it to be said that he was careless of a first voyage apprentice's life.'

Fifty-eight days out from New Zealand, the *Wairoa* crossed the Equator and the young apprentices became 'freemen of the Seven Seas'. Next day Worsley was able to demonstrate his navigational prowess when sighting St Paul's Rocks from aloft. After reporting the sighting, he added: 'Twenty-two miles distant', and when the mate demanded how he knew, Worsley explained: 'Sixty-four feet height of the rocks – nine miles. One hundred and forty-six feet up here – 13 miles. Twenty-two altogether, Sir.' The mate agreed and added: 'You'll make a navigator one of these days.'

Worsley was intrigued by this first sight of land in the northern hemisphere and imagined himself as an explorer on the rocks. Thirty-three years later he was working for the Admiralty and recalled then those first voyager's daydreams with some pleasure in their fulfilment. His later survey actually moved the St Paul's Rocks half a mile farther west than the charts of the day recorded.

The north-west trade winds were picked up and the *Wairoa* went 'bowling along over the deep blue sea day after day'. Now the work was scraping, cleaning and painting to present the ship at London in company-standard condition. And as the ship neared the English Channel Worsley said his heart 'thrilled tumultuously with excitement'.

> I was approaching 'Home.' The England that I had never set foot on was 'Home.' We English of New Zealand have a keen patriotism, more aware of itself than the equally deep but self-concealed love of country that pervades the home-born Englishman. Imbibed from our parents was the pathetic love of the exile for the kith, home and country that, in most cases, he was fated never to see.

Before the westerlies, 'we drew steadily on towards the famous island called Britain, to that mysterious haven called "Home" that I was about to discover'.

But still there was danger. The English Channel – a crowded waterway at any time – was doubly treacherous in the foggy conditions that now prevailed.

The air was raw and damp. The sails flapped heavily. Fog-horns were moaning, but for a sailing ship this was no protection against a steam liner which, thundering along at 15 knots, would be on top of a sailing ship before the fog-horn would even be heard.

The *Wairoa*'s fog-horn went on through the night and the captain stayed on the poop throughout, listening to steam whistles and fog-horns all around. In the early morning, with the fog as thick as ever, one steam whistle was sounding nearer and clearer. 'She was coming down on us and coming fast.'

'To each raucous five-second blast of the fast-approaching steamer, our fog-horn answered with pitiable bleating wails. It had been maddeningly loud all night; now it seemed a ludicrously inadequate sound to warn an approaching steamer,' wrote Worsley.

All hands stood by, facing the direction of the approaching danger. The captain got the steward to bring him his shotgun. He fired both barrels and to port the crew heard the wash of a bow and the thud of a propellor.

'The next moment a great blaring sound burst forth almost overhead. A glaring masthead light and red and green sidelights to port were bearing straight down for me standing at the break of the poop, 60 feet from our stern,' Worsley said.

The captain screamed for the helmsman to steer hard a-port, and as the *Wairoa*'s stern swung away the steamer 'scraped past our stern with a foot to spare', sending the sailing ship spinning. The captain's face was distorted with fury as he yelled, 'I've a mind to shoot you blasted murderers tearing at 15 knots through this fog.' All hands cursed the steamer. Worsley, although he later skippered steam boats, was never so comfortable as with sail. His distaste for steam may have been cemented by this experience.

In 24 hours the fog was gone and there appeared the hills and dales of Devon.

'My heart thumping with excitement, I thought: "So this is England – Home"…
so orderly and different from our untamed wildness in New Zealand. But I
recognised this scene: I knew it from my father's lips. In 1853 it was the last he
had seen of England.'

The *Wairoa* finally berthed at the West India Docks, and Worsley was dressing
to go ashore when there arrived a man whom he knew as Uncle Lawrence from
his brother Harry's experience. He had a month's leave, in which time he met a
series of aunts and cousins, 'all of whom delighted in my riotous behaviour …
I hugely enjoyed my English holiday.'

Back at work in London, Worsley lived at the company's lodging premises
close to the docks, where 60 apprentices from its 16 sailing ships were based in
May 1889, working to keep their ships clean and making minor alterations and
repairs. The youngsters occasionally broke out, most of them having acquired
what Worsley called 'a nautical thirst'. They enjoyed the local brew and sometimes
clashed vigorously with the cockney youths, often over local girls. The police
were sometimes involved but they viewed the young colonial sailors with a good
measure of tolerance. The worst excesses occurred at their boarding premises in
North Island–South Island confrontations, culminating in the apprentices being
kicked out and confined to their ships.

These fun-filled days and nights ended for Worsley when he was transferred
to the *Rakaia* for the voyage back to New Zealand, sailing in three days. The
company had decided that the ocean was a more suitable playground. And little
Worsley found himself the senior apprentice of the three on board, under Captain
Banks, who was also a Royal Naval Reserve lieutenant.

Two men, Captain Banks and the mate Mr Watson, buffed and polished
Worsley's seamanship and navigation on the voyage back to New Zealand via the
Cape of Good Hope.

The senior apprentice was meeting responsibility for the first time. He found
the mate was 'a diver',

> he made us work hard and thought nothing of keeping us on deck for the whole of a
> precious watch below if we had not done enough work to satisfy him. At the same
> time he treated us like men instead of puny first-voyagers and made us carry out,
> unaided, every job of seamanship necessary to keep the mizen-mast and its gear in
> perfect order and repair.

Captain Banks' hobby was navigation and he was determined that 'his boys' should
acquire the art. He conducted classes two afternoons a week, teaching so well,

> that we became expert with logarithms, Mercator's sailing, day's work and meridian
> altitude. Mr Watson reinforced the theory by handing the apprentices the log-book
> and the noon altitude of the sun with orders to produce the noon latitude and the
> ship's position by dead-reckoning.
>
> On one awful day Johnny Muir [another apprentice] placed the ship in the Transvaal
> by DR, while my astronomical calculation lost six days of the passage. Some of the
> things the mate said that day became classics.

The sturdy young apprentice, by now packing on muscle and weight and growing into his manhood height of 5 feet 7 inches (1.7 metres), had both the confidence and the will to exercise what he called his 'cat-like agility aloft, and strength of grip'. His greatest joy and release was doing the most dangerous acts he could think of, scorning to use the safety devices rigged. 'My chums looked on these antics with strong disapproval.'

Once he swung across the front of the bellying topsail by the reef points, 18 inches long and thinner than a man's finger. After crossing the sail from side to side, he jumped on to the fore-deck where the sailmaker gave him two tremendous cuts with a rope's end. 'If two of those reef points had drawn you'd have broken your damned neck. I wouldn't have minded that but I'd have got the blame and I'm too good a sailmaker to take blame for your tricks,' said Sails, who then showed the youngster something of his art. 'For my part, I never again swung across a sail by the reef points,' wrote Worsley.

He concluded later that 'these foolhardy exploits of mine were the result of overflowing animal spirits and a sheer intoxication of the joy of living that has lasted for more than 40 years at sea, but was strongest in the rough and happy days of the old wind bags'.

Back into the Roaring Forties and the *Rakaia* met the westerly swells, with two southerly busters that came howling up from the Antarctic for variety. On each of those two occasions, for 48 hours all hands 'strove and toiled, unbent burst sails and bent new ones, working like one man with the mates and the master to save the sails, masts, the ship and our lives'.

Worsley wrote: 'With the constant hauling on wet, hard, bitterly cold ropes, our hands became curved claws. We could not straighten them. They were admirable for maintaining a grip on anything, but not quite so ready to let it go. We 16-year-olds now realised that in the main essential, we were men and not boys.'

The *Rakaia* survived another huge gale after passing 'the Leeuwin' – Cape Leeuwin, the south-west corner of Australia – that had the crew labouring for 36 hours. During this storm there was trouble with the fore-royal sail in a snowstorm driven by a southerly buster. The seaman on duty took a blow on the nose and panicked. Worsley and one of his junior apprentices raced 130 feet (40 metres) above the deck as the ship rolled, lurched and pitched and for an hour fought to save the sail and the mast itself.

Their reward came when the storm passed: the tough bosun, known to all (and addressed to his face) as Sir Bevis, let them sleep an extra three hours before he turned them out from their bunks to the roar: 'What the hell are you loafing in here for?' But he also praised the youngsters as 'two little first-voyagers, not two spits high, not a dog-watch at sea, saving the royal after Dutchie had been driven to tears by a clout on the snout'.

South of Tasmania the *Rakaia* passed over the position of the Royal Company Islands, but no land was sighted. Until the end of the nineteenth century the islands were marked with 'P.D.' (position doubtful) on charts. Worsley noted that he had met at different times two old sealers in New Zealand who swore they had been on the islands to kill sea elephants and fur seals. But hundreds of sailing ships had seen no land, and finally the islands were removed from charts.

Theorising about lost islands became a hobby for Worsley, and he was happy to discuss them, along with pearl lagoons and treasure, with anyone keen to listen. He was to find a sympathetic ear with Shackleton.

Journey's end was close when the *Rakaia* rounded Stewart Island, the picturesque southernmost island of New Zealand, and hauled to the wind up the lee coast of Otago. 'The 1000-mile-long breakwater of the greatest island nation in the Southern Hemisphere lay out-thrust from the offing of the tropics into the stormy Southern Ocean to protect us from the howling gales and devastating seas of the Roaring Forties.'

Thirty hours later 'we were sailing under topsails into Lyttelton Harbour with the pilot aboard and the tug bearing down to take our tow rope'.

The apprentices were given leave. Worsley was walking towards the railway station when he saw 'a well-remembered figure approaching. I forgot that I was a full-blown sailor-man who had sailed round the world: I only remembered that I was a boy and that this was my father.'

The *Wairoa*, one of five sister ships built for the New Zealand Shipping Company, made about 20 journeys between New Zealand and England, the last for the company in 1894. She was bought by a Norwegian company and was later sold to Russian interests. She was lost in 1907 on a voyage from the United States to Argentina with a cargo of timber.

The *Rakaia* was the first ship build specially for the company. All the sailing vessels were named after New Zealand rivers, most of them in the South Island. She also did about 20 voyages for the company over the longest sea route in the world. She was sold in 1892, sank in 1906, was refloated and finally dropped off the Lloyds registry in 1919 when she had French owners.

The company operated sailing ships from its inception in 1873 until 1900, when it turned exclusively to steam. It is now part of the P. & O. Line.

CHAPTER 3

Pacific Command

Worsley went under sail again in New Zealand Shipping Company ships, in the *Piako* and the *Orari*. It was in the *Piako* that he performed what he called his riskiest trick aloft, on the tallest mast, on a fine day with a steady breeze abeam, the ship heeling slightly but not pitching or rolling.

High on the mast, the barefooted youngster drew himself up until his chest lay across the truck, the circular piece of wood 8 inches (20 centimetres) across that is placed on the extreme top of the mast. Standing from the centre is a copper spike, the point of the lightning conductor. Worsley placed one knee after the other on the truck, then one bare foot after the other and drew himself erect until he was standing without any support on the tiny platform 140 feet (42 metres) above the deck. 'A beautiful view…but I did not pause to admire it,' he said.

As he lowered himself to get off the truck, with his face close to the surface, he read the letters H.W. carved into the wood: his brother Harry had been there before him, at least as far as the truck, on the voyage back to New Zealand after the sinking of the *Waitara*.

Worsley stayed with the New Zealand Shipping Company until 1895, when he left. He was a third officer in rank, and a supremely experienced mariner under

The *Piako* at Wellington Harbour in the 1880s. Frank Worsley sailed in her and recorded that he performed his most dangerous 'trick' aloft by standing without support on the truck of the highest mast, 140 feet (42 metres) above the deck. His brother Harry also sailed back to New Zealand in this NZ Shipping Co. vessel after a tragic collision between two company ships in the English Channel.
Alexander Turnbull Library, No. F-38364-1/2

sail. His record of service read: apprentice (December 1887), third mate (October 1891), fifth officer (April 1892), fourth officer (January 1893), third officer (December 1895). The letter added that he was leaving at his own wish to join another service, and he was reported as being 'a strictly sober and good officer'.

The 'other service' was the New Zealand Government Steamer Service, and his first posting was as second mate in the 811-ton steamer *Tutanekai*, sailing around the Pacific Islands. The steamer started service in 1897 for the Marine Department. In 1913 she was transferred to the Post and Telegraph Service, and nine years later she took over from the *Hinemoa* duties of servicing the lighthouses of New Zealand.

The voyage of the *Tutanekai* to Samoa and around the islands of the group in 1899 was undoubtedly Worsley's liveliest, as it involved an incident at the capital Apia that went close to wrenching New Zealand–German diplomatic relations as violently as they were parted 15 years later at the outbreak of hostilities in the Great War.

The 1899 voyage was on behalf of the Samoan Commission, the members of which wanted the convenience of visiting the islands in a ship capable of coming close to shore to make landings more easy. The New Zealand Governor, Lord Ranfurly, put the *Tutanekai*, under Captain C.F. Post, at the commission's disposal. The mission accomplished, the ship was back in Apia in July of that year.

The incident involving Worsley has been told in three accounts by the historian James Cowan, who became a personal friend of Worsley and later sailed twice in the Pacific with him. Only one account names the young second mate and the ship. This is in *New Zealand Railways Magazine* (October 1933) in a series, *Famous New Zealanders*. The other reports concealed the identities: one was in the *Auckland Star* (1917) and the other was in Cowan's book, *Suwarrow Gold and Other Stories of the Great South Sea*.

They all centred on the disappearance of the Imperial German ensign that was flying outside the consulate on the beachfront headquarters of the colonial power in Apia. At the time, Samoa was ruled under a tripartite arrangement involving Germany, the United States and Britain. All three states had warships stationed there; the *Tutanekai* appeared to be the only merchant vessel in the harbour at the time.

Detail of the 'liberation' of the consular flag varies slightly in the different accounts, but there is no doubt that Worsley nabbed it and brought it back to New Zealand.

The *Railways Magazine* article says the centre of flag 'occupies a place of honour on the wall of a New Zealand museum today. It is popularly supposed to have been captured valiantly by the New Zealand Expeditionary Force in the taking of Samoa in 1914.' The *Star* article says the purloined flag 'came to fill a useful, if inglorious, place in the shape of covers for sofa cushions in a certain New Zealand home today,' possibly Worsley's family home, Ringloes, in Christchurch.

The version closest to the truth is probably the *Star* article, written by 'Orakau' (Cowan). The Scott Polar Research Institute at Cambridge has a clipping of the

The SS *Tutanekai*, built on the Clyde in 1896 for the New Zealand Government Steamer Service. Frank Worsley was second mate on an eventful voyage to Samoa in 1899, when he stole the German Consulate's ensign from outside the consulate in Apia.

D.A. De Maus Collection, Alexander Turnbull Library, No. G-3439-1/1

article, on which there are two notations in Worsley's handwriting, one of them stating: 'Slightly hashed and altered by Jim Cowan from F.A. Worsley's account.'

In it a young mate called Tommy Walsh (Worsley) was on his ship, the *Tembinoka* (*Tutanekai*), one hot afternoon observing the beachfront through binoculars and noting in the middle of the scimitar of the beach, 'the most-hated emblem in Apia, the Imperial German colours floating from a tall mast of a flagstaff in a paling-fenced compound'. He saw the armed blue-coated sentry marching to and fro with loaded rifle and fixed bayonet before the 'sacred mast-foot'. The sentry was relieved every hour. It was the German consulate, the origin and hatching-place for most of the plots and intrigues in Samoa.

'Walsh' persuaded the boatswain 'O'Shea' to join his venture, and that night they went ashore and surveyed the German establishment behind its picket fence. One German sailor was on duty tramping on his beat, 'no doubt wishing for his relief that would allow him to join his fellows and their supper of sausage and beer in the little guardhouse'. The sentry was starting another round when the New Zealand sailor pounced.

'Walsh' leapt over the fence and ran to the flagstaff. The newspaper report says he lifted the flag from a wooden locker at the base of the pole. In Worsley's second notation, this paragraph is over-written with the words 'Worsley hauled the flag down and removed the halliard.' He stuffed the flag under his jacket, jumped the fence and the two men started down the road.

Out of the dark loomed a figure and they were challenged: 'Vat you do here, eh?' It was one of the Germans from the guardhouse. 'O'Shea' lashed out with his fist and whacked the German's jaw, knocking him to the ground. The sentry's measured footsteps approached as the sailors raced for the beach and their boat.

Theft of the flag was not noticed until daylight, and the furious consul, in cocked hat and tight white uniform, went to the German Navy cruiser *Falke*. Soon after an armed German crew pulled alongside the '*Tembinoka*' and demanded to search the ship, an officer rightly complaining that as she was the only merchant ship in harbour it was likely that some of her sailors had the flag.

Captain Post angrily threatened to call over armed men from the Royal Navy cruiser *Royalist*, from which officers were observing the German advance with interest. A boat was launched from the *Royalist* and headed for the schooner. The Germans retreated and next day the New Zealand ship sailed for home.

Cowan said that one morning, with the Auckland coast in sight, the skipper found the mate hoisting the German colours under the Red Ensign in the morning breeze. 'Walsh' said he was 'just airing our flags, Sir'. The captain was astonished, but declared he might have been tempted to do the same; in any case, he would never have handed his young officer to the Germans.

About the time Worsley and his companion were raiding the German consulate, the leader of the Samoan Commission, C.N.E. Eliot, was writing a despatch (July 10, 1899) to Lord Ranfurly, acknowledging the service rendered by the *Tutanekai*. He added that the commission 'also desire to express their thanks to Captain Post for his courtesy and polite attention which have rendered the journey not only useful but agreeable. The *Tutanekai* intends to leave tomorrow at 10am.' He never knew how close to a diplomatic incident he had come, thanks to one of Captain Post's crew.

Worsley's career was unchecked by the flag incident: perhaps Captain Post kept the details to himself. Cowan said Captain Post 'thought a great deal of his alert young second mate, who was a careful and exact navigator'.

His next posting was as mate in the *Hinemoa*, also on New Zealand Government service in the Pacific. Cowan said he sailed twice with Worsley in the *Hinemoa*, a steamer of 542 tons that also did service late in her life on the lighthouse circuit. Cowan said that one of these voyages was to Samoa, and the other was a search in the Tasman Sea seeking a disabled and drifting steamer, the *Perthshire*.

Worsley now felt that he was ready to sit for his foreign-going master's certificate, after 12 years at sea and steady progress through the ranks to chief officer. He sat the examination in Wellington in June 1900 and was successful on his first attempt. The principal examiner of masters and mates in the Nautical Advisor's Office, H.S. Blackburne, later wrote of the young mariner: 'I have pleasure in certifying to having examined the papers of Frank A. Worsley who was a candidate for a foreign-going master's certificate on June 6, 1900. He passed very creditably at first attempt, all problems being correctly worked without having been returned for any correction.'

In the report on candidates that year was the following: 'In a few instances candidates have passed exceedingly well at the first attempt.' Worsley was one of two named as 'deserving especial mention for the very creditable manner in which they passed their examinations'. And in a personal note to Worsley, Blackburne added: 'I am glad to hear that you are keeping your hand in with the most useful problems in navigation.'

Worsley's first command was the *Countess of Ranfurly*, another New Zealand Government schooner, a three-masted 'handsome little vessel' built in New Zealand for the South Sea islands' trade, linking New Zealand dependencies. She was ideal for the work, being square-rigged on the foremast and with an auxiliary engine. The *Countess of Ranfurly* started her island duties in 1901, sailing into commercial storms as the New Zealand Government sought to break a grip on island trade held by private and foreign firms.

Worsley was never likely to be a conventional captain, according to Cowan, who was quoted in a National Broadcasting Service tribute to Worsley soon after he died in 1943. Cowan, a guest on the trial cruise of the *Countess of Ranfurly* on Hauraki Gulf, out of Auckland, added, 'But it would probably have gone hard with anyone who took liberties with him.'

Highlighting this, Cowan said that on the cruise one summer Sunday evening, with most of the crew of Cook Islanders gathered at the main hatch for a song, the young skipper led off with some shanties and sang happily with his crew until the wind came up and there was work to do trimming the sails.

On one of his earliest voyages with the *Countess of Ranfurly*, Worsley was host to Cook Islands royalty in the form of J.M. Saluum, husband of the Queen of the

The *Countess of Ranfurly*, Frank Worsley's first command, was an auxiliary three-masted topsail schooner. Worsley was said to delight in showing island folk and passengers what he could do under sail.

Scott Polar Research Institute, No. 1529/9/15

island group. In a letter to Worsley from the palace in Arorangi, Rarotonga, in October 1901, he thanked the young skipper for the kindness shown him by all on the vessel, and said that when answering a letter from the premier of New Zealand, 'I will mention your kindness and courtesy.' Worsley's lack of appropriate headgear for life in the tropics had also been the subject of conversation, for the Queen's consort added that 'my wife the Queen will make your hat herself'.

The British Resident Commissioner in Rarotonga, Colonel W.E. Gudgeon, writing to the New Zealand Government on the Cook Islands' accounts ended March 1902 and the operations of the *Countess of Ranfurly*, said,

> I have never supposed that this schooner will pay her way, for the reason that the competition of the Union Company is now unremitting and there are still a few schooners taking part in the trade on behalf of certain firms. But it is well known that prior to our schooner coming on the scene the Union Company boats would only call at the outlying islands on a 50-pound guarantee. Now these islands have the same trade opportunities as Rarotonga, and this fact has done much to improve the circumstances of the said islands and benefit the public.
>
> …indirectly, she is invaluable for the reason that the government of the northern islands cannot be carried on effectively without a schooner of this type, and the Cook Islands Government can well afford to pay 1000 pounds per annum for a boat that reduces the price of freight and passages, gives prompt and certain communications between all the islands, and retains money in the group that would otherwise go into the pockets of foreign firms.

In his *New Zealand Railways Magazine* article, Cowan said Worsley's delight in his white schooner knew no bounds and he showed the island folk and his passengers what he could do under canvas. He now had full play of the sail-handling lore of his 'brassbounder' days as he cruised all over the New Zealand sector of the South Pacific, as far north as the coral-atoll outpost of Penrhyn Island.

'Robert Louis Stevenson wrote of one of his sailor-characters in *The Wrecker* that he could put his schooner through a Scottish reel. I can quite believe that Worsley could lead his pretty Countess just as neat a dance,' Cowan said.

Worsley himself, though he wrote little about his years in the Pacific, mentioned in lecture notes for the London celebrity circuit he exploited in the 1930s that he 'made thousands of landings in small boats'. His expertise in handling such tiny craft was clearly honed during these years, along with his navigational skills in making landfall at small islands in all weather conditions.

Private shippers in the Pacific were not pleased with the appearance of the *Countess of Ranfurly*, and they tried to bring pressure on the New Zealand Government by querying the cost of maintaining the schooner on Pacific duties. Questions asked in New Zealand, in the press and in Parliament, were directed to Gudgeon for reply.

He said, *inter alia*, 'The services of the government schooner are not to be gauged by actual earnings, and though the cost is heavy, it falls on the people of the Cook Islands only, and they do not complain. That the firm of Donald and Edenborough or the Union Company should not approve of the schooner is only natural for their ancient monopoly has been broken down by that vessel.'

After one trip, Worsley reported on what was required to construct moorings for a 200- to 300-ton vessel at Niue. The moorings would 'undoubtedly be of great benefit to trade,' he wrote.

In a reference to Penrhyn and Manihiki islands, a Cooks Group administration report on business prospects referred to pearl-shell lagoons, and in 1903 it was agreed that Aitutaki Lagoon would be seeded with the best available pearl-shell, from the Scilly Islands, in the hope that a local industry procuring 40 tons of shell a year would be cultivated. Worsley would certainly have known of this development; perhaps it was the basis for his pearl lagoon stories that so captivated Shackleton.

While commanding the *Countess of Ranfurly*, Worsley also joined the Royal Naval Reserve and earned the distinction of wearing the letters RNR following his name in formal designation. On the strength of his proven seamanship, he was appointed a sub-lieutenant RNR on 1 January 1902.

As the services provided by the *Countess of Ranfurly* grew, but the schooner continued to run at a loss, it was suggested that costs should be shared by the various island administrations. In slack times she was being chartered to private firms at about five pounds a day.

But in a few years Gudgeon was having second thoughts about the value of retaining the *Countess of Ranfurly* in service. He had two reasons.

Frank Worsley in his uniform as a captain in the New Zealand Government Steamer Service, taken in 1903.
H.J. Schmidt Collection, Alexander Turnbull Library, No. G-4931-1/2

Reporting in a letter to the New Zealand Minister of the Islands, C.H. Mills, in February 1904, he said he would prefer to sell the vessel. If sold tomorrow 'the Union Steamship Company would replace her at once and at least one other schooner would be placed in the trade. Traders are now alive to the value of the outlying islands.'

Niue's Resident Commissioner, C.F. Maxwell, did not agree, and suggested that Niue might buy the *Countess of Ranfurly*. In fact, New Zealand was eager to sell the vessel, and she was later purchased by the islands' administrations, the cost being met by the Cooks (three-fifths) and by Niue (two-fifths) with a loan over a 15-year period at 3 percent interest.

Gudgeon's second reason for wanting to sell the vessel, he told Mills, involved Worsley, although he was not named. Gudgeon said that 'under the management of the present captain, the government schooner cannot pay'. He was changing his tune about the need to make a profit and seemed to hold Worsley responsible.

In his 4 March 1904 reply to Gudgeon's point about the 'present captain', Mills said, 'The problem will disappear entirely when the schooner arrives in Auckland.' This was probably a reference to the impending sale of the vessel and the end of Worsley's contract.

When his pretty little *Countess* moved into direct control of the islands' administrations, Worsley left the government steamer service, handing over the vessel to Captain William Champion. He was ready for new adventures.

'He was a thoroughly well-qualified master mariner and was not likely to be long without a post, and he decided to seek his luck outside the Dominion,' Cowan wrote. 'He was fit for anything; hard-trained, compact and muscular of build, all steel and india-rubber…'

But before he left New Zealand, Worsley had one further local engagement. With his old skipper Captain Post from the *Tutanekai*, and a scratch crew, Worsley sailed to Sydney to bring the Goldfinch class Royal Navy gunboat *HMS Sparrow* to Wellington.

The *Sparrow* (805 tons), built in 1879, was rigged as a three-masted barquentine. She had been in action in both West Africa and East Africa, operating from South Africa. Between 1900 and 1904, *Sparrow* was part of the Royal Navy's Australian station based at Sydney. She visited New Zealand several times, but had been idle at Garden Island, Sydney, for a year when the New Zealand Government, seeking a ship suitable for training boys for the sea, showed interest in buying her.

Worsley was chief officer to Captain Post for the delivery voyage to Wellington, arriving there in March 1905. Captain Post then returned to the Lighthouse Steamer Service, and Worsley stayed with *Sparrow* which lay at anchor for most of the year while she was examined by Marine Department inspectors. Technically, he was in command of a Royal Navy vessel while only a sub-lieutenant in the naval reserve.

While the assessment process was still in progress, Worsley left for England in early 1906. *Sparrow* was finally bought by the Government from the Admiralty for 800 pounds in July the same year. She was stripped of guns, converted at

Wellington into a training ship, and renamed the *Amokura*. She was commissioned as such in early 1907 and sailed on her first cruise on 2 November that year with 60 boys aged 13 and 14, under the command of Captain S. E. Hopper. The *Amokura* served as training ship until 1922.

The *Countess of Ranfurly* continued to operate at a loss. In his yearly report in 1907, Gudgeon said the loss was more than 400 pounds, and he considered this good and sufficient reason why the boat should be sold. He said he would lay the *Countess* up after a July trip to Maldern Island, pending her sale. The Niue administration agreed, and the vessel was sold to Australian interests in October 1907. She was wrecked near New Caledonia in February 1910.

Worsley reached England in April 1906 and before resuming a merchant service career in probably the most trying sea-service in the world, the North Atlantic, he offered himself for further training in the Royal Naval Reserve. He was promoted to lieutenant in May the same year while serving in harbour on *HMS Psyche* (RNR).

The Royal Navy had always looked to the merchant service for its men: every English seaman was liable to serve in the navy when wanted. At the time Worsley was doing his training, junior officers entered either as midshipmen or as sub-lieutenants, according to age, but always on a probationary basis. They had to

The NZ Government training ship, *Amokura*. Frank Worsley was chief officer of the crew that sailed the vessel to Wellington, New Zealand, from Sydney in 1905. The *Amokura* was then HMS *Sparrow*. In Wellington, during the period when the Government was assessing *Sparrow* for suitability as a training ship, Worsley was in command. He left for Britain some months before *Sparrow* was bought and renamed the *Amokura*.
F.H. McClusky

pass a medical test almost as strict as that for the regular navy, and they had to be British-born, of British parents, and of pure European descent as far back as could be traced. Applicants for entry as sub-lieutenants had to have at least one Board of Trade certificate of competency.

There was no question of probation for Worsley, who already held commissioned rank; he was an experienced and competent sailor who had held a command, so there were no entry problems. What he lacked was the specialist training such as in applied gunnery, torpedo work and navigation in the navy manner. He easily qualified in all the esoteric areas at the Nautical College at Pangbourne, Berks.

He then had to serve full-time on Royal Navy vessels, service he performed during the remainder of 1906 on a number of ships, sometimes in harbour and sometimes at sea, culminating in a year-long duty on *HMS Swiftsure*, from November 1906.

Swiftsure was then a modern fighting vessel, being just three years old. She was later in action in the Great War in the early stage of the Gallipoli campaign, when the task of breaching the Turkish defences along the Dardanelles and capturing Constantinople (now Istanbul) was a Royal Navy operation. Sadly, the navy was not up to the task, and its failure led to the land invasion of the peninsula and the crippling and disastrous nine-month campaign that so touched Worsley's fellow New Zealanders.

Worsley was to stay with the reserve all his sea-going career, rising to the rank of lieutenant-commander in May 1914, that momentous year by the end of which he was sailing to the Antarctic in command of Shackleton's boat, the *Endurance*.

From time to time he was called back for RNR duty. In 1911, for instance, he served for a month at sea on *HMS New Zealand*, the newly launched battle-cruiser gifted to Britain by the people of New Zealand.

Three months after he completed his service in *Swiftsure*, Worsley married for the first time. His bride was Theodora Blackden of Tunbridge Wells, and the marriage was conducted on 20 December 1907. Worsley then went back to sea in the merchant service, with the Allan Line Royal Mail Steamers, sailing across the North Atlantic to Canadian ports, often encountering testing icy conditions, and occasionally to South America.

In London, in the cause of securing work, Worsley solicited from the High Commissioner for New Zealand a letter of recommendation. It outlined Worsley's career with government vessels, starting as second officer and ending with his command of the *Countess of Ranfurly* – eight years' service in all. The letter added, 'The Prime Minister of New Zealand speaks of Lt Worsley as a first class seaman and navigator.'

And Worsley continued to impress his skippers, one of them, Henry Blanchard, of the steamer *Sardiniare*, in 1910 stating that he took 'great pleasure in certifying to the ability of Mr Frank Worsley.'

Worsley was second officer on another of the line's vessels and was in London in 1914 on leave between voyages when he had a dream.

CHAPTER 4

On the Ice with Shackleton

It was an extraordinary episode. Most books about the life of Sir Ernest Shackleton touch on the subject of Worsley's dream, which had the New Zealander virtually sleep-walking into the greatest polar adventure of the century. It changed Worsley's life totally; it brought into Shackleton's life a consistently loyal companion whose skills far outweighed his defects, and on whom the explorer's life depended in the most dramatic stages of the Imperial Trans-Antarctic Expedition of 1914–1916.

After the excitement of Roald Amundsen's success in beating Captain Robert Scott to the South Pole in 1911, there seemed little left in Antarctica to explore. But Shackleton, who had failed by 97 miles to reach the pole three years earlier, still thirsted to go south. He noted Amundsen's generous comment that had Shackleton been able to start his attempt from the Bay of Whales as originally planned, as the Norwegian did, Shackleton would have been first to the pole. He believed in himself, and he also believed that Amundsen's achievement would not end Antarctic exploration: there remained the challenge of a trans-continental crossing, from sea to sea, via the South Pole. He made that journey his next target.

Shackleton set up the expedition's headquarters in London, at 4 New Burlington Street. There he interviewed some of the 5000 men who hoped to join the expedition, men whose enthusiasm was whipped along by the pleasure expressed by the popular press that Britain, after the disappointment of Scott's failure, was once more focusing on a polar undertaking of challenging substance.

For his boat the *Endurance*, Shackleton wanted as captain a fellow Anglo-Irishman, John King Davis, who had been chief officer and later skipper of the *Nimrod* for the 1907–1909 expedition. But Davis had no confidence in the enterprise and refused the post.

This was when Frank Worsley had his famous dream, and reacted to its message. Worsley described the event thus:

> One night I dreamed that Burlington Street was full of ice-blocks, and that I was navigating a ship along it – an absurd dream. Sailors are superstitious, and when I woke up next morning I hurried like mad into my togs, and down Burlington Street I went. I dare say that it was only a coincidence, but as I walked along, reflecting that my dream had certainly been meaningless and uncomfortable and that it had cost me time that I could have used to better purpose, a sign on a door-post caught my eye. It bore the words "Imperial Trans-Antarctic Expedition", and no sooner did I see it than I turned into the building with the conviction that it had some special significance for me.

Worsley met Shackleton. They spent only a few minutes together, Worsley said, 'but the moment I set eyes on him, I knew that he was a man with whom I should be proud to work'. They were similar in age – the New Zealander was the elder by two years – and both had apprenticeships in sail. Worsley had commanded small vessels and was an experienced navigator.

Shackleton soon satisfied himself that Worsley was competent and sensed that in him, he would have a friend. They quickly agreed on terms and Shackleton told Worsley: 'You're engaged. Join your ship until I wire for you.'

Worsley, then second officer in a transatlantic freighter, wrote: 'I was committed to my fate. Not a superfluous word had been spoken on either side, but we knew by instinct that we were to be friends from that hour…'

As the Great War loomed in August 1914, the *Endurance* sailed from London for Plymouth, but not before many on board, including Worsley, had indicated that they believed the expedition should be postponed, and the crew should disband to join the armed forces. Worsley, as a Royal Naval Reserve officer, naturally expected to be called up for duty. He was eager that Shackleton should seek Admiralty clearance at this late hour and at a crew muster he agreed that Shackleton should place the ship at the disposal of the Admiralty. Shackleton also told the Admiralty that if his ship were not required, he would have to sail immediately to take advantage of ice conditions in the Weddell Sea. The Admiralty told him to proceed.

Although the explorers were cleared to go, the chief officer, D.G. Jeffrey, and Worsley, went ashore at Plymouth, war by then having been declared, and approached Royal Navy authorities. They were told there was nothing to do at that

The *Endurance*: a sketch by 'W.E.H.'. Frank Worsley 'sleep-walked' into this command after a curious incident in London in which he dreamed he was navigating a ship through ice-blocks along Burlington Street. Sir Ernest Shackleton hired him next day.
Bamford family

time, as all the Royal Naval Reserve had not been called out. Jeffrey still felt that his first duty was to await a posting to a fighting ship, and he quit the *Endurance*. Lionel Greenstreet was called in at 48 hours' notice to take his post. (Jeffrey, incidentally, did finally sail with Shackleton and Worsley, in the *Quest* in 1921.)

So at noon on 8 August 1914, Worsley sailed the *Endurance* from England. Shackleton and the expedition's second in command, Frank Wild, were not on board: there were last-minute arrangements to be made. They would join the vessel at Buenos Aires, travelling by a much faster mailboat.

Worsley had no time for the Germans, the enemy, as he amply expressed in peacetime in the incident over the German consul's flag at Apia, Samoa, 15 years earlier, so when at Madeira (a neutral port) in mid-August a German ship berthed next to the *Endurance* swung foul of the British ship, Worsley reacted violently. He took some of his crew and boarded the German vessel.

The motor expert, Thomas Hans Orde-Lees, recorded the episode in his diary: 'During the night a German vessel which had anchored too near to us swung into us and damaged our bowsprit.' Worsley took Orde-Lees – who was born in Germany and understood the language – with him when he stormed on board. Orde-Lees wrote, 'They sent two engineers and a carpenter and repaired it for us in spite of the fact that we are at war with each other.'

It was an incident that probably coloured the estimation in which others on the *Endurance* – particularly the scientists – were to hold Worsley. It was reckless and impulsive and out of place for a ship's captain; it was certainly not out of character for Worsley.

Greenstreet later commented that Shackleton was vulnerable to a good story and would fall for it. It is suggested he was referring to the hiring of Worsley as captain. Orde-Lees, the only regular force officer on board, while he recorded in his diary that he found Worsley 'a remarkably nice man', also expressed disapproval of the lack of discipline among the crew on the way to Buenos Aires, in the absence of Shackleton.

On 13 August he wrote that the crew was 'insufficient for the ship's needs', and the scientists (he grandly considered himself one of that elite group, although on the ranking list he was placed between the artist, George Marston, and the carpenter, Harry McNeish) had to pull ropes when a sail needed altering.

He found this dirty work that made the hands sore, but conceded that it was good exercise. 'I suppose I shall be up aloft next,' he wrote.

Another task assigned to the scientists was scrubbing the deck each morning. 'This is work I should not mind a bit except for the disgusting way everyone spits all over the deck, which would not be tolerated for a moment in a man-o'-war. Still it has to be done and one can always have a bath afterwards and I suppose it is good for one from a disciplinary point of view,' Orde-Lees recorded on 17 August.

While the behaviour on board was doubtless standard for the merchant service, Orde-Lees as a marine officer was capable of comparing it with the Royal Navy. He strongly disapproved of Worsley's control of the crew.

There was one other incident at Madeira, when four of the *Endurance*'s crew 'kicked up a row in a cafe and after doing much damage were taken to gaol, where one was flogged,' Orde-Lees wrote on 22 August. He called the flogging an outrage and said that he and Worsley spent much of the day trying to get the Portuguese authorities to take up the matter.

Orde-Lees' greatest criticism was the degree to which Worsley allowed liquor to be consumed at sea. An example was the crossing of the Equator on 16 September:

> The captain let us get up a concert; nearly everybody contributed. Captain Worsley also 'spliced the mainbrace' and unfortunately let out rather too much liquor, with the result that one or two of the men were mad drunk at the end. One of them tried to throw himself overboard and made a dive off the quarterdeck but was caught by one leg by Tom Crean, our Irish giant.
>
> The man was screaming and using the most awful language. He wanted to fight everyone, especially the captain. So the matter ended, which shows the difference between the merchant service and the navy. In the navy, he would have got three months; here it was looked upon as nothing. I am afraid there is too much liquor about the ship altogether; it does not occur on the 'lower deck' only.

A week later, Orde-Lees recorded another complaint:

> Last night [27 September, a Sunday] we had a drinking concert and it seems as if there is about to be another tonight. I dare say it is a bit priggish of me, but I do wish the liquor did not run quite so free…it will be all right when Sir Ernest comes, as he is a teetotaller and will soon put his foot down on it…really the only recognition of Sundays on board seems to be that no-one plays cards.

He also regretted that a good proportion of the 'dainties', such as asparagus, petits pois and lobster, were consumed early in the voyage.

Alfred Lansing, in his book, *Endurance: Shackleton's Incredible Voyage*, wrote this assessment of the New Zealand skipper:

> Temperamentally, Shackleton and Worsley had some of the same characteristics. Both were energetic, imaginative, romantic men who thirsted for adventure. But while Shackleton's nature drove him always to be the leader, Worsley had no such inclination. He was fundamentally light-hearted, given to bursts of excitement and unpredictable enthusiasms. The mantle of leadership…did not rest too comfortably on his shoulders. He felt it was his duty to play the part of commander, but he was woefully out of place in the role.

The difficulties that Worsley and his crew experienced in getting to Buenos Aires were ignored in Shackleton's *South*, but Orde-Lees recorded them in his diary. The main problem was the shortage of coal a week out from the port. Without coal as a ballast, the vessel behaved badly in high winds, and little progress could be made under sail. Worsley had to steam against unhelpful winds and finally all the coal was gone two days out from Buenos Aires. 'There was nothing for it but to start burning all the available wood on board,' Orde-Lees wrote. 'It is a race against time to keep the fire supplied. We are making for Montevideo for all we are worth…we shall get 10 tons of coal and go on to Buenos Aires about 100 miles further on. We have just burnt our spare spars and mast…'

The *Endurance* reached Montevideo on 8 October, and to be certain of reaching

Buenos Aires without further trouble, Worsley took on 20 tons of coal.

Shackleton did apply a firm hand when he reached the ship at Buenos Aires in October. The reports he received doubtless prompted the comment in a letter to his wife Emily, 'I do not trust Worsley enough to be sure he would get to the station next season to bring out the remainder of the shore party.' And to Ernest Perris of the *Daily Chronicle*, with whom he kept in regular contact, he wrote that Worsley had 'a rather curious, tactless nature'.

With crew problems resolved – Shackleton dismissed the worst of them, which included the cook, and hired replacements – the *Endurance* sailed south, for South Georgia, on 26 October 1914, reaching the desolate South Atlantic island on 5 November and anchoring at the Norwegian whaling station at Grytviken.

Worsley called South Georgia 'a wild and barren land covered by hurricane-swept ice, savage and unfriendly to man', but socially, with the friendly Norwegians, 'we found it quite delightful…hospitality the more striking because it was so ill-matched with the surroundings.' With the Australian photographer, Frank Hurley, and Greenstreet, Worsley also climbed one of the peaks surrounding the whaling station. He made the height 1611 feet (499 metres), giving them a fine panorama, 'a wilderness of jagged, snow-clad peaks dominated by three imposing mountains…I heard that nobody had ever crossed the island.'

Shackleton learned then that the ice-pack was farther north that year than the

On the *Endurance*, Sir Ernest Shackleton's ship for the Imperial Trans-Antarctic Expedition. The photograph shows most of the crew. The two figures in white sweaters in the centre are Shackleton (left) and Worsley (in white cap). Between them is Frank Wild.
Dulwich College, London

Frank Worsley is second from the right, as Sir Ernest Shackleton (left) welcomes Norwegian whalers on board the *Endurance* at South Georgia in November 1914. The whalers warned Shackleton that the ice was unusually far north that year; they doubted the *Endurance* could get through to make a landfall on Antarctica.

Karl Skontorp

whalers working out of Grytviken could remember. The whalers doubted that the *Endurance* could get through the ice in the Weddell Sea to Antarctica and land the shore party.

Worsley took the *Endurance* out of the whaling station on 5 December, and three days later she met the first of the pack-ice, which was easily worked around. But by 11 December, the ice-pack was unavoidably in the path of the ship, 600 miles from the nearest coastline of Antarctica and 1000 miles from Shackleton's designated landing place, Vahsel Bay, from which he would launch his trans-continental party.

The *Endurance* had to work through heavy masses of snow-capped ice to find open water. Worsley said Shackleton would point out to him where the floes had been most smashed up, and Worsley steered the ship for it. 'Great blocks of ice, fantastic shapes of blue, green and white, rose and fell with amazing swiftness and violence on all sides of us.' It seemed impossible that the ship could live through it, but by careful manoeuvring the *Endurance* wove a passage south, covering about 3000 miles as she turned this way, then that.

Worsley enjoyed the excitement of ramming the floes. He wrote:

One never quite knew what would happen. The weakest floe that barred our way was always attacked. Great discrimination and experience were needed; judgment was all-important...the floe, sometimes 3 feet thick, would be approached at our full speed of eight knots. Just before striking the ice, the engines were stopped to save jarring them badly and with the helm amidships the ship's steel-shod cut-water would be made to crash into the ice, cutting out a large V. Then with engines reversed, she would back astern for 100 yards.

A man on the platform slung over the stern closely watched the propellor, which could be badly damaged in contact with the hard ice when revolving. Again the ship would charge full speed ahead, and the engines stopped a second before impact in the V previously made, to enlarge the incision. Another charge, and the ship usually split the floe for several hundred yards ahead, into which she was driven at full speed and hopefully into a patch of open water. Worsley, Wild and Shackleton, with one ship's officer each, maintained three watches while the ship worked through the pack-ice.

The chief surgeon, Alexander Macklin, wrote, 'Each watch had its characteristics. Worsley specialised in ramming and I have a sneaking suspicion that he often went out of his way to find a nice piece of floe at which he could drive at full speed and cut in two; he loved to feel the shock, the riding up, and the sensation as the ice gave and we drove through.'

Macklin noted that 'We had no Worsley thrills in Wild's watch.'

The scientists had to do their share of the work. The carpenter, McNeish, rigged a 6 foot wooden semaphore on the bridge to enable the navigating officer to give whoever was at the wheel the appropriate direction and the exact amount of helm required to avoid collision with solid pieces that might damage the propellor and the rudder.

During one run Worsley set the semaphore showing hard-a-port. Nothing happened. He shouted at the scientist manning the wheel, 'Why in paradise don't you port?' The answer came in indignant tones, 'I am blowing my nose!'

Shackleton in *South* recorded for 7 December, 'The situation became dangerous that night. We pushed into the pack in the hope of reaching open water beyond, and found ourselves after dark in a pool which was growing smaller and smaller.

The *Endurance* enters loose pack ice on the way south into the Weddell Sea. The photographer, Frank Hurley, had rigged a platform on the bowsprit from which he took photographs and cine film. Shackleton called the loose pack 'nature's gigantic jigsaw puzzle'.

The ice was grinding around the ship in the heavy swell…Worsley and I were on deck all night, dodging the pack. At 3am we ran south, taking advantage of some openings that had appeared, but met heavy rafted pack-ice, evidently old…then we steamed north-west and saw open water to the north-east. I put the *Endurance*'s head for the opening, and, steaming at full speed, we got clear.'

Shackleton on 15 December, 'Long leads of open water ran towards the south-west, and the ship smashed at full speed through occasional areas of young ice till brought up with a heavy thud against a section of older flow. Worsley was out on the jib-boom end for a few minutes while Wild was conning the ship, and he came back with a glowing account of the novel sensation. The boom was swinging high and low and from side to side, while the massive bows of the ship smashed through the ice, splitting it across, piling it mass on mass and then shouldering it aside.'

Throughout December, the *Endurance* stop-started her way towards the continent. Worsley took to conning and working her from the crow's nest, finding it much the best place from which to see ahead and work out the course. With solid pack-ice barring the way in early January, Shackleton ordered the ship to be moored to a solid floe. Some enthusiastic footballers played on the floe until about midnight, Worsley, as goalkeeper, distinguishing himself by dropping through a hole in rotten ice while retrieving the ball, and having to be retrieved himself.

On 10 January the first land was sighted, with a lead of open water along the barrier edge. Following the coast to the south-west, the expedition passed the farthest south reached by William Bruce in the *Scotia* in 1902, and new land was being charted. Shackleton named this new land Caird Coast, after Sir James Caird, his main financial backer.

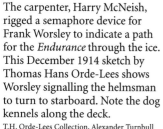

The carpenter, Harry McNeish, rigged a semaphore device for Frank Worsley to indicate a path for the *Endurance* through the ice. This December 1914 sketch by Thomas Hans Orde-Lees shows Worsley signalling the helmsman to turn to starboard. Note the dog kennels along the deck.
T.H. Orde-Lees Collection, Alexander Turnbull Library, No. M-SP00405-04

Shackleton was watching for possible landing places, 'though…I had no intention of landing north of Vahsel Bay, except under pressure of necessity. Every mile gained towards the south meant a mile less sledging when the time came for the overland journey.' Vahsel Bay was named by the German explorer Wilhelm Filchner, after the captain of his ship. In 1910–1912, Filchner reached the farthest south of the Weddell Sea.

On 15 January an excellent landing-place was noted. Shackleton named the place Glacier Bay, 'and had reason later to remember it with regret.' Worsley also recorded the occasion: 'It looked as though it would afford an ideal track to the interior of the continent. Shackleton afterwards regretted that he had not landed here instead of endeavouring to go 100 miles further south. He mentioned this to me next day, but it is easy to be wise after the event.'

A gale swept down on the ship and Shackleton had her shelter in the lee of a stranded iceberg until early on January 18. Worsley took the *Endurance* under sail through a lane, with the engines stopped to prevent damage to the propellor, making 24 miles. Pack-ice again forced the *Endurance* to the north-west until Shackleton decided to lie to for a while to see if the pack would open again with a change of wind.

Next morning, 19 January, at latitude 76° 34' S, longitude 31° 30' W, no progress could be made. The ice had closed around the ship during the night. No water could be seen in any direction from the deck. Next day it was clear that the ship was firmly beset. 'The ice was packed heavily and firmly all round the *Endurance* in every direction as far as the eye could reach from the masthead,' Shackleton recorded.

The ship was about 60 miles from Vahsel Bay, but she would never see land again: this was her first and only voyage. The *Endurance* was in the grip of a force that would not release her. Worsley wrote, 'Strong north-easterly winds drove all the ice in that part of the Weddell Sea down to us, and packed it solidly around the ship. In this manner we drifted off the coast during the remainder of January.'

Worsley said the temperature fell in February to 50° below zero, noting that this was supposed to be the height of summer. The ice-pack consolidated into a solid body around the vessel, and 'we were never able to free the ship sufficiently to navigate her again'.

Later in the month Shackleton made one big effort to move free. All hands were sent on the floe with ice-chisels, saws and picks. Steam was raised ready to drive the *Endurance* through the slightest hint of a path. Shackleton wrote, 'We worked all day and throughout most of the next day…the men cut away the young ice before the bows and pulled it aside with great energy.' But still there was about 400 yards of heavy ice separating the ship from a beckoning lead. 'The task was beyond our powers,' he said.

Shackleton knew that without extracting his ship from the drifting ice-pack that year, there was no hope of crossing Antarctica. Worsley said, 'We all shared his disappointment. But he did not permit himself to display the regret that he felt, or to admit defeat, and talked continually of making another attempt during the following year.'

The *Endurance* tried to force her way through pack ice, using sail, steam and on occasions, man-power. The official photographer, Frank Hurley, took the picture.

By the end of the month, the brief Antarctic summer was officially over; but for Shackleton and his men it had hardly begun. He mused on what might have been: 'If I had guessed a month ago that the ice would grip us here, I would have established our base at one of the landing places at the great glacier [Glacier Bay].'

On 24 February the ship routine was abandoned and the *Endurance* became a winter station, drifting slowly north away from the land. All hands were on duty during the day, and slept at night except for a watchman. Worsley took a party to

Another celebrated Hurley photograph. By now the *Endurance* was beset in the ice, never to get free. Hurley rigged up lamps to illuminate the doomed vessel for this dramatic shot.

T.H.Orde-Lees Collection, Alexander Turnbull Library, No. P-AC2094-028

the floe and started building a line of ice cairns and 'dogloos' around the ship; he may not have had a ship to sail, but the energetic New Zealander was not about to put his feet up and rest. He also took a particular interest in taking soundings of the depth of the ocean, and in dredging up specimens for the biologist, Robert Clark.

Worsley's report, *Biological, Soundings and Magnetic Record, Weddell Sea, 1914–1916*, is a meticulous daily recording of events other than ship's business that occurred on the journey south from South Georgia, and then during the drift around the Weddell Sea. Among the entries are glimpses of Worsley's love of verbal expression and his deep fascination of the life around him. Samples:

26 September 1914, on the way to Buenos Aires: 'A young gentleman from Brazil flew aboard wearing a brilliant red waistcoat, bottom button fashionably undone, red epaulettes and whitey-yellow stripe on either side of his cap. Despite his gorgeous uniform, I believe he was some kind of starling.'

15 January 1915: 'Clark secures a half specimen of an alepidosauridie, allied to the mackerel. It has extraordinarily long sharp jaws and long thin teeth, slightly recurved and a very beautiful silvery colour all over.' Worsley sketched the fish: it looks remarkably like the nose of the Concorde aircraft in flight.

21 February: 'Shot four crab-eater cows. Each cow had a foetus, the first we have found. The cows had no bull with them; blood around the hole they had come up rather pointed to the unfortunate Mr Bull having been assimilated by a killer [whale].'

9 May: 'Of the two kinds of seal we use for food up to this date we infinitely prefer the crab-eater, as it appears to be a much cleaner and healthier animal than the Weddell [seal]. The latter is a very sluggish beast and many that we killed, besides smelling very high, are unhealthy looking and sometimes positively diseased. These last we feed the dogs with; they appear to thrive quite well.'

In the spring, in the northern part of the Weddell Sea, Worsley found that the Weddell seal's condition improved. The crab-eater remained in prime condition.

20 July: 'Killed four penguins and stomachs of three contained small stones and cuttle fish beaks, but were otherwise quite empty. The other had been fishing today as live amphipods were found in its stomach, besides three interesting fishes, one of them unknown to Clark.'

On 29 March, Orde-Lees wrote: 'James, the physicist, had the task of tinkering with the still-developing wireless system of communication. Before leaving South Georgia, arrangements were made for the powerful station at the Falkland Islands to transmit a time signal and a little news on the first of each month. James had established an aerial, but on three occasions no signals had been received.' With assistance from Greenstreet and Hurley, he created a new aerial in preparation for a new attempt on 1 April. It again failed. No wireless contact was ever established.

McNeish converted the interior of the ship into winter quarters as the dreary winter progressed and the *Endurance* gently edged further from land. Shackleton kept a careful eye on the men, looking for signs of distress. He was particularly keen on all hands getting plenty of fresh meat to fight off scurvy, and Worsley was one of those who enthusiastically took part in killing anything that could be attacked. Orde-Lees's diary notes that on one dinner 'menu' there appeared 'Stewed Clubbed Seal à la Worsley'.

The scientists and the sailors occupied the hold cubicles. Worsley, Wild, Marston and Crean lived in cubicles which McNeish established in the ward room, just above the hold, and Shackleton took sole occupancy of Worsley's cabin, which he had been sharing with the captain since the ship left Buenos Aires. When the new sleeping arrangement had been established, all meals were taken in the hold.

Orde-Lees described the ward room accommodation as being divided into four cubicles that 'look like little horse-boxes, so are always alluded to as "The Stables". Marston…has fixed up a sort of opium den settee about 4 feet by $4^1/_2$ feet which really occupies almost the entire available space…he is by no means tall, which is lucky, and so he probably fits diagonally'.

The cubicles in the hold accommodated two men each, though the occupants of two of them – Hurley and Hussey, and Drs Macklin and McIlroy – took down

The *Endurance*'s artist, George Marston, leads the dogs from the ship to the ice-floe for exercise during the period when the *Endurance* was beset. Shackleton is standing on the platform overlooking the gangway. Six teams were formed from the pack of dogs, none of which survived the journey.

their partition to create one large room 12 feet by 7 feet, which, Orde-Lees said, was called 'The Billabong' from the word in 'an amusing song which Hurley often sings'.

Cards were a popular pastime, and Orde-Lees wrote of a poker school comprising Shackleton, Wild, Crean, Dr McIlroy, Worsley and McNeish. For gambling chips, Shackleton dismantled a walking stick made from hundreds of small whale bones threaded on an iron rod, a gift from South Georgia whalers.

Worsley also diverted his shipmates early in the winter when he stripped and ran on to the snow naked and had a brief snow-bath in a temperature of 29° below freezing, probably the first voluntary skinny-dip in Antarctica. Worsley said Crean was particularly shocked, thinking the captain had gone 'wrong in the napper'.

Orde-Lees described a curious sight during testing on 29 and 30 April of the motor-sledge, for which he was responsible. 'Sir Ernest and Captain Worsley accompanied it and it was as much as they could do to keep up with it.' During one breakdown, Shackleton and Worsley danced together on the floe. They performed a one-step while another of the party sang or whistled 'The Policeman's Holiday'. It was, Orde-Lees said, 'most amusing and not a little incongruous to see the great polar explorer thus gyrating on the Antarctic ice. That is Sir Ernest all over though. He is always able to keep his troubles under and show a bold front…'

On 1 May the sun disappeared as midwinter approached. The month passed quietly. Worsley spent a lot of time aloft, taking sightings when he could, always peering into the horizon. Orde-Lees recorded (2 May): 'Captain Worsley has wonderful eyesight. From the masthead he spied a seal about $3^1/_2$ miles away.'

In his diary for 7 June, Orde-Lees made another critical comment about Worsley, recording how the captain was night watchman on the night of 6 June, and 'somehow managed to let the temperature in the cubicles drop to 28deg, so he was not at all popular this morning. He said it was due to the strong south wind blowing down the hatches and so on. We don't think so.'

The drift of the *Endurance* continued quietly through June. McNeish recorded on 8 June: 'We have drifted 12 miles nearer home and the Lord be thanked for that much, as I am about sick of the whole thing.' He noted also that Hurley had been taking some flashlight pictures; the best of these became the most famous photographs ever taken on the ice.

Midwinter came on 22 June, and was celebrated with the best dinner the cook could provide and speeches, songs and toasts. The Antarctic Derby dog-sledge races were held. Worsley was judge, and while Wild's team won the race, he awarded the honours to Hurley's team because Wild failed to weigh in correctly: Shackleton, on Wild's sledge, had fallen off 50 yards short of the winning-post.

In early July the sun started to re-appear and some sounds of pressure on the ship were heard. A huge blizzard swept in and temperatures dropped as low as minus 33.5°F. When the weather cleared, the nature of the surrounding ice-pack had changed. Masses of ice thrown up by pressure could be seen in all directions.

There were distant rumblings, the areas of disturbance approaching the *Endurance*. Shackleton, Worsley and Wild resumed night watches as the ship was shaken by heavy bumps from the pressure wave. Shackleton wrote, 'Our long months of rest and safety seemed to be at an end.'

Next day he ordered stores of sledging provisions and other essentials to be placed handy for any sudden emergency. The pressure would return. The triumvirate of Shackleton, Wild and Worsley met on 13 July in Shackleton's cabin, and the Boss told his skipper that he was going to lose his ship. Outside, the blizzard was still howling as Worsley asked, 'You seriously mean to tell me that the ship is doomed?'

He said Shackleton knew 'far better than I: he had been in the Antarctic ice-fields before. I had not.' Shackleton knew that the party was just at the start of its troubles. 'The ship can't live in this, Skipper,' he said. 'You had better make up your mind that it is only a matter of time…what the ice gets, the ice keeps.'

Worsley recorded that the days and nights which followed 'were the most trying, perhaps, that I have ever lived through… there was nothing that I, the ship's commander, could do to save the ship. I had to stand passively by as she drifted to meet her doom.' The party was by then 400 miles from the Antarctic continent, 1000 miles from South Georgia, in the heart of the Weddell Sea in abysmal conditions with the currents and the winds piling ice up on the land, which threw back more ice on the *Endurance* despite the distance. 'There was no room for it all, and the result was that it got even more closely jammed than usual.'

At their next conference, the three men discussed preparations for what might follow abandoning the ship. 'The men seemed to know that the game was up,' Worsley wrote. The blizzards were never-ending and the ice-floes 'seemed to be fighting each other, hurling against one another and uniting only to use their mighty force to attack the poor little *Endurance*.'

The next scare was on 1 August, when during lunch there was a noise 'as of 1000 guns going off' and the ship was squeezed up and out of the ice, on to her side. 'We slithered on to the wall of the dining saloon,' Worsley said. The ship gradually righted herself, and the rest of August was comparatively uneventful. The next wave of pressure came with September, and all through the month the *Endurance* suffered in the unstable ice.

She began to leak badly. The time came when the crew had to pump continuously for 72 hours without sleep, with the main engine running, in an effort to get her dry. The water gained and a coffer dam was built across her hold to confine the water to the stern. Coal was starting to block the pumps; Worsley led a team into the hold to shift the coal.

It was, he said, the most eerie and nerve-wracking job he had experienced to that time. Freezing water swirled about their legs as they shovelled the coal away, and as the ship lurched wildly, the beams cracking loudly, more coal was hurled on and around them. After many hours, the coal seemed to be secure; the pumps were working again.

Worsley's diary for 26 October reads:

Very heavy pressure with twisting strains racking ship fore and aft, and opening butts of planking 4in and 5in on starboard side; at the same time the stout little ship could be seen bending like a bow and gallantly recovering against titanic pressure. Lowered boats, gear, provisions and sledges on floe. All hands pumping all night.

A strange occurrence was the sudden appearance of eight emperor penguins, at the instant that the heavy pressure came on the ship. They walked a little way towards the ship, then halted and after a few ordinary calls or cries, proceeded to sing what sounded like a dirge for the ship.

Even the sparse wildlife seemed to appreciate that something was dying on the ice. His diary for 27 October:

Pressure throughout day, increasing to terrific force at 4pm, heaving stern up, smashing rudder, rudderpost and sternpost. Decks breaking up. 7pm: Ship too dangerous to live in. We are forced to abandon her. Water over-mastering pumps and coming up to engine fires. Draw fires and let down steam. Men and dogs camp on floe but have to shift camp twice with the floe cracking and smashing underfoot. Get little sleep.

The ship was abandoned just in time. Soon after camping on the ice, the crew heard the crushing and smashing of her beams and timbers. 'Subsequent examination showed that only six cabins aboard had not been pierced by floes and blocks of ice,' Worsley wrote.

With the ship in her death-throes – and cinematographer Hurley busy recording the event for posterity – Shackleton examined the situation. The *Endurance*, trapped for 10 months, had drifted 1300 miles through waters where nobody was believed ever to have been. He said he would lead the men over the pack-ice to land, which Worsley had previously calculated was just over 300 miles away. There should be a hut stocked with stores for just such an emergency. He planned to drag two lifeboats all the way over the rough, broken ice.

It sounded reassuring, but Worsley had other ideas. He thought the boats would be damaged on the journey; and besides, two boats were not enough for the whole party. He suggested camping on the nearest flat iceberg and drifting to open water, where the boats could be launched.

Shackleton, of course, had his way. Two lifeboats were rigged on sledges, all but vital gear was dumped, and on 30 October the march began, the first team trying to find a way through the chaos of ice ridges and pinnacles. Worsley had command of the two boats, with 15 men hauling them in relays. A huge stumbling effort of two hours in the late afternoon achieved an advance of one mile; the next day they travelled another mile. On the third day, Shackleton decided to find a solid floe and camp there until conditions were better before making a second effort to haul themselves out.

They established what became known as Ocean Camp, and moved the third boat up from the previous camp, much to Worsley's relief: there would now be enough room for all 28 men on the boats when they reached open water.

Life on the floe became boring and frustrating as they drifted vaguely north. The men lived in five tents that had to be moved from time to time as the surroundings became squalid and the snow a dirty quagmire.

As December arrived Worsley logged the drift, and to break the developing

Enduring no more. It is November 1915, and the *Endurance* is in her death throes, crushed by the ice. She sank on 21 November after the crew had abandoned her the previous month and waited for the inevitable.

T.H. Orde-Lees Collection, Alexander Turnbull Library, No. P-AC2094-025

ennui Shackleton proposed another sledge march with the boats. As before, the going was appalling and the progress negligible. On Christmas Eve, leads in the ice were opening in the soft summer conditions, and in two days they made no more than three miles.

Next day Shackleton and Wild returned from their morning route survey to find a state of near mutiny involving Worsley and McNeish. The carpenter had decided to stop work, and he refused Worsley's order to resume duties.

McNeish had never liked the idea of hauling the boats over the softening snow. Actually Worsley agreed that it was wasteful labour and possibly damaging to the boats. This was, however, a situation in which an officer's command had been challenged.

McNeish's point was that now the ship had been lost, Ship's Articles, the contract binding the crew, had lapsed; he was no longer obliged to obey the captain's orders. The crew – most of whom also loathed the hauling operation, and some of whom certainly agreed with McNeish – watched with interest. It was Shackleton's move.

The Boss put on a convincing performance with a shaky case, for McNeish may well have been right. However, Shackleton called the crew together and read from Ship's Articles about the duty to obey the lawful commands of the master, whether on board, in boats or on shore. He explained that he was in fact the master, and Worsley was the sailing master. This was not true, but it gave Shackleton the chance to assert his authority from two fronts – as leader of the expedition and as master of the *Endurance*.

His most convincing argument was that because Ship's Articles had not terminated with loss of the ship, in his opinion, neither had wages ceased; thus pay would continue until they reached port, he said in another improvisation. The crew accepted this, and McNeish was on his own. Face to face with Shackleton, in private, he still argued until Shackleton indicated that he would shoot the Scotsman if he continued. That ended the incident.

Sir Ernest Shackleton at first planned to drag his lifeboats 300 miles across the ice to the Antarctic Peninsula. The crew made several attempts, this one recorded by Frank Hurley, but the terrain was too rough. The boat is the *James Caird*. Harry McNeish rebelled and challenged Frank Worsley's authority to order the men to do the work. Shackleton had to intervene and at one stage threatened to shoot McNeish.

Dulwich College

Neither Shackleton nor Worsley mentioned it in their books; McNeish did not enter it in his diary. But Shackleton never forgot what the crotchety carpenter did, recording in his own diary, 'I shall never forget him in this time of strain and stress.' And he didn't. He paid McNeish back when he had the opportunity.

One possible reason for McNeish's bloody-mindedness was the loss of his well-loved cat, Mrs Chippy. The cat was a real character, a creature of substance, very idiosyncratic and a great favourite among the crew. Worsley was a fan of Mrs Chippy (in reality, a male), and he wrote of her: 'She is wonderfully lithe and gracefully active like a miniature tiger. She is full of character and no-one ever knows what she will do next…'

While on the ship Mrs Chippy was protected, safe from the 50-odd sledge dogs chained on the deck. On the ice, however, the savage dogs were in their element, and Mrs Chippy would soon have been torn to pieces. Shackleton deemed it more humane to kill her there and then, and she was shot.

Worsley later wrote that many in the crew 'felt this badly', and McNeish 'shed a bitter tear'.

On 23 December, during a period when the men were trying to sledge the two boats in the march to the west aimed at Paulet Island, Shackleton recorded that the weather for a time was fine and warm, and several men slept out in the open. 'One night however a slight snow-shower came on, succeeded immediately by a

The castaways camped on the ice. Frank Worsley is standing on the platform at the rear. He was responsible for charting their drift around the Weddell Sea. Sir Ernest Shackleton is the figure marked X, under the flags.

T.H. Orde-Lees Collection, Alexander Turnbull Library, No. P-AC2094-041

lowering of the temperature. Worsley, who had hung up his trousers and socks on a boat, found them iced-up and stiff; it was quite a painful process for him to dress quickly that morning.'

The sledging operation continued for only a few more days before Shackleton gave up the labour and decided to settle on a solid floe and wait until the ice broke up. Worsley and McNeish were among those who were pleased with this prudent decision. Worsley was even happier when the third boat was brought up from Ocean Camp. The new site, which was to be home for nearly three and a half months, was named Patience Camp.

Worsley's biology record contained this item for 1 January 1916: 'One sea leopard killed, a savage beast 12 feet long. Her weight is over 1000lb. Teeth are cusped like a crab-eater, but she also has four formidable fangs in the front of her jaws. They attack without provocation, evidently looking on men as on penguins or seals.'

Orde-Lees was the only man in the party who could claim to be an expert skier, and he recorded in his diary (8 January) how he took Worsley out for a run as 'passenger, standing on the back of the skis, moving his legs in unison'. Next day Worsley, who enjoyed the experience, got his own skis and went seal hunting with Orde-Lees. Such outings helped to break the monotony of their lives.

The lifeboats by now had names: the whaler was the *James Caird* and the two cutters were the *Dudley Docker* and the *Stancomb Wills*, all named after prominent supporters of the expedition. McNeish was working on the boats, which had been damaged in the hauling operation as he and Worsley had feared. He raised the freeboard with material salvaged from the *Endurance*, and was coating the seams with seal blood to hold in caulking.

And he was still complaining on 20 January: 'We can't get our sleeping bags dried as they are soaking wet as the heat of our body cause the snow under us to melt.' On 11 February: 'There is nothing for it but get into the sleeping bags and smoke away the hunger…' Next day: 'I smoked myself sick through trying to stifle the hunger this afternoon.'

And 14 March, as the men now knew that soon they would have to take to the boats and try to sail or row to safety: 'Still we have some that don't wish to get in the boats. They want to drift ashore, which we can't do. I notice those are the ones who have never done a day's work in this world and don't intend to as long as they can act the pharasite [sic] on somebody else. They know themselves to be useless and I expect they won't be much more use in a boat.'

Orde-Lees' diary for 20 February: 'Captain Worsley and Blackborrow were sent out to kill penguins…the surface, covered with freshly fallen snow, was terribly cloggy and they had much harder work than they had anticipated to tow home the loaded sledge, especially as Worsley was "took queer" through eating an experimental milk pudding which was the dish for luncheon. They were wet through when they arrived in camp, not through falling in the water but with perspiration, although they were lightly clad. It is quite unusual for anyone to sweat perceptibly here.'

Orde-Lees wrote on 25 February: 'Worsley thinks he can see Mt Haddington, on Ross Island, 114 miles away. We doubt it, but he has wonderful sight. The mountain is about 7000 feet high.' And on 27 March: 'Close to huge berg we call Mt Haddington Berg, because Worsley mistook dome at top for the mountain – though he won't admit it, of course.' By now the party was killing penguins by the hundred. Three hundred Adelies were killed on 23 February, and another 300 on 3 and 4 March.

Orde-Lees recorded another penguin round-up on 31 March, during which half of the flock escaped slaughter 'because of the impetuosity of one or two of the less-experienced hunters'. Worsley led the chase and the birds were finally killed and loaded on a sledge. Then they found to their dismay that what had been a 3 foot gap in the floe had widened to a big lead more than 50 yards wide.

'We found a splendid square slab of hard floating ice and on this Captain Worsley and Greenstreet ferried across, using boards from the sledge as oars,' Orde-Lees said. Shackleton saw their peril and tried to launch a boat to assist, but could not reach the party because of slush, and had to haul the boat back on the ice. Finally Worsley got a rope across the gap, and a sort of pontoon bridge of ice slabs was constructed, over which the hunters crossed to safety with their booty. 'We expected that Sir Ernest would have been extremely vexed about it but strange to say that apart from saying he would send out no more hunting parties, he merely seemed pleased at our safe return,' Orde-Lees said.

Patience Camp had been drifting northwards with the pack-ice to the edge of the Weddell Sea, and the continent was at last sighted, Joinville Island at the northernmost point. But the castaways, five months now drifting in endless monotony, as Worsley expressed it, were still too far away – about 60 miles.

And danger was coming from a new quarter: icebergs. Worsley recorded that two swept in and 'came charging towards us, ploughing through the great masses of pack-ice as though this had been tissue paper'. Shackleton ordered preparations to get out of the way, even if that meant abandoning supplies.

The mountains of ice approached. Shackleton and Worsley stood together watching them. Worsley said, 'He was quite cool, and smoking a cigarette.' Suddenly the current swept the icebergs off that line to remove the threat; but surely there would be more. It was time to launch the boats.

Shackleton had not made up his mind where the boats would head. The crews had to manoeuvre the small boats in and out of leads among charging floes. Shackleton's boat led, followed by Worsley's and then that of the navigating officer, Hubert Hudson. They camped on a small floe for one sleepless night, and finally rowed clear of the world of ice that had gripped them for so long. Shackleton led in the *James Caird*, with Worsley bringing the *Dudley Docker*, followed by the *Stancomb Wills*.

The sailor at last had a boat of sorts under his feet again. Worsley sailed his boat faster than the others, and so went back to assist Hudson, tying the boats together to help him draw clear of the ice.

Worsley recorded 'A wet, cold, rotten night. All hands wet by snow and sleet showers...no sleep and not enough pulling to keep us warm.'

The crews of the boats were:

James Caird: Shackleton, Wild, Clark, Hurley, Hussey, James, Wordie, McNeish, Green, Vincent, McCarthy.

Dudley Docker: Worsley, Greenstreet, Kerr, Orde-Lees, Macklin, Cheetham, Marston, McLeod, Holness.

Stancomb Wills: Hudson, Crean, Rickenson, McIlroy, How, Bakewell, Stephenson, Blackborrow.

The *Endurance* crew breaks free from the ice. In *South*, Sir Ernest Shackleton wrote, 'A big ice-floe resting peacefully ahead caught my eye, and half-an-hour later we had hauled up the boats and pitched camp for the night. It was a fine big blue berg with an attractively solid appearance and from our camp we could get a good view of the surrounding sea.' The expedition's artist, George Marston, painted the scene.

T.H. Orde-Lees Collection, Alexander Turnbull Library, No. P-AC2094-044

The first target in Shackleton's mind, according to Orde-Lees, was the South Shetland Islands. But when Worsley did manage to get a sight, on 12 April, this showed that the little flotilla was as far from land as when it started from the ice; the crews had hoped for something much better, particularly as Worsley's dead-reckoning to that point had been exceptionally accurate. A second sighting confirmed the bad news, and after Shackleton had joined Worsley on the *Dudley Docker* for a conference, the leader abandoned the effort to reach the South Shetlands, and decided to take advantage of the prevailing north-west wind and run for Hope Bay, in Louis Phillippe Land, about 180 miles to the south west.

But the next day (13 April) the wind changed again, and once more it was favourable to make for the South Shetlands. Clarence Island, on the eastern extremity

of the group, was by then about 40 miles away and was sighted at dawn on 14 April.

As it grew lighter, Elephant Island appeared through the mist and another conference suggested that this offered the best choice of all. The reasoning was that the steepness of Clarence Island might preclude a landing there, and with unfriendly winds and/or currents, the small boats might miss it altogether. Elephant Island was no more distant and should the party fail to weather it, Clarence Island would still be under the lee. Making a run at the central point made good sense.

CHAPTER 5

To Elephant Island

About two hours before dawn on the fourth day, with the sea freezing around the boats, the men were shivering so badly they huddled against each other for warmth under the flimsy covering of the tent. They lay on top of a chaotic pile of stores at the bottom of the *Dudley Docker*. Worsley crawled out to survey the morning. The three boats were tied together, and Worsley and Shackleton spoke – or rather shouted – frequently during the day. Shackleton said that as no cooking was possible, the men should eat as much as they wanted to compensate for lack of sleep, warmth and shelter.

'Some are unable to take much advantage of this owing to sea-sickness,' Worsley later wrote. 'I am sorry for these poor beggars…however our amusement is roused by the dismay of one man who is fond of accumulating food, and now gazes impotently at us ravening wolves.'

That man was Orde-Lees, already an unpopular figure through his task of dispensing stores. His performance in the boat, when it came to his turn to row, further divorced him from his fellows. Orde-Lees, according to Alfred Lansing, sometimes had to be shamed into taking his spell with the oars, when he would 'exhibit an ineptitude which won him a speedy relief'. He would keep out of rhythm and 'curses, threats – nothing had any effect on him'.

When unlimited food was available, and Orde-Lees was too sick to partake, the men in the *Dudley Docker* taunted him to make sure he saw them eating, 'in the hope that it would sicken him further'.

Orde-Less recorded (11 April) 'another horror – a large school of killer whales which surrounded us on every side'. He said their blood-curdling blasts came from the darkness alongside the *Dudley Docker*. 'Every now and then we could see their sinister black forms diving like submarines beneath our frail boats. These deadly creatures, more rapacious than sharks, would have made short work of a boat's crew had they chanced to upset us.' It was, he said, 'a miserable spent night, with sea-sickness added to the other horrors for some.'

The three little pitching open boats made some progress during the awful day. The meteorologist, Leonard Hussey, later wrote in his book *South With Shackleton* that he was constantly asked about the temperature. 'When I reported it as being well below freezing, I used to get some pretty rude comments hurled at me.' He said Worsley suffered, as he did, for the faults of their special departments. 'I got black looks when the temperature was low, as though I was responsible for it. Worsley too was hero when he had something good to report in the way of progress; he would even be given small presents, such as a cigarette or a piece of chocolate.'

The conditions were such that if the men faced aft they had the freezing wind directly in their faces; by facing forward, they were stung by the freezing spray breaking over the side. On the *Dudley Docker*, there was only room enough to sit upright. Their clothing was soaked down to their felt boots. To keep their feet from freezing they had to work their toes all the time.

In the *Stancomb Wills*, conditions were worse. She shipped a lot of water. Percy Blackborrow, the young seaman who had stowed away on the *Endurance* in Buenos Aires, was wearing leather boots. After a few hours he lost all feeling in his feet. Hudson, in charge of the boat, had been at the tiller for almost 72 hours. He had severe frostbite in his hands.

Blocks of ice swept on the boats from all directions, and had to be poled off with the oars. The *James Caird*, in spite of the care taken, was holed in the bows. The crew patched her as best they could with sealskin. The sea was so cold that small fish were lying on the surface, trapped in the sea-ice as it froze.

Hussey said, 'All night long we were almost frozen, our beards white with frost and our breath forming clouds of vapour. The temperature fell to four below zero.'

There was ice everywhere but before nightfall on 14 April all the men were thirsting for water. They had left the ice-pack so hurriedly that they took no ice to melt into drinking water. Mouths were dry, lips were swelling and cracking, and it was becoming hard for some to swallow. Worsley said, 'We resorted to chewing some raw seal meat for the sake of the blood. This assuaged our thirst for the time being, but afterwards it became more acute than ever. To be unable to take our food was a serious matter, for the cold was intense.' Shackleton ordered that the salty seal meat should be served only at stated times, or when thirst seemed to threaten the reason of any individual.

In the *Dudley Docker*, Greenstreet's feet were found to be badly frost-bitten. It was the rather despised Orde-Lees who acted to save him, in a gesture of charity that few could have imagined. He massaged Greenstreet's feet for a long time; then he opened his shirt in the freezing temperature and placed Greenstreet's feet, two cold blocks of freezing flesh, against the warmth of his body, and rubbed life back into them, Greenstreet finally reporting pain in his limbs as the blood began to circulate.

The boats were all thick with ice. The *Stancomb Wills*, her eight men linked with the *James Caird* by a single line, had ice forming in masses around her bows, even as she dipped into each sea. The weight was so great men had to go forward regularly to chip the ice away. And so the awful night passed. When it came to freeing the boats, the line could not be untied: it had to be chopped with an axe.

Shackleton wrote, 'In the full daylight Elephant Island showed cold and severe to the north-north-west. The island was on the bearings that Worsley had laid down, and I congratulated him on the accuracy of his navigation under difficult circumstances, with two days' dead reckoning and after drifting during two nights at the mercy of wind and waves.' Worsley said of the sighting of Elephant and Clarence Islands, 'We were enormously cheered' and he recorded proudly, 'They are both exactly on the bearing I had said they would be.'

The *Stancomb Wills* came up to the *James Caird* and Shackleton was told that Blackborrow's feet were now very badly frost-bitten. Shackleton was keen to move, to try to make a landing that day, but there were problems. All the men were exhausted. The *Dudley Docker* and the *Stancomb Wills* were iced up, inside and out; it took more than an hour to chip the ice away. Oars were frozen to the sides of the boats and had to be broken free. The boats finally got under way at 7am, and were moved by both sails and oars for Elephant Island, about 30 miles away.

Hussey wrote, 'With the help of a gentle breeze we made slow but sure progress. Gradually Elephant Island drew nearer. We all took our turn at the oars, even though some of us now had not slept for 80 hours. During the afternoon a heavy sea was running, and after dark the wind increased to a gale. This meant another terrible night.'

All that day Worsley had towed the other boats alternately, but when the weight of the wind increased, Shackleton in the *James Caird* took over towing the *Stancomb Wills.*

Worsley wrote, 'We soon realised that we were not going to touch land that night. Driving snow-squalls and treacherous, lumpy seas – far more dangerous to our small deep-laden open boats than a big true sea, with large regular swells which they could ride – bombarded us all night from various directions, one following the other, so that the boats could never settle down. To steer became a work of art.'

The gale blew so hard the boats were separated. 'The last we saw of the other two was shortly after midnight, when Shackleton shone his compass light on the *James Caird*'s sail, to which I replied by lighting our compass candle.'

Shackleton never saw the reply from Worsley, and he recorded that the separation 'caused me some anxiety during the remaining hours of the night…I could not feel sure that all was well with the missing boat. Under such conditions, in an open boat, disaster might overtake the most experienced navigator.'

Worsley's boat had got into a bad rip-tide which, combined with the heavy sea, made it almost impossible to prevent swamping. The *Dudley Docker* shipped several bad seas over the stern. Worsley lowered the sail and unstepped the mast. He ordered all hands to row, including Orde-Lees, who cried off and sat in the bottom of the boat, according to Lansing.

With the others at the limit of their capacity to row further, Worsley risked hoisting sail again, swinging the boat into the teeth of the wind. It was a delicate position, and it took all his experience to hold the *Dudley Docker* there. She became sluggish under the weight of water shipped, and Orde-Lees, suddenly realising that the boat was sinking, grabbed a pot and began to bail. He kept at it for hour after hour, and Worsley later warmly credited the enigmatic soldier, rotten oarsman though he undoubtedly was, with stopping them from foundering.

All night Worsley fought the gale. 'I had been steering unrelieved for 18 hours. The air was so thick with snow and spindrift that although we were close to land we could see nothing of it,' he said. Continuous peering to windward, watching for seas that might swamp the boat to strike, gave him a cold in the eyes. 'I could not longer see properly and was constantly falling momentarily asleep at the tiller.'

Greenstreet relieved him, and Worsley had to be pulled amidships and straightened out like a jack-knife, the men rubbing his thighs, groin and stomach to restore some circulation. Worsley promptly fell asleep.

Lansing wrote that Worsley's performance through the five-and-a-half-day ordeal put him in a new light to his companions. He had exhibited 'almost phenomenal ability, both as a navigator and in the demanding skill of handling a small boat. There wasn't another man in the party even comparable with him, and he had assumed a new stature because of it.'

Land was sighted an hour later and Greenstreet did not know which way to steer. He told the men to waken Worsley, 'but their most strenuous efforts failed'. One crewman was afraid he was dead, and urged Macklin to examine Worsley, which the doctor did, pronouncing him alive. Thomas McLeod, a fireman on the *Endurance*, knew what to do: he woke Worsley by giving him a couple of hearty kicks on the back of the head.

Worsley wrote that he never knew how he had been awakened until Macklin told him when they were serving in North Russia with the army years later.

Of the night before landing on Elephant Island, Shackleton wrote: 'It was a stern night…but the land looming ahead was a beacon of safety.' Also in *South* is this quote from Worsley: 'In the height of the gale that night Cheetham was buying matches from me for bottles of champagne, one bottle per match (too cheap; I should have charged him two bottles). The champagne is to be paid when he opens his pub in Hull and I am able to call that way…'

Ahead of the *Dudley Docker*, out of sight, the other boats were approaching Elephant Island. Shackleton, by good fortune, had avoided the following sea that so threatened Worsley's boat through the night. By 7am his two boats were under the cliffs of Elephant Island. The crews grabbed pieces of ice that had fallen and sucked them eagerly.

Two hours later, at the north-west end of the island, Shackleton spotted a narrow beach and decided to risk landing there. 'Two days and nights without drink or hot food had played havoc with most of the men, and we could not assume that any safer haven lay within our reach,' he wrote.

Shackleton called the *Stancomb Wills* alongside, intending to take her to the beach first. As he climbed on board, the *Dudley Docker* was sighted coming up astern under sail. 'The sight took a great load off my mind,' he recorded.

Shackleton decided that Blackborrow, as youngest member of the expedition, should have the honour of making the first-ever landing on Elephant Island. He told the young man to jump ashore, and 'to avoid delay, I helped him, perhaps a little roughly, over the side of the boat'. Blackborrow promptly sat down in the surf, not moving: Shackleton had forgotten that both his feet were badly frostbitten. Others jumped out to pull him to a dry place. Shackleton remarked, 'He is now able to say he was the first man to sit on Elephant Island.' Blackborrow later lost his toes in the first and only medical operation performed on Elephant Island.

With all three boats aground, Shackleton recorded a curious spectacle. Some of the men were reeling about the beach as if drunk. They were laughing loudly,

The three lifeboats at the first landing on Elephant Island. They are the *Stancomb Wills* (foreground), the *Dudley Docker* and the *James Caird*, around which the men are gathered. This landfall was soon abandoned after tide marks were found at the base of the cliffs.

T.H. Orde-Lees Collection, Alexander Turnbull Library, No. P-AC2094-050

picking up stones and dribbling pebbles through their fingers 'like misers gloating over hoarded gold'. Smiles and laughter caused cracked lips to bleed.

Two seals on the beach were killed and the cook soon had hot drinks and seal steaks ready. Hussey said, 'We ate to capacity and were also able now to drink as much water as we wished. It was a wonderful time.' Shackleton, who had not slept for 100 hours, 'must have felt particularly relieved in knowing that he had brought every single member of the expedition safely through. This was a tremendous achievement.'

By 3pm a camp had been prepared and and most of them men crept into their sleeping bags, and apart from a turn at watch, slept around the clock.

While they rested Shackleton, with Wild, Worsley and Hurley, inspected the beach and found to their distress clear signs that in a gale, waves would break against the sheer sides of the rocky wall behind them at high tide. The cliffs behind the beach were inaccessible; their safe haven could be a death-trap.

Early next morning, 16 April, the sun shone brightly and wet gear was set out to dry. Shackleton sent Wild along the coast in the *Stancomb Wills* to find a new campsite. It had to be a place where the party could live for weeks – even months – in safety. Wild returned after dark, reporting a sandy spit seven miles to the west, the only possible site he had seen. The weather was good, and Shackleton was keen to move early next day. Another seal was killed and fresh meat was on the supper menu. Spirits were high.

Conditions were still fine early next day, but a change seemed to be bearing

Frank Worsley's boat, the *Dudley Docker*, reaches the second landfall on Elephant Island. Sir Ernest Shackleton wrote in *South:*, 'I was very anxious about the *Dudley Docker*, and my eyes as well as my thoughts were turned eastward… within half-an-hour the missing boat appeared labouring through the spume-white sea.'

T.H. Orde-Lees Collection, Alexander Turnbull Library, No. P-AC2094-048

down from the south. Some of the men, after the terrible experiences they had so recently survived, were reluctant to move back on to the water. Shackleton rushed them through breakfast, loaded the boats floating in the shallows, and by 11am they were away. Within half an hour the southerly gale struck and the boat crews were straining at the oars to keep off the rocks.

The boats had to keep close inshore to avoid the raging seas. It was impossible to hoist sails: they had to row and row, and two of the boats were short of oars, several having been broken in the loading of the boats when the oars were used as rollers.

After two hours, when the boats were about halfway to the new site, they came to a tall rock a quarter of a mile offshore. The *James Caird* and the *Stancomb Wills* rowed inside the rock; Worsley, in the *Dudley Docker*, went outside it. It was a bad decision soon appreciated as the boat was caught by the full force of the wind.

He swung his boat around and urged his three rowers to put their backs into it. The oarsmen could barely hold their own against the wind. Worsley gave Greenstreet the tiller, grabbed an oar and, being fresh, set a tremendous pace, according to Lansing. The other two men on the oars matched his cadence and foot by foot they won their way back to the rock, nearly being wrecked on it.

The other two boats were already at the new site, with a fire going and seals being cooked, when the *Dudley Docker* appeared through the mist in mid-afternoon. One last blast from the storm threatened the boat. Worsley again took to rowing, and the boat was beached.

Macklin wrote of his new home: 'A more inhospitable place could scarcely be imagined.' Worsley was sufficiently alert to record 'countess cape pigeons flying in and out of dwellings in the towering cliffs above'.

That night, in a snow-storm, the men had to turn out to move the tents. Two bags of stores were lost in the surf, and the biggest tent was blown to pieces. The blizzard continued through the day and into the next. Better shelter had to be provided, and the *Dudley Docker* was turned upside down for protection for the men from the destroyed tent. It was also the basis of the hut that was constructed by using both the *Dudley Docker* and the *Stancomb Wills* in tandem for a more permanent hut.

The men gave the site a name, after its discoverer: it became Cape Wild, or sometimes Cape Bloody Wild.

Cape Wild was about seven miles to the west of Cape Valentine, the first landfall. Cape Wild was a sandy spit about 200 yards long running out at right angles to the coast and ending at the seaward end in a mass of rock, 'by no means an ideal camping-ground,' commented Shackleton, 'but some of the larger rocks provided a measure of shelter from the wind…' A snow-slope joined the spit at the shore end. Wild believed it was the only possible camping site.

CHAPTER 6

The Boat Crew

Shackleton knew that a party would have to leave Elephant Island and seek rescue: the island was uninhabited, inhospitable, and, more importantly, unlikely to be touched even by adventurous whalers who could well be in dire straits themselves. There was almost no chance of being saved by doing nothing: nobody in the world knew whether Shackleton and his men were alive, and where they could be found. The Great War was well into its second year: who would be looking for the men Winston Churchill later derisively referred to as 'those penguins'?

To fail to make an effort to save themselves meant slow starvation on a bleak and icy piece of rock.

The mental, as well as the physical, condition of some of the party had deteriorated badly, though the extent of this tends to be glossed over in books written by those involved. Leonard Tripp, in Wellington, New Zealand, a lawyer who became a trusted confidant of Shackleton, however, learned much of this in conversation with Shackleton and Worsley years later, and recorded some of the information.

In a letter to a British MP friend, R. J. S. Neville – they had been at Cambridge together – when Tripp was seeking a British Government grant to assist Shackleton's rescue of the *Aurora* crew in 1917, he mentioned a conversation in which Worsley had spoken of the 'terrible time' Shackleton had endured in getting to Elephant Island. 'Some of the men were mentally affected and did not want to save themselves,' Tripp wrote. 'Shackleton forced them to save themselves.'

And in another letter, to Hugh Robert Mill for his book on the life of Shackleton, Tripp wrote: 'He has not mentioned in his book – and it cannot be mentioned – but on the ice in the Weddell Sea the men were not normal; some of them wanted to commit suicide and he had to force them to live.'

After a very short time on Elephant Island the only questions to be answered were the direction the small-boat party would take in a desperate attempt to effect a rescue, and the make-up of the boat crew.

Compared with the ordeal the full party had just survived – bare existence on a floating iceblock drifting the most inhospitable sea on Earth, followed by a brief but terrifying journey in small open boats – Elephant Island at least offered a stable position. Shelter of a sort was available from the barren and ugly land mass, and refinements to this would come from wise use of the two boats to be left behind. The island was known to be attractive to sea-elephants, though there was none to be seen when the party arrived, and there was the hope of plenty of seals and penguins for fresh meat and fuel. With winter near, Shackleton noted, however, that the animals seemed to have deserted the beach, and he could not count on supplies of fresh meat and blubber. Meat from game was essential to supplement the dwindling supply of other rations; blubber from slain animals, and seal skins were essential for fire and, to some extent, light. Without fresh meat, death through scurvy was inevitable.

The decision therefore seemed to rest on the state of other rations, and examination of the stores showed full rations available for the whole party for only five weeks. Worsley wrote: 'Food, insufficient for 28 men, might still nourish 22.' The boat journey to seek help was obviously necessary and something that could not be delayed.

Worsley noted the possibility of fatal shortages of food if seals and penguins failed to land from pack-ice or the sea, or abandoned the rookery 'where such a dangerous neighbour as man had suddenly settled'.

Shackleton, while making up his own mind about this, turned to his two lieutenants, Wild and Worsley, for support. The news came as no surprise to anyone: the subject had been openly discussed during the previous weeks, when the planned dash to Elephant Island was becoming the only sensible next move.

Worsley recorded the occasion: 'The day dawned when Shackleton had to face the fact that he would not be able to feed his men through the winter…he asked me to walk with him to our usual look-out promontory and there he confided to me his ever-growing anxiety. 'Skipper,' he said, 'we shall have to make that boat journey, however risky it is. I'm not going to let the men starve.'

Worsley hoped that Shackleton would stay ashore in command of the main party, seeing this as the most responsible action, having in mind the authority that Shackleton exercised. Worsley asked, 'Will you let me take the boat?'

But Shackleton refused. 'That's my job,' he said. Worsley argued. He pointed out his broad experience in small boats and surf landings, and dared to suggest that in this regard at least he was better equipped than his leader.

Worsley wrote: 'He stopped me by clapping me on the shoulder and saying, "Don't worry Skipper, you'll be with me anyway".' He added that 'it was certain that a man of such heroic mould and self-sacrificing nature as Shackleton would take this most dangerous and difficult task himself. He was in fact unable by nature to do otherwise. Being a born leader, he had to lead in the position of most danger, difficulty and responsibility: he had to be in the forefront.'

The decision to delegate a huge area of responsibility – that of minding the lives of the 22 men to be left behind – weighed heavily on Shackleton, who at the best of times found delegation difficult. As always, he was thinking ahead when he confided to Worsley, 'It's hateful to have to tell the men that we've got to leave them. If things went wrong it might be said that I had abandoned them.' And Worsley said Shackleton was not reassured to be told, 'Nobody who knew you would ever say or think that.'

Before the *Endurance* was crushed and sunk, Worsley had worked out the courses and distances from the South Orkneys to South Georgia, and from Elephant Island to Cape Horn, to the Falklands and to South Georgia. The great westerly system of winds that might take a lifeboat as far as South Georgia, 800 miles away, seemed to offer a better chance than trying to beat against the prevailing north-westerlies in a frail and weakened boat to the nearest port, which was Port Stanley in the Falklands, only 540 miles away.

'It was not difficult to decide that South Georgia must be the objective,' wrote Shackleton.

When it came to selecting the boat party, Shackleton said that while he decided to call for volunteers for the five to accompany him, 'as a matter of fact I pretty well knew which of the people I would select.' The first of these was Worsley, 'for I had a very high opinion of his accuracy and quickness as a navigator, and especially in the snapping and working out of positions in difficult circumstances.' He added that this opinion 'was only enhanced during the actual journey', the only time in his book *South* that he acknowledged Worsley's remarkable skills.

Wild was the only other man Shackleton could trust to hold the Elephant Island party together for what he hoped would be no more than a month, perhaps six weeks. He told his second-in-command that if the rescue mission had not succeeded by the spring, he should try to reach Deception Island, to the south off the coast of the Antarctic Peninsula, where there had once been a whaling station.

He should use the two small boats left behind, though everyone knew that these would barely be large enough for 22 men, and one had to be partially gutted to strengthen the *James Caird*, the lifeboat Shackleton chose for the journey. It was distressingly obvious that the South Georgia rescue mission was the only realistic chance of survival.

There are several accounts of how Shackleton chose the other four men for the dash to South Georgia. Worsley wrote that immediately after Shackleton told the men of his decision, and the 'forlorn hope' that the small boat journey offered, 'every man volunteered'. This is a somewhat glamorous version. Orde-Lees, the Royal Marines officer and the expedition's motor expert, certainly had no desire to step into a small boat again. 'I decided to excuse myself,' he wrote. And there were others, though the majority certainly did volunteer.

In *South*, Shackleton said he chose Second Officer Tom Crean, who 'begged so hard to be allowed to come in the boat that, after consultation with Wild, I promised to take him'. In fact, Shackleton had earmarked the Antarctic veteran Crean to stay on Elephant Island as right-hand man for Wild. Huntford says in his biography of Shackleton that he took Crean 'perhaps also because he was Irish too', a reason he gives also for the selection of Timothy McCarthy, a seaman.

Lansing wrote that, while Crean was a tough and seasoned sailor who did what he was told,' Shackleton was not sure that Crean's rough, tactless nature would lend itself well to a period of enforced and perhaps long waiting.'

McCarthy was perhaps the most popular man in the crew, known to be cheerful, helpful and never likely to cause trouble. Lansing says Shackleton picked him simply because he was an experienced seaman and built like a bull.

McNeish the carpenter, an experienced Antarctic sailor and the oldest man in the party, was a whole-hearted volunteer. The *James Caird* needed a lot of work, and McNeish had the skills to make the small boat as sound as any man could in the circumstances. McNeish had serious doubts that the crew left on Elephant Island would live to tell the tale. In his diary (20 April) he wrote: 'I don't think there will be many survivors if they have to put in a winter here.' The small-boat crew would obviously have a huge task ahead, but he preferred to take his chances on the sea.

When Shackleton outlined what he needed for the *James Caird*, the carpenter cannily first asked if he was to be part of the crew. The stage was set for another drama like that on the ice, when McNeish had challenged Worsley's authority to order the crew to drag sledges over the ice-floes. But it never developed because Shackleton really wanted the Scot on board for several reasons: McNeish 'had a good knowledge of sailing boats and was very quick', and given his skills as a carpenter, and the danger of having a wooden craft holed by ice, it was sensible to have a man of his ability on hand.

Perhaps more important was the desire to make Wild's task as easy as possible: the cantankerous McNeish had shown signs of mutiny once, and, drawn by the strain of bare existence on the island, might crack again. McNeish was one of several in the crew who keenly felt the loss of alcohol and tobacco.

Shackleton recorded that McNeish 'seemed quite pleased when I said "yes".'

The sixth man, John Vincent, started the expedition as bosun, but he had lost his seniority for bullying. He was, however, young and strong, and a good sailor, showing his best qualities at sea and his worst while ashore. Taking Vincent with him also meant that Shackleton was further helping Wild by removing another potential troublemaker.

There were several who felt that the *James Caird* was too flimsy to survive the worst ocean in the world, and one of them, the official photographer Frank Hurley, who packed some of his precious photographic plates for Worsley to carry on the journey, thought about the survival and ultimate exploitation of the remaining plates, should the *James Caird* rescue fail and by some miracle, the men on Elephant Island be saved in some other way. He persuaded Shackleton to sign a letter in Hurley's diary, witnessed by John Vincent. Dated 21 April 1916, it read:

> To whom this may concern viz, my executors assigns etc. Under is my signature to the following instructions. In the event of my not surviving the boat journey to South Georgia I here instruct Frank Hurley to take complete charge and responsibility for exploitation of all films and photographic reproduction of all films and negatives taken on this expedition, the aforesaid films and negatives to become the property of Frank Hurley after due exploitation, in which the moneys to be paid to my executors will be according to the contract made at the start of the expedition. The exploitation expires after a lapse of 18 months from date of first public display.
> I bequeath the big binoculars to Frank Hurley.

Shackleton wrote one more letter. It touched on the future publication of his book. This was in his own log, in his final official instructions to Frank Wild:

April 23 1916, Elephant Island

Dear Sir,

In the event of my not surviving the boat journey to South Georgia you will do your best for the rescue of the party. You are in full command from the time the boat leaves this island, and all hands are under your orders. On your return to England you are to communicate with the Committee. I wish you, Lees and Hurley to write the book. You watch my interests. In another letter you will find the terms as agreed you to do England Great Britain and Continent. Hurley the USA. I have every confidence in you and always have had. May God prosper your work and your life. You can convey my love to my people and say I tried my best.

yours sincerely

E H Shackleton.

CHAPTER 7

Preparing the Boat

The *Endurance* came from Norwegian builders, and was constructed specially for work in the ice. When Shackleton bought her and she was delivered to London, she had two ship's boats. Shackleton wanted more. Worsley had another boat constructed to his orders at a Thames boatyard near where the *Endurance* was berthed in Millwall Dock, Isle of Dogs.

In July 1914 Worsley took delivery of this boat. Like the other ship's boats it had no name then but later became the *James Caird*, named in honour of the wealthy Scottish manufacturer Sir James Caird, who had given Shackleton 24,000 pounds at a time when the expedition was faltering for lack of finance.

The *James Caird* was double-ended and carvel-built: she was pointed at bow and stern, and the planks used to build up the sides were butted one on top of the other, with the spaces between caulked with hemp and sealed with pitch. A motorboat, to be the responsibility of Orde-Lees, the designated motor expert, was also purchased. This boat was never used, however, and was left to sink with the *Endurance*.

The two boats that came with the *Endurance* from her builders became the *Dudley Docker* and the *Stancomb Wills*, named after two other supporters of the expedition. They were slightly smaller than the *James Caird*, had square stems, and were clinker-built: their planks overlapped and self-sealed. When in water each plank swelled and compressed against the next plank.

The carpenter, Harry McNeish, directing work on the *James Caird* on Elephant Island. The lifeboat was built in London to Frank Worsley's specifications, and Shackleton chose it as the best of the three boats to attempt the 800 mile journey to South Georgia. McNeish traded off his boat-building skills for a place in the boat. He had already build up the side with two strakes, and he added a makeshift decking.

T.H. Orde-Lees Collection, Alexander Turnbull Library, No. P-AC2094-064

Worsley gave the inside measurements of the *James Caird* as 22 feet 6 inches long with a 6 foot beam. The planking was Baltic pine, the keel and timbers were American elm, and the stem and stem-post were of English oak. She was more lightly constructed than was required by the Board of Trade, and this made her 'springy and buoyant'. As a lifeboat, she had to have metal water tanks fitted.

With McNeish firmly on side, work preparing the *James Caird* for the journey to South Georgia, slightly more than 800 miles to the north-west, progressed well. The accomplished carpenter had already raised the freeboard of all three small boats with wood salvaged from the *Endurance*. It was said of McNeish that he never had to measure timber with anything other than his eye. McNeish raised the gunwale of the *James Caird* by 10 inches (25 centimetres), giving her a depth of 3 feet 7 inches (109 centimetres).

The carpenter constructed a 'flimsy covering' over the forward half of the boat with pieces of board, lids of boxes, sledgerunners 'and other oddments'. There was not enough timber to cover the whole boat, so McNeish completed a framework by dismantling the extra freeboard on the *Dudley Docker*. All that could be done now was to sew pieces of old canvas together and nail this to the decking. The canvas, which was frozen stiff, had to be thawed first and stitched slowly and painfully with frostbitten and bleeding fingers using a needle that had to be pulled through with a pair of pincers. Shackleton said, 'It bore a strong likeness to stage scenery.' A pump was contrived from part of the ship's compass.

All who could contribute did so: to ensure the *James Caird* was as watertight as possible, the seams were caulked with an improvised putty of cotton lamp wick and the artist George Marston's oil paints, finished off with smears of seal blood. 'Probably the first time in history that an artist's colours were used for "paying" a boat's seams,' said Worsley.

But the real hero of the preparation was McNeish, who worked on through ferocious weather, until a blizzard proved too severe even for him. The prospect of getting off the island was the spur: he had no confidence that any left behind would survive.

They all recognised the danger of the huge seas of the Southern Ocean 'bending' the *James Caird* and breaking her back, so McNeish took the mast from the smaller *Stancomb Wills* and secured it as best he could inside and along the keel to increase strength. The *Stancomb Wills* sail was also cut down to make an extra sail for the larger boat. Worsley listed the rigging: 'Her sails were jib, standing lug and a small mizzen.' McNeish's work gave the *James Caird* final external measurements of 23 feet 6 inches, a beam of 7 feet 3 inches and a depth of 4 feet 7 inches.

All that remained before loading the *James Caird* was to ballast her. The water tanks were removed, and at Shackleton's insistence ballast of more than a ton was loaded, some as shingle and the rest stones. Worsley disagreed with him over the weight of ballast required, but Shackleton had his way. Old blankets were sewn into bags, into which the shingle, about 100lb to a bag, was put. On top of these bags, loose stones from the beach were placed to make up the weight.

The rescue party loaded enough food for about 30 days. Glacier ice was melted

McNeish's additions to the *James Caird* can be clearly seen. McNeish also took the mast from the *Stancomb Wills* and secured it along the keel for added strength. The picture shows the launching of the *James Caird* for the 800-mile journey to South Georgia.

T.H. Orde-Lees Collection, Alexander Turnbull Library, No. P-AC2094-067

over the blubber stove and two 'breakers' containing 36 gallons of water in all, were filled. Large blocks of glacier ice were also put into both ends of the boat for drinking water. During loading, one of the breakers was dropped in the sea. It seemed unaffected, and was stored without further thought, though this was to have nearly disastrous consequences later. With the six-man crew on board, with all their gear, Worsley estimated the freeboard – height above waterline – at a mere 2 feet 2 inches (66 centimetres).

To even the most optimistic of the desperate castaways, the *James Caird* must have looked flimsy. They still had vivid memories of the nightmare three days from the ice-floe to Elephant Island; how much more dangerous was the long voyage to South Georgia. In *South*, Shackleton recorded his feelings when it was decided to make the rescue attempt: 'The boat had never looked big; she appeared to have shrunk in some mysterious way when I viewed her in the light of our new undertaking.'

Of all the men in the party, Worsley probably had best knowledge of the conditions they would encounter. He had first rounded Cape Horn under sail as a 16-year-old. He knew of the danger of the southern storms, and of island-size icebergs looming in the night on to which any sailboat could be driven by the prevailing wind. In particular, he was aware of constant danger from the tremendous swells that endlessly rotated around the Antarctic Continent, moving west to east.

In his book, *First Voyage*, and in writing about the boat journey, Worsley recorded the ferocity and the majesty of these relentless swells:

They are the offspring of the westerly gales, the great unceasing westerly swell of the Southern Ocean, rolling almost unchecked around this end of the world in the Roaring Forties and the Fierce Fifties. The highest, broadest and longest swells in the world, they roll on in circumnavigation until they reach their birth-place again and so reinforcing themselves and their brethren, they sweep forward in fierce and haughty majesty.

Four hundred, a thousand yards, a mile apart in fine weather, silent and stately, they pass along, rising 40 to 50 feet and more from crest to hollow. They rage in apparent disorder during fierce gales while fast clippers, lofty ships and small craft are tossed on their foaming, snowy brows and are stamped and battered by their ponderous feet; the biggest liners are but playthings for these real Leviathans of the deep with a front of 1000 miles.

Smitten, battered and smothered by them, many a good ship has foundered with all hands, a hencoop, a grating or a lifebuoy tossing along to mark their grave.

At times rolling over their allotted ocean bed two or three miles deep, they meet a shallow of 30 to 100 fathoms. Their bases, checked by these banks, are retarded and their crests are swept up in furious anger at this resistence until their front forms an almost perpendicular wall of green frothing water that smashes on a ship's deck, flattening steel bulwarks, snapping 2in steel stanchions and crushing deck houses and boats like eggshells.

These blue water hills in a very heavy gale move as fast as 27 statute miles an hour, but striking the banks, the madly leaping crests falling over and onward probably attain a momentary speed of 60 miles. The impact of hundreds of tons of solid water at this speed can only be faintly imagined.

In his vivid prose, Worsley told how even when 'combed' by south-westerly squalls, 'they keep, in the main, to their easterly course…they hold mightily on their way, their great crests blown back in long white streamers: the manes of galloping white horses.'

Worsley's task was to plot a course that would enable the *James Caird* to ride these monsters across hundreds of miles to South Georgia. He had to get the navigation right in what he knew would be the worst possible conditions. Any miscalculation and they would sail past South Georgia and into the South Atlantic Ocean, meaning sure death for all 28 men.

Worsley was ready for the challenge. He had Hudson's sextant as well as prismatic compass, charts and chronometers. Above all, he had his great experience as a navigator and a small-boat seaman.

The *James Caird*, re-built and ballasted and with all but last-minute loadings to be stored, was ready. McNeish had a few final checks to make. For Shackleton it was a matter of waiting for a break in the ice.

Monday 24 April 1916 dawned fine. There was a way clear through the ice to open water. McNeish re-checked the boat at daybreak and by 10am he was satisfied. All hands were mustered. A heavy surf came in unexpectedly and the *James Caird* almost capsized as the last stores and crew were ferried out on the *Stancomb Wills*. McNeish and Vincent were tossed overboard. They had to swap some of their soaked garments with dry clothing from the men waiting to see them off.

Then the boat started to fill with water. A point of rock had struck and driven the plug of the boat inwards. Worsley groped around in darkness under the canvas

Frank Worsley steers the *James Caird* from Elephant Island at the start of the great journey to South Georgia. The lives of 22 men left on the island, and the six crew of the lifeboat, depended on his navigational skills.

and could not find it. The *James Caird* was already a third full of water. 'I took a treasured possession – almost the last thing remaining to remind me that I had once been a civilised man: a handkerchief now black with soot and grime – and jammed it in the hole with a marlin spike,' he wrote. 'We then bailed the boat dry.'

Shackleton was the last man to step aboard. He shouted, 'Good-bye boys!' It was just after noon. Worsley wrote of the 'pathetic group' ashore:

> As we drew away from them the forlornness of their appearance as they stood out against the overhanging glacier front flanked with jagged crags of massive black rock was pathetically striking, and I felt that whatever hardships we might be called upon to face, we were the fortunate ones. Inactivity and uncertainty would come harder to men of the type of my shipmates than the unknown adventure that was before us. We had in fact started on the greatest adventure of our career.

CHAPTER 8

The Boat Journey

It was a strange time for Shackleton to confess that he had no expertise in small-boat sailing: he had just begun a journey that if successful, would rank among the greatest of its kind in sailing history, as great as William Bligh's epic journey across the South Pacific after the mutiny on his ship, *Bounty*, in 1789.

Bligh sailed much further – 4000 miles compared with the 800 facing Shackleton – but in much more benign seas, a much kinder climate, and with a crew in far better physical condition. His boat, incidentally, was about the same size as the *James Caird*, and packed 18 men into comparable space. However, Bligh was able to replenish his supply of food and water at one island after four days at sea, again after another 14 days on an island off the northern coast of Queensland, and once more after that resting point, before his final run to Timor to conclude the extraordinary 46-day voyage, on which one life only was lost.

Shackleton would never have admitted his failing in the presence of the *James Caird*'s crew, but he did so to Worsley on the first night out from Elephant Island, when the two of them sat together after Worsley had steered the boat clear of the thick, chaotic line of ice from floes that had broken or melted into disparate shapes and sizes, some chunks much taller than their small craft. The ice created the worst danger to the enterprise on that first day out: there was a high risk of being smashed by a lump being pitched about in the heavy seas. The risk grew so great that Shackleton ordered the sails down, and late in the day the crew rowed the *James Caird* gradually to open water.

Once clear, as night came and the strong westerly wind sent sea after sea over the boat, drenching everything and everyone, Shackleton sent the other four men 'below', which meant to the sleeping area in the bow, potentially the driest part of the boat. Worsley had the rudder yoke lines, and he and Shackleton sat huddled together for warmth, yarning quietly and smoking while they kept watch for stray pieces of ice.

In that moment of confidence, he told Worsley, 'Do you know, I know nothing about boat sailing?' Worsley laughed and replied, 'All right Boss, I do. This is my third boat journey.'

Shackleton was leader of the rescue mission, and he was by no means such a sailing boat tyro as he stated – he had the yoke lines through one of the most terrifying moments of the journey – but he may have been telling Worsley in an oblique way that the New Zealander was the man in charge of the *James Caird*; that the Boss, while accepting his overall responsibility, was looking to the skipper to take them through.

While Worsley had doubts about the wisdom of ballasting the *James Caird* to the degree that Shackleton had demanded, he believed in himself and the crew all had faith in his ability as a boat sailor and as a navigator. Worsley's skills were the factors that gave them and the 22 men left behind on Elephant Island their only chance. The ballast question at worst would no more than vary the degree of discomfort they might experience.

They struck north at first, as Shackleton was anxious to get clear of the ice and its chilling, potentially deadly cold. At that early stage he was still not wholly convinced that South Georgia would be the target. Worsley said Shackleton again discussed with him the possibility of making for Cape Horn, which would reduce the distance by one-third, but Worsley knew that the south-east wind that now favoured them would not last the distance. It had to be South Georgia.

They were blessed with the favourable wind for the first two days and Worsley said the first night was the quietest they were fated to spend on that journey. Already their sleeping bags were sodden, and there was no comfort in the boat, but they seemed to be clear of the ice danger, and soon it would be possible to turn to the east and lay a course for South Georgia, seeking advantage from swells circumnavigating Antarctica, and the prevailing winds which were known to gust to hurricane velocities.

The ordeal proper began when a northerly gale arrived and threatened to drive the *James Caird* back to the ice-pack, 'a virtual death sentence, not only upon

A sketch showing the ballasting of the *James Caird*. The sleeping bags were in the bows. Worsley and Shackleton disagreed on the amount of ballast. Shackleton got his way, but said later that Worsley was probably correct.
Dulwich College

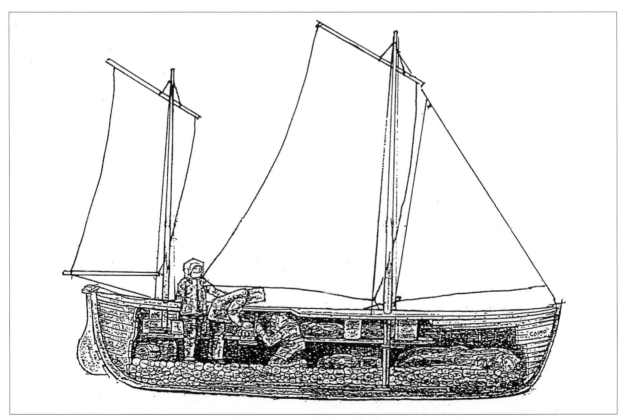

ourselves but upon the waiting men marooned on Elephant Island,' as Worsley said. Shackleton was aware of how close they were to early failure. Worsley recorded that 'between drunken lurches of the boat', Shackleton told him, 'Skipper, if anything happens to me while those fellows are waiting I shall feel like a murderer.'

The northerly, striking after the south-west gale, produced a heavy swell and a dangerous cross-sea that found the weak spots in the boat with water running into the bilges and seas washing over the canvas covering. 'We got wetter and wetter and colder and colder,' Worsley said, 'and gradually began to gauge the magnitude of the task.' By the second night everyone except Worsley and McCarthy had been seasick, 'and even we felt squeamish from the extraordinary switchback leaps of the boat'.

The six men shared duties at the yoke lines of the rudder. The watches, Shackleton with Crean and McNeish, and Worsley with Vincent and McCarthy, were four hours on, four hours off. On duty, one man had the helm, one looked after the sails and the third bailed as necessary. Those off duty sought the comparative shelter of the bows, where the sleeping bags were placed on top of cases of food, and the ballast of sharp angular boulders and bags of shingle in an area 7 feet long and 5 feet wide tapering to nothing.

There was little room between the stores and the canvas cover above, and those going off duty, and those coming on, had to crawl under the thwart as the *James Caird* bucked and pitched. It was an operation that had the potential to shorten tempers to breaking point, so Shackleton took to directing traffic.

Shackleton wrote, 'There was no comfort in the boat. The bags and cases seemed to be alive in the unfailing knack of presenting their most uncomfortable angles to our rest-seeking bodies. A man might imagine for a moment that he had found a position of ease, but always discovered quickly that some unyielding point was impinging on muscle or bone.' The Southern Ocean, he said, 'lived up to its evil winter reputation'.

Worsley said that within the bows, 'our unfortunate bodies were swung up and banged down on mountainous seas as we rushed up hills and plunged down valleys, shivering as we were slung from side to side…to our imagination she seemed to wag like a dog's tail or flap like a flag in a gale.'

But there was consolation in the extra decking and the canvas cover, even though it was by now leaking at every sagging point where it was not nailed to the wooden frame. Without it, they could not have used the Primus cooker and taken hot food and drink. The problems of cooking were soon evident: it took three men, one to hold the lamp and two to guard the pot, which had to be lifted clear every time the boat bucked. Shackleton recorded the laughter caused by a Worsley effort to place the hot aluminium pot back on the Primus after it fell in a heavy roll: 'With his frost-bitten fingers he picked it up, dropped it, picked it up again and toyed with it gingerly as though it were some fragile article of lady's wear.'

It was three days before Worsley the navigator got his first observation. To that point he had worked on dead reckoning, and he expected to be 'very wide of

An impression of Frank Worsley, supported by two of the *James Caird* crew, taking a sun sight. Worsley managed only four sightings in 16 days but was still able to accurately navigate the lifeboat 800 miles to the small island of South Georgia.
Dulwich College

the mark'. He set the course each day at noon, calculating progress made in the previous 24 hours. At night, the helmsman steered by the feel of the wind and the angle at which their small pennant blew at the masthead. The erratic course was confirmed with that first observation, when he knelt on the forepart of the cockpit, propped up by Vincent and McCarthy to stop him going over the side as the *James Caird* pitched and tossed, and he caught the weak sun. Shackleton, protected under the canvas, took the time by the only chronometer left in working order.

The observation said they were 128 miles from Elephant Island and into the dreaded Drake Passage, where they could expect to be attacked by the worst seas imaginable in a boat of any size, let alone one scarcely 23 feet long. However, their position enabled them to turn to the north-east and head for South Georgia, assisted by the prevailing conditions.

Every necessary chore seemed designed to try their patience. Pumping the vessel was a day and night job. 'Hateful', was Worsley's succinct comment. The pump had been made by Hurley from the case of the *Endurance*'s standard compass. It was effective but labour-intensive. Worsley described the operation:

One man with bare hands had to hold the brass tube hard down on the bottom of the boat, while the other man had the less-detestable task of working the handle up and down. A third man (the helmsman) caught in our cooking pot the water thus pumped and emptied it overboard. The man who had to hold the tube, without mittens,

invariably became chilled to the bone by the stream of icy-cold water which came up through the pump, some of which also ran over his hands. To make it a little less difficult, the operators would change places every five or six minutes.

Towards the end of the watch, one man would light the Primus stove and fill the bowl with ice, melting it in preparation for Crean, who was acting as cook, to prepare what Shackleton called 'hoosh', a mixture of beef-protein, lard, oatmeal, sugar and salt, cooked into the consistency of pea soup. This was eaten every four hours in the daytime, as a watch finished. At night, again every four hours, a drink of hot milk was prepared. Sometimes Shackleton would add to the ration with a nougat-type nut piece, or with nourishing biscuits that he had had prepared for his trans-continental sledge trip.

Worsley said the Boss was alert to the condition of all his crew. If he thought this man or that seemed extra cold, or showed uncharacteristic signs, he would immediately produce a hot drink served to all; he would never let the man he was concerned about know that it was on his account. 'It was due solely to Shackleton's care of the men in preparing these hot meals and drinks every four hours day and night, and his general watchfulness in everything concerning the men's comfort, that no-one died during the journey; two of the party at least were very close to death.'

Shackleton said, 'Our meals were regular, in spite of the gales. Attention to this

The *James Caird* crew was sustained by a blend of beef protein, lard, oatmeal, sugar and salt, cooked to the consistency of pea soup. The sketch shows how Frank Worsley and Tom Crean sat with their backs to the boat, balancing the Primus stove between their feet.
Dulwich College

81

point was essential since the conditions of the voyage made increasing calls on our vitality.'

Worsley was the 'scullion' to Crean. They pared the task down to the two of them. To cook the hoosh, they each put their backs against the sides of the boat and jammed the Primus between their extended feet. Worsley held the pot on the stove while Crean broke up and melted lumps of ice, then added the hoosh ingredients which he stirred until it boiled. Worsley held the pot, lifting it when the *James Caird* made her wild leaps, and setting it back cautiously so that none of the contents spilled. Crean would call 'ready' and mugs would be filled swiftly and consumed fast. The first man to finish would relieve at the rudder lines for the helmsman to get his mug while the hoosh was still hot.

On Day 4, a severe south-westerly gale forced them to heave-to. 'The sea was very high and the *James Caird* was in danger of broaching to and swamping…during that afternoon we saw bits of wreckage, the remains probably of some unfortunate vessel that had failed to weather the strong gales south of Cape Horn,' Shackleton wrote. Worsley put out the sea-anchor to help keep the boat's head up to the sea, but they were all conscious of the time being lost. As they were hove-to, the heaviest seas broke over the boat even though it rode the waves. And it did not improve for the fifth day at sea, with the cold becoming so bitter that some of the water froze as it struck the canvas covering.

The conditions were creating a new danger, and it was some time before the crew realised it: a casing of ice was forming on top. Worsley recorded the dilemma:

> Wave after wave broke over us, at first pouring through the slightly turtle-backed canvas and rushing down our necks and backs as usual. We were so accustomed to it we paid little attention: indeed we had come to regard these drenchings as part of our daily existence and had got rather beyond feeling irritation at discomfort; but after we had been there for an hour or two, we noticed that there was a decrease in the violence of the cascades of water pouring in from the top. Soon we were getting only little drops – a change that was perhaps the most agreeable thing that had happened to us…

They were still sitting there, but they were not being drenched. They thought that the ice would melt, as they were now in a warmer latitude. The prospect of a relatively dry night 'appeared…as a glimpse of paradise', said Worsley. Shackleton announced that there would be no night watch and hopefully, all hands would get a good night's sleep.

The six men all seemed to wake at the same time, about five hours later. Worsley said, 'I don't know who woke first but within a few minutes…a feeling of uneasiness seemed to have communicated to every man aboard. Not a word was spoken as we turned out of our sleeping bags and put on our boots, but every one of us had a strange conviction that something was wrong.'

And it was. The movements of the boat were unfamiliar. She laboured as she climbed the rollers, and seemed to lack buoyancy. There was less water among the ballast, yet she seemed heavier. 'There was a palpable and sinister difference in this dragging movement.'

Worsley was pumping aft when Shackleton looked though the gap in the decking and in the darkness, saw that the hull of the *James Caird* was enveloped in a heavy sheet of ice. With this accumulation she was not only top-heavy but also she was settling lower in the water and could either founder or capsize.

'We must get rid of that sharp. It's sinking her,' said Shackleton.

The ordeal of getting the boat free of ice began. Worsley described it thus: 'While one man, standing in the gap in the decking, picked with a knife at the ice breast-high in front of him, another man undertook the hazardous job of cutting a hand-hold and a foot-hold in the ice on top and then, with nothing more to depend on than these slight indentations, crawled up on the slippery mass and, with the boat bucking about all the time, chopped away at the encumbrance.' Ice was even forming inside the boat, with water slopping in the bottom close to freezing.

Four minutes at a time outside was the most any one man could take: contact with the ice had a paralysing effect. But as each man slid back into the boat, another took his place. With hands frostbitten within minutes, it was a miracle that none simply slid over the side to his death; nobody on board could have prevented it.

Once Vincent did slide when the *James Caird* gave one huge lurch, and Worsley said he threw himself forward instinctively to grasp the seaman, but he was beyond reach. 'He managed to grasp the mast just as he was going overboard. In the momentary relief of seeing that Vincent was safe, I felt the blood rush to my head. Furious with him, I yelled at him…I know now why mothers invariably spank lost children upon recovering them.'

Another anxiety was the danger of slicing through the canvas protection with a blow from a knife or axe: this would allow more water to pour into the boat, and would also expose them more to the cruel elements. But after two hours' dangerous work, they felt the boat rising again and riding the seas correctly.

They were all chilled to the marrow; some were shivering badly. Shackleton and Crean put new life into them with hot drinks, and as an insipid dawn highlighted their miserable condition, the Boss had the Primus relit and instigated a smoking, yarning session to ease the tension.

On the afternoon of the same day, the operation had to be repeated. The oars lashed outside the decking were catching the spray and holding up masses of ice; all but two oars, which were taken inside, were thrown overboard. And two of the sleeping bags, so wet for so long that they had become sodden lumps, also went over the side, leaving four bags for six men.

The sleeping bags were described by Worsley as 'wretched bits of sodden wetness, hairy and chill' but two of the men, watching their sleeping bags float away, 'looked as if they had lost the last thing on earth that mattered'.

Worsley recorded that at this time, with the *James Caird* doing her usual 'roll, bowl or pitch: generally all three together', it became impossible to keep his log diary going, so he wrapped it carefully and stowed it in the driest part of the bows. 'Even there it was much damaged by the seas,' he said later. He stowed with the log some photos that Hurley had given him.

That night the gale was still too strong to run before it, so they remained riding to the sea-anchor, but late next morning the *James Caird* rose to one very high sea, was struck by a breaking wave, and did not swing back up into the wind: the sea-anchor had gone, and she rolled badly to starboard and fell into the trough. She could have rolled so violently that she would either have filled and sunk, or foundered under a breaking beam sea. They needed to get some sail up quickly.

Shackleton wrote: 'While the *James Caird* rolled heavily in the trough, we beat the frozen canvas until the bulk of the ice had cracked off it, and then hoisted it. The frozen gear worked protestingly but after a struggle our little craft came up to the wind again and we breathed more freely.' Worsley summed it up: 'A bad day.'

They held the boat up to the gale all day 'enduring as best we could discomforts that amounted to pain', Shackleton said. They were all troubled by frostbite and developed large blisters on fingers and hands. Constant soaking caused legs and feet to swell and turn white. Surface sensitivity was lost. Early next day ice had formed on the deck for a third time, though it was not as bad as previously. But it had to be removed, again at great risk. However, sea and wind conditions were improving, enabling the voyage to South Georgia to be resumed. They all worried about the time lost in weathering the storm.

Now there was, briefly, sunlight, and Worsley got another sight: they had covered 380 miles. The wind freshened and blew hard for three days and early on 3 May Worsley got a third sight – 403 miles out, more than half-way. But Shackleton was recording disturbing signs. 'We still suffered severely from the cold for though the temperature was rising, our vitality was declining owing to shortage of food, exposure, and the necessity of maintaining cramped positions day and night.'

It was now 'absolutely necessary' to prepare hot milk for all hands during the night to sustain life until dawn. Vincent and McNeish were in the worst condition, the younger seaman Vincent even worse than the veteran carpenter. McNeish was suffering badly from exposure; Vincent, according to Shackleton, seemed to have mentally collapsed and 'ceased to be an active member of the crew'. On the tenth night out Worsley could not straighten his body after a spell at the tiller. He was so cramped that he had to be dragged 'below' and massaged until he could unbend himself and crawl into a sleeping bag.

Next night Shackleton was steering when at midnight he noticed a line of clear sky to the south. He called to his watch that the sky was clearing 'and then a moment later I realised that what I had seen was not a rift in the clouds but the white crest of an enormous wave. During 26 years' experience of the ocean in all its moods, I had not encountered a wave so gigantic. It was a mighty upheaval of the ocean, a thing quite apart from the big white-capped seas that had been our tireless enemy for many days'.

Shackleton shouted, 'For God's sake, hold on! It's got us!' One of the freak waves that Worsley knew frequented the high latitudes had indeed caught the *James Caird*, which rose higher and higher until she met the broken crest that flung the little boat forward like a cork in surf. 'We were in a seething chaos of tortured water; but somehow the boat lived through it, half-full of water, sagging to the dead weight and shuddering under the blow,' Shackleton wrote.

Crean and McNeish were on watch with him. Worsley's watch struggled from sleeping bags to join them. They had to lighten the vessel before another wave struck to finish them.

'We bailed with the energy of men fighting for life, flinging water over the sides with every receptacle that came to our hands, and after 10 minutes of uncertainty we felt the boat renew her life beneath us,' Shackleton said. It took two hours to get all the water out; then they had to re-adjust the ballast that had shifted. Crean found his Primus stove, clogged with debris. It took him another half-hour to clean it and they lit it and had some hot milk.

The weather improved next day. Worsley got a glimpse of the sun and his observation showed they were 91 miles from the north-west corner of South Georgia: two more good sailing days, they thought, to the promised land. But something spoiled the mood and added to their torture. The last cask of drinking water was broached and was found to be contaminated with saltwater, doubtless from the accident when the casks were loaded on Elephant Island. Reindeer hair from their disintegrating sleeping bags further contaminated the brackish water, making it difficult, though not dangerous, to drink after being strained through gauze from the medical supplies.

Shackleton now had to deny his suffering crew the essence that should have slaked their thirst, but instead would make it worse: at the same time, all the men had to drink some of the tainted water to relieve their agony He allowed them one-quarter of a pint a day, and had to be firm to 'refuse to allow anyone to anticipate the morrow's allowance, as I was sometimes begged to do'.

On the thirteenth day, Worsley knew they must be close to land. It was essential that he should get observations. The morning was foggy. He could not see the horizon, so he kneeled on the stones on the bottom of the boat and took a rough observation.

At noon, to observe for latitude, he could make out the sun only as a dim blur. He measured the centre 10 times, using a mean of the observations as the sun's altitude. With his tattered, soaked and nearly unreadable navigational books and tables, the pages of which had to be carefully peeled apart, he worked out a position that gave them 68 miles to go.

Worsley said later that the navigation tables had the cover and front and back pages washed away, while the *Nautical Almanac* disintegrated so rapidly before the onslaught of the sea that it was a race to see whether the pages for the month of May would last to South Georgia. They just did: April had vanished completely.

Shackleton's original plan was to run up the east coast of South Georgia to his Norwegian whaling station friends, but the water shortage and the rapidly deteriorating condition of the men suggested that he should not spend more time at sea than was necessary. Only a landing, and soon, on the uninhabited west coast would save their lives.

At 4am on 8 May, with Worsley's watch on duty, Shackleton stayed up to help keep a lookout. By 7am they should have been 12 miles out, but still there was mist around them and no sign of land. Both watches were now alert and looking. Vincent spotted seaweed about 10.30am. At noon McCarthy pointed dead ahead. The fog was nearly gone, and a gloomy cliff with snow was visible about 10 miles away.

Worsley wrote, 'Happily my calculations proved correct…we saw the peaks of South Georgia straight ahead. It looked nearly as uninviting as Elephant Island.' They took the *James Caird* closer, and Worsley made a rough sketch of the contour of the land. It was probably the area of Cape Demidov, about 16 miles from the western tip of the island, which had been their target.

Worsley's navigation, born of four far-from-ideal sightings in 15 days, was close to faultless. Baths, clean clothes, real beds and proper food were the main subjects of conversation. But in the spirit of the whole journey, something had to spoil the occasion.

It came at 2.30pm about three miles off the coast as they admired patches of tussock grass on the steep headlands, the first growing things they had seen in 16 months. Then the deep crashing, rumbling sound of heavy surf reached them. In many directions Worsley saw blind rollers, suggesting shoals and breaking seas, all indications of reefs. He sensed dirty weather ahead, and while he favoured a run to the shelter of King Haakon Sound, Shackleton – ever cautious – gave the order to come about. They headed seaward once more to lay-off until morning in the hope of finding a way through the reefs.

Crean prepared hoosh with water from near the bottom of the contaminated cask; the food was particularly foul and it took an effort to swallow. Worsley said, 'We were painfully thirsty owing to the brackishness of the last few drops of water…unhappily we were to undergo further ordeals before we touched the land.'

It started during the night. The wind was rising every hour. The rain came and then hail. By 11pm the storm reached gale force, and the *James Caird* was slammed about in a cross-sea. The wind shrieked though the night, and by dawn there was a mountainous westerly swell sweeping inland before the gale. 'It was a gale of extraordinary violence,' wrote Worsley. 'None of us had ever seen anything like it…Every few seconds the roaring seas dashed into the boat and sent up spray to thicken the air for 100 feet above us…the wind was blowing us straight on to an iron-bound coast.'

The one defence against cold, wet and exhaustion was denied the six men: they were out of water and could not cook a hot meal. Their tongues were swollen with thirst and their lips were cracked and bleeding. Some tried cold sledging rations but they lacked the saliva to swallow properly. They had to get ashore for water and warmth, but dared not try in the mounting hurricane; rather, they had to fight all the elements and keep out to sea before the little boat was swept into unseen cliffs by the great breakers.

The gale and the sea were winning and the *James Caird* was being swept to disaster, along with the hopes of rescue for 22 men left on the desolate rock of Elephant Island. Worsley wrote: 'I remember my thoughts clearly. I said to myself, What a pity. We have made this great boat journey and nobody will ever know.

We might as well have foundered immediately after leaving Elephant Island. Then I thought how annoying it was that my precious diary, which I had been at such pains to preserve, should be lost too. I don't think that any of us were conscious of actual fear of death. I know that I did have, however, a very disagreeable, cold sort of feeling, quite different from the physical chill that I suffered. It was a sort of mental coldness.'

Huntford, in his book *Shackleton*, says this of Worsley: 'In the crisis, Worsley showed his true stature. It was not only that he displayed no fear: he became possessed of a fierce detachment out of which he was able to apply his knowledge of boats and experience of the sea. A sense of being above the battle was the quality he concealed under the adolescent wildness of himself ashore or on bigger ships.'

Worsley was now in sole charge. The navigator in him had got the *James Caird* to South Georgia; the seaman now had to save the enterprise from disaster. He trimmed the sails to get the boat's maximum capacity to face the wind and beat to sea in spite of the helm. Shackleton took the tiller lines while Worsley and Crean pulled themselves on their stomachs over the decking to the main mast to get the jib off and secure it to the forestay. McCarthy helped with the mainsail and it was made fast and reefed, as well as the mizzen. This work, that would normally take less than 10 minutes, on the *James Caird* that awful morning took an hour. Below, McNeish and Vincent shifted the ballast, piling the boulders on the starboard side.

A virtue of their position was that the boat was by now so low in the water the wind could not push her. They then had to trust that the little sail they dared show would be sufficient to claw the boat out of danger. The impact of the on-rushing seas was like striking a stone wall, Worsley said, and the boat bucked and skewed

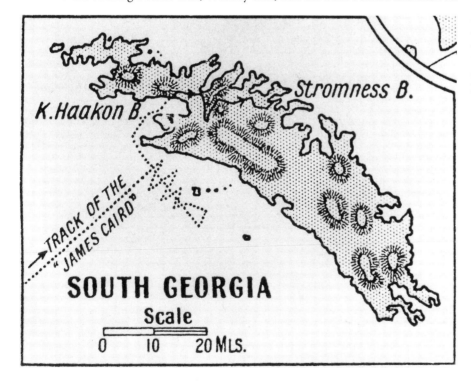

Close-up map of the last stages of the *James Caird* voyage, showing the desperate manoeuvrings of Frank Worsley to keep the boat from being driven ashore in the hurricane.

with bow planks opening and closing to let in squirts of water. Seas crashed over the *James Caird* and soon she was even lower in the water. Three men working the pump were not enough: two others had to bail while the sixth man had the rudder lines.

But slowly the little boat was winning. They were holding their own offshore; now they had to get clear of Annenkov Island. Worsley looked up at black rocks that 'seemed to tower almost above us', and said to Shackleton, 'She'll do it.'

Just after 6pm the *James Caird* was in the backwash of the rocks of Annenkov Island with the surf close when the wind suddenly shifted. Only the man at the helm could actually see what was happening: the others were all below pumping and bailing. One after the other the helmsmen in turn shouted down: 'She'll do it!' And she did. They were safe for another night.

They had fought the hurricane for nine hours, a hurricane so fierce that it sank a 500-ton steamer bound for South Georgia from Buenos Aires, with the loss of all hands.

Early in the morning, Shackleton spoke quietly to Worsley, saying two of the men were weakening. 'We must get water or ice.' Worsley suggested a landing spot six miles to the north, then making for the whaling station on the east coast. Shackleton thought it would be mad to take to sea again and risk being blown to the east of the island. He had already planned to land at the first possible site and, if necessary, walk across the virgin centre of South Georgia.

About noon, a gap in the reef surrounding King Haakon Bay was sighted. But the capricious wind shifted again and blew right out of the bay. Five times the *James Caird* was tacked and as dusk approached a small cove with a boulder-strewn beach was spotted. The entrance was so narrow they could not use the oars, but the swell carried them in and they touched the beach.

Worsley wrote: 'We leapt from her bows and hauled her up.' They found themselves standing in a stream of pure water. While some men held the boat, they took turns drinking the water which, while coming from a swamp and perhaps peaty or muddy, was nectar to them. The date was 10 May 1916.

The boat was bumping heavily on boulders. In the darkness the rudder was torn off and disappeared. The weary crew had to haul the *James Caird* beyond the highest-reaching seas. Exhausted though they were, the six men formed a chain and stripped the boat. The work 'could only be done slowly', Worsley said. 'We had almost lost the use of our limbs through the constant wetting and lack of normal movement due to the confined space in the boat. We had not been able even to sit upright for a meal, so that every muscle was cramped; we were in the condition that one might expect to find in sick or bedridden men.'

Only when the boat had been stripped and made fast to a large boulder did they rest and eat in a small shingle-floored cave. About 2am Crean, on watch, yelled for assistance. A big sea had moved the boulder and threatened to sweep the boat away. Crean was holding the rope, but was losing ground. It took the combined strength of the six men to drag the boat. They spent the rest of a miserable night holding the rope.

In the daylight, refreshed with more hot food, they got the boat above the high-water mark after stripping the topsides to lighten her. The wood was useful for their fire, and at last they could relax and examine their surroundings. The four strongest – Shackleton, Worsley, Crean and McCarthy – climbed above the swamp and found baby albatrosses on nests. They killed three chicks and had what Worsley called 'super chicken broth' that strengthened and nourished them. There were plenty of chicks about, and Worsley also killed a sea elephant, stunning the 7 foot beast with a blow on the nose and then cutting its throat.

Shackleton and his men rested, ate, yarned, mended and dried their clothing and their near-shattered bodies for several days, during which the Boss and Worsley also plotted the next move.

It was agreed that the state of the *James Caird* – even though the lost rudder quite miraculously had drifted back into their grasp – precluded going back to sea for the 150-mile voyage around the coast to the whaling station at Stromness. The only alternative was to walk where no man had ever gone before: they had to traverse the unknown interior of a terrifyingly bleak, storm-lashed and forbidding island of peaks, glaciers and cliffs. Shackleton, Worsley and Crean, three sailors with no mountaineering skills, would attempt to cross what had long been considered impassable.

But they did move the *James Caird*, on 15 May, a sparkling, sunny day, from

Frank Worsley's map showing the landfall on the west coast of South Georgia. To reach the spot marked 'Cove' the *James Caird* had to survive one last ordeal, a screaming hurricane that blew for nine hours, threatening to throw them against cliffs. Worsley's skill kept them at sea until the weather changed and they could pick their landing place. They later moved the boat across King Haakon Bay to a better site, which they called Peggotty Camp.
Dulwich College

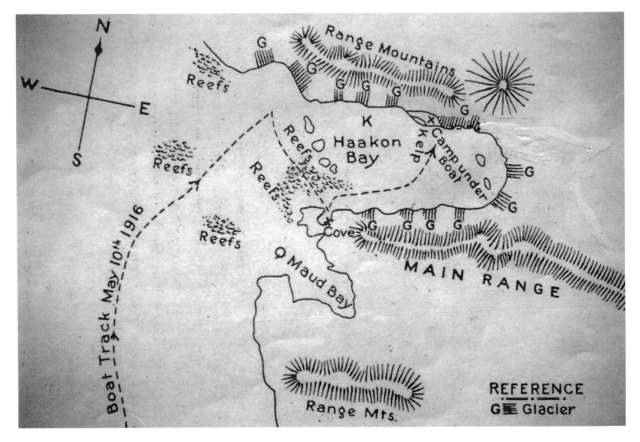

the small cove to the head of the bay, where a more comfortable and secure camp was established by turning the boat on its side and using it as a cabin. They christened the site Peggotty Camp.

Duncan Carse, who in 1956 duplicated the crossing of South Georgia, wrote an appreciation of Worsley's skills in a foreword to the Folio Society edition of Shackleton's Boat Journey:

> In his book *South, the official record*…Shackleton compresses the boat journey into 16 gripping but inadequate pages. It was left to Worsley to shape an account that better matches its subject…Looking for the historic landing beach, I found Worsley's description as good as a map.
>
> Of the boat journey, there are only two eyewitness accounts and neither the Boss nor the Skipper give themselves their due. Without Shackleton's extraordinary nursing of his companions, not all would have lived to see the land. Without Worsley's equally extraordinary navigation, there would have been no land to see.
>
> The landfall, when it came, was spot on…that the skipper could command the triumvirate of sun, horizon and sextant do his bidding with such assurance and precision is for me the most remarkable individual achievement of this remarkable voyage.
>
> I think Frank Worsley's share in the saga of the *James Caird* has been undervalued, never on purpose, but because fewer and fewer seafarers have the knowledge and experience to appreciate how great his contribution must have been.
>
> I think it unlikely that the *James Caird*, minus Worsley, would have foundered; I think it likely that she would have flunked her landfall…

Shackleton and Worsley on 17 May went on a 'pioneer journey' to examine the sort of country they must cover to reach the east coast of South Georgia. Worsley worked out from the chart that the distance on a direct line was 17 miles.

Frank Worsley's map of Cave Cove, the first landfall on South Georgia after the small boat voyage. Worsley did all the maps published in Shackleton's book *South*, but his name (as map-maker) was removed.

Scott Polar Research Institute, No. 1529/9/15

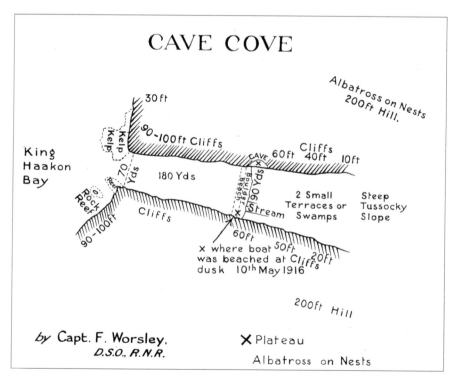

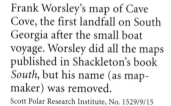

Shackleton had McNeish construct a sledge, and next day, with Crean, they tried to haul it; the task was too great for them, the sledge being too heavy and cumbersome.

They then decided to abandon all heavy gear, including sleeping bags, and travel light, each man carrying his three days' rations. The only other gear would be McNeish's small axe, a 50 foot length of knotted alpine rope, a lamp and a small cooker, and a box of matches. McNeish patched their boots with screws taken from the *James Caird*: these would give the climbers some purchase on ice. Worsley also carried two compasses and the chronometer.

They all turned in early that night, but Shackleton's mind was busy and he did not sleep. He was leaving behind a still-weak party. Vincent had not recovered from his mental lapse and McNeish was 'pretty well broken up'. Only McCarthy had the strength to forage. But still he put the older man, McNeish, in charge, writing in the carpenter's diary a letter which McNeish cherished for the rest of his life. It read:

> May 18, 1916
> South Georgia
> Sir:
> I am about to try to reach Husvik (the closest whaling station in Stromness Bay) on the east coast of this island for relief of our party. I am leaving you in charge of the party consisting of Vincent, McCarthy and yourself. You will remain here until relief arrives. You have ample sea food which you can supplement with birds and fish according to your skill. You are left with a double barrelled gun, 50 cartridges, 40 to 50 Bovril sledging rations, 25 to 30 biscuits, 40 Streimer Nutfood. You also have all the necessary equipment to support life for an indefinite period in the event of my non-return. You had better after winter is over try and sail around to the east coast. The course I am making towards Husvik is east magnetic.
> I trust to have you relieved in a few days.
> yours faithfully,
> E H Shackleton.

Worsley noted that Shackleton, straining to get started, seemed to gain strength and vigour from the challenge ahead. He was excited all that day and talked about how long it would take to get back to Elephant Island. 'He was the old Shackleton again.'

Worsley and Shackleton woke early next morning to look at the weather. At 2am the moon was shining brilliantly. It was fine and clear. Shackleton said, 'We will start now, Skipper.' They woke the others and by 3am they were away, McNeish walking about 200 yards with them. It was the most he could manage.

CHAPTER 9

Over the Island

Shackleton chose wisely when he selected Tom Crean for the boat party. Apart from himself and Worsley, Crean was the only other man available who had demonstrated the level of physical and mental toughness that the little party would need for their arduous journey.

Crean had been a Royal Navy petty officer, and had twice experienced the Antarctic with Scott. It was on Scott's second voyage that Crean distinguished himself with an act of heroism by helping drag one of Scott's officers, Lieutenant Teddy Evans – later Admiral Lord Mountevans – many miles to safety after he collapsed with scurvy. Crean walked the last 20 miles alone to fetch help, and was awarded the Albert Medal for gallantry. Replaced by the George Cross in 1971, the Albert Medal was the highest civil honour that could be conferred for acts of courage.

Shackleton, Worsley and Crean were, however, badly undernourished after an ordeal that had by then lasted 16 months, from the day the *Endurance* was beset in the ice. Their only fresh food had been seal meat, without which they would have long been dead from scurvy. They had lived in wild and cold conditions virtually without shelter, and their clothing was pathetic: Worsley was using safety pins to patch holes in his trousers – a pair from a dinner suit.

Their bodies were so tired that it was an effort to carry even the sparse supplies required for three days. Without the screws from the *James Caird* in their tattered boots, they could not hope to keep their feet on ice, of which there was much to cross. What they shared was an unbending spirit that would not allow thoughts of failure, and this they drew from Shackleton, whose ability to face odds that would daunt lesser beings was by now totally inspirational. His power was evident in his bearing, as Worsley had noted. They were three mature men, two just over 40 and the third, Crean, aged 39, who had faced danger most of their adult lives and on whom the lives of their comrades depended. The seamen knew what they had to do, and if they had any doubt about their ability, they were men who kept such thoughts to themselves. They had a duty, and duty was well understood.

Shackleton took his rightful place at the head of the party; Worsley, as navigator, took the rear. They had a sketchy chart of the island, just an outline, the interior being blank, without any detail: none had ever been recorded. Worsley's compass was small enough to rest in his hand and he was often able to use it to take bearings without stopping the group.

For about two hours they climbed a pass from the bay, and in the moonlight they caught a glimpse of the 'high peaks, impassable cliffs, steep snow-slopes and sharply descending glaciers', as Shackleton recorded. Near the top of the slope a thick fog drifted in. 'We could not see a step ahead,' said Worsley. 'Suddenly we found ourselves on the very edge of a strange dark pit that was more than 100 feet deep…it looked as though an enormous meteorite had ploughed its way through the ice-sheet.'

The fog was now so thick that Worsley believed they had had a 'wonderful escape' from falling into the hole. 'Never have I felt so puny, nor realised so clearly the helplessness of man against nature…I became conscious of nerves in my body that I had not known existed.'

'Better rope up after this,' Shackleton said, and they proceeded, Worsley at the rear calling 'starboard' or 'port' or 'steady' as required to keep them on a more-or-less straight path for Stromness Bay and the whaling stations.

At the top of the saddle, still in a mixture of moonlight, mist and snow, they saw to the east what looked like the smooth surface of a frozen lake, which

Shackleton, Worsley and Crean traversing the island of South Georgia. Painting by Arthur Shilstone.
NZ Geographic

Shackleton thought might offer easier travelling. But as they climbed down they met crevasses that suggested a glacier.

Dawn came, the mist dissipated and the 'lake' was exposed as Possession Bay, an arm of the sea on the east coast. There was no point in proceeding all the way to the bay: there was no possibility of following the coastline to reach Stromness Bay. They had wasted at least one precious hour on this wrong trail and had to retrace steps to the slope that would take them into the range of mountains that constitutes the backbone of South Georgia.

While the weather was wonderfully mild, this softened the snow at lower levels and made the going hard. At they reached higher, the cold became apparent but the going was firmer. They stopped for a hot meal after six hours, digging a hole 3 feet deep in the snow for the Primus. Crean and Worsley shared the task of lying over the hole to prevent the wind from blowing out the flame. Worsley said they ate by taking turns at dipping their spoons into the hoosh, and he recorded this quirky exchange between the irrepressible Irishmen:

Shackleton: 'Crean, you've got a bigger spoon than we have.'

Crean: 'Doesn't matter – the skipper has a bigger mouth.'

They marched towards a feature of five rocky peaks with spaces between, what Worsley said looked like four gaps between the stumpy fingers of a giant hand, one of which might be a pass to the south. The right-hand gap was nearest to the course Worsley had set, but at the crest they found it fell away in precipices and cliffs to a glacier a thousand feet below.

The cold was by now intense, and the weakened men had to halt every 20 minutes for a rest. 'We would throw ourselves flat on our backs, with legs and arms extended, and draw in big gulps of air so as to get our wind again,' Worsley said.

They climbed to the crest of the second gap and found conditions almost as bad as the first: a dazzlingly beautiful view in brilliant sunlight, a view never seen by another human, but an impassable landscape. They climbed back down to tackle the third gap. This one was steeper and Worsley said that to reach the pass, at about 5000 feet, was 'very exhausting'. It was much like the first one. 'So, down again and up again!'

The fourth and last pass. Darkness was approaching. This time they had to cut steps in the ice with McNeish's adze. They had no tent, no sleeping bags, tatty and weather-worn clothing: it would mean death to be caught at such an altitude. Fog was creeping up the slope behind them as they peered down another daunting slope. They could not see where it ended: the slope could lead to a sheer drop of possibly thousands of feet. There was a good chance of death ahead; there was a certainty of it behind.

Shackleton dealt with what followed in a most matter-of-fact way: 'There was no turning back now so we unroped and slid in the fashion of youthful days,' he wrote in *South*. Worsley told it better. He said Shackleton, who had started to cut steps in the ice to climb down, realised that such a slow and painful operation was hopeless. He proposed instead that they should slide down; but to what? None of them knew.

They had, said Shackleton, a small chance. 'All right,' Worsley said aloud, but perhaps not very cheerfully, he confessed later.

> It seemed to me a most impossible project. The slope was well-nigh precipitous and a rock in our path – we could never have seen it in the darkness in time to avoid it – would mean certain disaster.

Still it was the only way. We had explored all the passes…to go back was useless…to stay on the ridge longer meant certain death by freezing. It was useless to think of personal risk. If we were killed, at least we had done everything in our power to help our shipmates. Shackleton was right. Our chance was a very small one indeed, but it was up to us to take it.

Each man coiled his section of the rope until it constituted a pad on which they would launch themselves. Shackleton sat in front. Worsley was next, straddling his legs around the Boss and clasping him around the neck. Crean did the same with Worsley and when they were locked as one entity, Shackleton kicked off without hesitation.

Worsley wrote:

> We seemed to shoot into space. For a moment my hair stood on end. Then quite suddenly I felt a glow and knew that I was grinning. I was actually enjoying it. It was most exhilarating. We were shooting down the side of an almost precipitous mountain at nearly a mile a minute. I yelled with excitement and found that Shackleton and Crean were yelling too. It seemed ridiculously safe. To hell with the rocks!

The sharp slope started to level slightly. 'Little by little our speed slackened, and we finished up in a bank of snow,' said Worsley. They shook hands all round as Shackleton commented, 'It's not good to do that kind of thing too often.' Worsley judged that they had descended about 3000 feet in about three minutes; Shackleton estimated the drop had been 'at least 900 feet'. Above them the ridge disappeared in the killer fog. The worst casualties of the slide were their trousers: they were now very badly torn instead of just torn.

They paused long enough for a hot meal at 6pm, Shackleton and Worsley lying on their sides to protect the little Primus. The fair weather continued, and by 8pm there was a brilliant moon to guide them. Their path seemed to lie between two crevassed areas that should lead them to another bay – possibly Stromness Bay. After about six hours of reasonably easy passage, they suddenly found themselves among crevasses, clearly a large glacier; and there were no large glaciers at Stromness Bay.

'The smoothness and easiness of that long slope to the bay had lured us on and deceived us,' Worsley wrote. 'After the difficulties and hard climbing that we had experienced we had accepted too readily the promise held out by what appeared to be the easiest way. Now we had to pay for it; it was not until 5am that we regained our former altitude and resumed our proper course.'

He recognised the degree of exhaustion which now threatened to overcome their gallant effort. Nerves were on edge; each man had to be careful not to irritate the others. 'We treated each other with a good deal more consideration than we should have done in normal circumstances,' Worsley said. 'Never is etiquette and "good form" observed more carefully than by experienced travellers when they find themselves in a tight place.'

They sat in the lee of a rock to rest, close together, with their arms around each other. Shackleton suggested half an hour's rest while they felt a little snug. 'Within a minute my companions were fast asleep,' Shackleton said. Merciful sleep also beckoned Shackleton, but he knew that if they all slept, the relaxation would probably merge with death. He gave Worsley and Crean five minutes' slumber, shook them awake and told them the half-hour was up. The march resumed. 'We were so stiff that for the first two or three hundred yards we marched with our knees bent,' Shackleton said.

They made for a line of peaks with a gap like a broken tooth, passing through the gap about 6am. As dawn opened, they saw thousands of feet below the dark water of Fortuna Bay. Beyond were two more mountains, the formation that they knew embraced Stromness Bay. For the third time in 27 hours they shook hands in quiet congratulation at another obstacle being beaten.

While Worsley and Crean dug a hole for the Primus and a hot meal, Shackleton climbed a ridge above them and at 6.30am he thought he heard a whistle: it could be the signal to the whaling station men to get out of bed. As the three men ate, they listened carefully as the minutes ticked off to 7am. On the dot, another whistle was heard – the signal to start work. 'It was the first sound created by an outside human agency that had come to our ears since we left Stromness Bay in December 1914,' said Shackleton.

They began the descent, intending to go around the head of Fortuna Bay. It looked straightforward. Worsley suggested a route which he thought was safe, though less direct than the one Shackleton wanted to follow. Worsley had always praised Shackleton as being the most cautious man he knew. Now, 'for the first and only time in my memory of him', Shackleton seemed less cautious than Worsley. In fact he was thinking well ahead, as usual, and was anxious to save time. In his mind, they had already won through; now he had to get back to Elephant Island.

Shackleton's route became alarmingly steep and they had to cut steps on an ice slope. They were so exposed now that a blizzard would simply lift them off the slope and throw them down a virtual precipice, but the unusually benign weather held. Shackleton turned on his back and used one heel after the other to smash steps in the ice, with Worsley taking his weight on the rope. Worsley followed Shackleton, with Crean supporting his weight, enlarging the steps and literally walking on his back. 'It was not an agreeable experience,' Worsley said. 'I was afraid to lift my head off the ice, feeling that if I did I might fall outwards.'

It was, however, a faster way to descend than facing the ice and cutting steps, and by 10am they were on the shores of Fortuna Bay, ankle-deep in mud pushed out by a giant glacier. By noon they were well up the other side of the bay, on what they thought was a fine piece of level ground, when Crean broke through the ice and they realised that they were on a frozen lake. They threw themselves flat to distribute their weight, and worked their way off the treacherous surface, Crean soaked to the waist.

At 1.30pm they climbed the last ridge above Stromness and looked down 2500 feet at the whaling station, where minute figures were moving around and a little steamer was entering the bay. Worsley said, 'Unconscious of the absurdity of our actions, we yelled and waved, but of course no-one saw or heard us.'

They struck out cheerfully down a ravine that seemed to get steeper and more narrow, until they were walking ankle-deep in a stream of water. The stream ended at a waterfall, 25–30 feet high, with what seemed to them to be impassable cliffs on both sides. 'To go up again was scarcely thinkable in our utterly wearied condition,' Shackleton said. If the rope were long enough, they would go over and through the icy waterfall.

It was a relief to see the rope touching the rocks below. They made one end of the rope as secure as they could around a disturbingly smooth boulder. Worsley and Shackleton lowered Crean, the heaviest of the three. He disappeared in the falling water and emerged gasping at the bottom.

Shackleton went next, sliding down the rope, and Worsley, the lightest weight, conscious that nobody was above holding the rope for him, went down 'sailor-fashion', avoiding putting his full weight on the rope but letting it slide freely through his hands until just before he reached the outstretched hands of his companions. His loop around the boulder held, and they abandoned the rope.

By now the brass screws which McNeish had fixed in their boots had worn flat, so when they came to smooth ice they slithered without control, each man taking many falls. Worsley thought this was also due to the fact that 'our legs

Frank Worsley's map of South Georgia, showing the route he, Shackleton and Crean took in their pioneer crossing of the rugged and wild island.
South

97

were a bit tired'. By 3pm, when they reached the whaling station, they had been fighting the elements without proper sleep, halting only occasionally for food, and crossing an unknown and hostile island, for 36 hours; they had every reason to be 'a bit tired'. It was something of a miracle that they had achieved, and this had registered with each of them in their worst moments.

Shackleton said, 'We tried to straighten ourselves up a bit, for the thought that there might be women at the station made us painfully conscious of our uncivilised appearance. Our beards were long and our hair was matted. We were unwashed and the garments that we had worn for nearly a year without a change were tattered and stained. Three more unpleasant-looking ruffians could hardly have been imagined.' Worsley produced his safety-pins and made some repairs.

Of the several whaling stations in the bay, they made first for that at Stromness. The first humans they had seen for almost 18 months were two youngsters who 'bolted at the sight of us', said Worsley.

At the house of the station manager, Thoralf Sorlle, where the *Endurance's* crew had been entertained so long ago, they were not recognised as they stood on his doorstep, 'but after food, hot baths and clean clothes we became civilised beings once more', Worsley said.

They were also able to inspect their bodies, which they had not seen for many months. Neither Shackleton nor Worsley recorded this experience, but Orde-Lees did when his time came.

He wrote:

Some of us rather expected to undress black, but as a matter of fact one's skin was in just the same condition as it would be if one had not had a bath for a fortnight; a little bit greasy, and that is all. Just what a garment worn next to the skin looks like after all that time is not quite so easy to describe, but generally speaking it seems that a layer of

'After the Bath' is Frank Worsley's caption on the reverse of this historic photo, thought to be the only one in existence of a bathed and shaved Sir Ernest Shackleton (centre), Worsley (right) and Tom Crean taken after their crossing of South Georgia in May 1916. The gloom is probably due to the late afternoon light of 20 May. Soon after the picture was taken, Worsley sailed off in a whaler to pick up the three men from Peggotty Camp.
Bamford family

dead skin has rubbed off and adhered to the inside of the garment, which is clogged with a sort of greasiness, but nothing so terribly offensive as one would imagine, and of course there are no vermin in the cold climate.

Following the bath, which Worsley said was 'really wonderful and worth all that we had been through to get', came the shaving, after which they hardly knew each other.

Worsley had the same problem next day when he went ashore at King Haakon Sound to pick up McNeish, McCarthy and Vincent: they greeted their rescuers happily but McCarthy complained that he expected the skipper, at least, to return for them. Worsley said he told them, 'Well, I am here.' They looked at him in amazement: he had left them a hairy, dirty figure and returned spruce and shaven.

Worsley sailed for the other side of the island the first night they reached Stromness, sleeping in the Norwegian whaling vessel the *Samson*, while Shackleton and Crean rested at the station, catching up with the depressing news that the war was far from over. Shackleton also learned of problems in the Ross Sea with the *Aurora*.

Before Worsley left, he gave Shackleton the Hurley photographs which he had preserved so carefully in the bows of the *James Caird* with his log. Some of the photos showed the *Endurance* squeezed up on the ice. All were eroded at the edges from the soaking they had received. Shackleton sent them to England at the first opportunity, where they were reproduced in that state by the *Daily Mirror*. These first photos from the nearly-forgotten expedition created a sensation in war-weary England.

Back on South Georgia, at King Haakon Bay, the Norwegians from the whaler hoisted the *James Caird* on deck, Worsley returning to Stromness from Peggotty Camp on 22 May. At the whaling station, the workers inspected the small boat with what Shackleton called 'professional interest'. Worsley said every man wanted to share the honour of hauling the *James Caird* ashore. 'We were not allowed to touch her.'

Shackleton also said the rescue was just in time for McNeish, who looked woefully thin. The strain had told on the older man more than the others.

At a gathering of whalers and sailors that evening, at another whaling station in Stromness Bay, Husvik, described by Worsley as occurring in a large room 'full of captains and mates and sailors and hazy with tobacco smoke', Shackleton told their story. There were no formal speeches, but Shackleton, Worsley and Crean were aware that they were being given a rare accolade in the ceremony of shaking hands with men who recognised courage and fortitude and wanted to express their admiration with simple sincerity.

'I enjoyed this more than any other honour bestowed on us afterwards,' Worsley said. Congratulations from such fine seaman, the 'men of the Viking brand', meant something special. One white-haired veteran who spoke for the others said he had never heard of such a feat of daring seamanship, crowned by tramping across the island. He finished with a dramatic gesture: 'These are men!'

At that time, each of the three survivors held secret thoughts that they had been assisted across South Georgia. They believed there was a fourth person present in their worst moments of despair.

Shackleton made a brief reference to the 'fourth presence' in his book *South*, saying he had 'no doubt' that Providence guided them not only across the snow-field but also the sea between Elephant Island and South Georgia. 'I know that during that long and racking march of 36 hours over the unnamed mountains and glaciers of South Georgia it seemed to me often that we were four, not three.'

He said nothing until Worsley confessed to him that he had had 'a curious feeling' on the march that there was another person with them. Crean said the same.

Their conclusion seemed to be that, when more dead than alive, and sustained only by their own indomitable spirit, they were assisted by a force that they all, as seamen who had witnessed the mysteries of nature in all its strength and majesty, would believe in: the guiding hand that sometimes chooses to protect poor sailors in distress.

In a letter years later to Shackleton's biographer, Dr Hugh Robert Mill, the explorer's friend Leonard Tripp wrote from New Zealand: 'As to the religious side of Shackleton's character there is no question. He was absolutely convinced that he could not take credit for all he had done, but that it was due to the Almighty…although he would tell me everything when I asked him, if I started to praise him he always would say quietly, "I am not entitled to all the credit".'

The 'extra person' experience is now a well-documented phenomenon, but in 1916 this was not so, and the sensation described attracted much attention.

The poet T. S. Eliot, explaining some lines in a poem called *The Waste Land*, said he was inspired to write them by Shackleton's account of the presence of one more member in the little party than could actually be counted. The excerpt reads:

> Who is the third who walks always beside you?
> When I count, there are only you and I together
> But when I look ahead up the white road
> There is always another one walking beside you
> Gliding wrapt in a brown mantle, hooded
> I do not know whether a man or a woman
> But who is that on the other side of you?

A measure of the greatness of that crossing of South Georgia by three desperate and enervated men comes in the account of the 1956 British survey expedition that set out to cover the same ground. This was a well equipped and prepared group of expert climbers.

The leader, Duncan Carse, described what he considered were the only two possible routes across South Georgia. He called them the High Road and the Low Road. Carse and his team chose the High Road; Shackleton, Worsley and Crean took the Low Road.

Carse commented at the time, 'I don't know how they did it, except that they had to – three men of the heroic age of Antarctic exploration with 50 feet of rope between them, and a carpenter's adze.'

Carse, in an article in *Geographical Magazine* in 1974, said Worsley's positions and descriptions of wind and sea 'are precise and reliable', and his account in *Shackleton's Boat Journey* 'easy to follow'. The landfall was correctly identified as Cape Demidov. Carse said that from his calculations, both Shackleton and Worsley 'tend to improve on the distances, and they blow up the heights out of all recognition'. Carse concluded that the explorers had lived so long with only the sea and pack-ice for horizon that they had lost all sense of a vertical scale.

Three days after they stumbled into Stromness, Shackleton, Worsley and Crean were back at sea in the *Southern Sky*, a large steam whaler that Shackleton hired to attempt to pick up Wild and the other Elephant Island castaways. McNeish, McCarthy and Vincent were to return direct to England. Shackleton recorded in *South* that he was not sad to see the back of McNeish and Vincent.

One hundred miles from Elephant Island, the sea was smooth and the air cold, the right conditions for pack-ice to form, and 60 miles out their way was blocked. The unprotected steel-hulled whaler was not capable of forcing through, and with fuel low Shackleton made for the Falkland Islands, where he cabled a message to the King and to his friend Ernest Perris, editor of the *Daily Chronicle*.

The Admiralty cabled Shackleton that it would be October before it could get a suitable rescue boat out to him. Shackleton cabled back that October would be too late for Wild and his men. He would have to try again from the South Altantic with whatever craft he could find.

The Uruguayan government offered a trawler, the *Instituto de Pesca No. 1*, and the second attempt at rescue started from Port Stanley on 10 June. This time they reached within 20 miles of the island before having to turn back because of ice. 'Shackleton was nearly heart-broken,' Worsley said. 'At one time we were actually facing the camp and had it not been for white, low-lying mist they would have seen us.'

Back at the Falklands, Shackleton decided to try to get a more suitable vessel from Punta Arenas, Chile, where British residents raised 1500 pounds to charter a small 70-ton schooner, the *Emma*. Worsley was first mate and navigator. The *Emma* was towed in part by the small Chilean steamer, the *Yelcho*, for three days. The ice was struck within 100 miles of Elephant Island, and Shackleton, by now desperate, tried to force her through, but stopped when he realised that the vessel was actually lighter than the lumps of ice around her. The engine broke down, and Worsley had to sail her against the prevailing westerlies back to Cape Horn.

The *Emma* arrived at Port Stanley after three weeks at sea. Worsley said Shackleton was 'taking his disappointment very badly'. For the first time in three years he drank whisky, 'and it affected him at once'.

Worsley thoughtfully wrote a letter to George Marston's wife from Punta Arenas between the second and third rescue attempts, telling Mrs Marston that when the *James Caird* party left Elephant Island, 'your husband was quite well and fit and cheerful. I am firmly of the opinion that the party of 22 men as a whole are all right…you may have no fear of George being anything but fit and hopeful.'

He added that on the boat journey from the floe to the island: 'he was in my boat and stood the wet, cold exposure, toil and thirst as well as or better than anyone else in the whole party. His cheeriness and good humour were a great help to me in pulling the boat through and I am sure that the same cheeriness and good humour will pull him through the long and trying wait for our relief. We have made two attempts to get them off and are now arranging for a third, from Punta Arenas.'

Shackleton was having a hard time with the Admiralty, many of whose officers were men who favoured Scott over him in the inevitable rivalry and taking of sides which existed between them as representatives of the Royal Navy and the Merchant Navy. There was no chance that Shackleton would have command of a navy ship sent to effect the rescue. If he was to have a part in the final stage of the adventure, he had to get fast help from another quarter.

He found it in Chile, where his determination to rescue his own men was appreciated. Shackleton was open about his emotions. 'I begged the Chilean Government to let me have the *Yelcho* for a last attempt,' he said.

And fortune favoured him at last. The vessel left Punta Arenas on 25 August with Worsley navigating, and made a fast run south in comparatively fine weather. 'Our spirits rose,' Worsley recorded. 'Shackleton was confident that at last we should get our men off the island. He was a different man – vigorous and alert, urging the engineers to drive the little ship hell-for-leather.'

Sixty miles from the island the *Yelcho* ran into thick fog that cautioned Shackleton to order half-speed. Early next morning it was evident that the ice had cleared, at least temporarily, though conditions were still foggy. Worsley stationed himself at the bow, searching for a change in the colour of the water to indicate the depth. Suddenly the northern land mass was straight in front of them. Shackleton, said Worsley, 'said nice things about the accuracy of my landfall'.

An hour later, as the *Yelcho* edged east by south, the fog cleared and the familiar shape of the peninsula became evident. Worsley concentrated on steering the *Yelcho* clear of reefs and shoals, while Shackleton, peering through binoculars, muttered in a low, strained voice, 'There are only two, Skipper…no, four…I see six – eight.' Then in a voice ringing with joy, 'They are all there! They are all saved!'

Shackleton, with Crean and some sailors, rowed ashore and greeted the castaways. Worsley stayed on the *Yelcho,* watching the weather. Shackleton was on edge, aware that the weather could close on them. Wild asked his leader to come to the camp and see how they had improved the boat-shelter at Cape Wild. The loyal lieutenant must have had a huge sense of relief at his own achievement of holding together the 22 men and delivering them safely to Shackleton.

But there was no room for sentiment in their situation. The *Yelcho* was totally unsuitable for work in the ice; Shackleton had to get everyone away as fast as possible. He refused to leave the beach immediately, instead hurrying the castaways into the boat for delivery to the waiting vessel, taking only the remaining records of the expedition.

This was Shackleton's other concern, according to Worsley: 'It was imperative to get on board the records of the expedition and the photographs and films that Hurley had made, as herein lay his only chance of paying off the expenses of the expedition, which fell on his shoulders.'

It took three boat trips. Everyone was on the *Yelcho* within an hour, and she steamed north at the best possible speed; the weather was still favourable and the ice was still open. It was 1pm on 30 August 1916, 128 days after the *James Caird* had sailed for South Georgia. They had hoped to be rescued in four weeks, not four months.

Orde-Lees later recorded that he, Wild, Clark and Greenstreet had gone back to the boat-hut (nicknamed 'The Sty') to 'square up a bit'. Orde-Lees stayed behind, waiting to show Shackleton over the premises. Only after the last boat-load had left the island and was pulling for the *Yelcho* did Orde-Lees realise that he was in danger of being left behind. Shackleton turned the boat around when the marines officer was seen running frantically along the beach, waving his arms and screaming with alarm. He leaped into it from the rocks even before it reached the shore.

Greenstreet was first on board the *Yelcho*, greeting Worsley with the comment, 'We knew that it would be all right if you were on board, Skipper…you weren't born to be drowned!'

For the first hours on the *Yelcho*, the *Endurance*'s officers and the scientists

The Chilean steamer *Yelcho* finally reaches Elephant Island. It took Shackleton four attempts and more than four months to get back to pick up his 22 stranded men. The beacon at left was lit after the *Yelcho* was sighted.
T.H. Orde-Lees Collection, Alexander Turnbull Library, No. P-AC2094-069

remained on deck with Shackleton, who brought them up to date with world and war news. They munched gratefully on apples and oranges which he had thoughtfully brought with him, while the crew had a meal below, 'and rather too much wine,' Orde-Lees said. Later the positions reversed, and while the wardroom gentry ate, the sailors relaxed on deck, with the smokers seemingly making up for lost time as they puffed incessantly to feed their habit, one man smoking two pipes at once – with a cigarette in the middle.

The Chileans were almost as happy as the *Endurance* crew. They took great pleasure in having supplied the boat and crew to make the rescue. At Punta Arenas,

the *Yelcho* was offered to take the whole party to Valparaiso for a national welcome, what Worsley described as 'a magnificient reception' by more than 30,000 people.

The *Yelcho* reached Punta Arenas on 3 September, and the party stayed for nearly two weeks, resting and being entertained by the local people. Blackborrow was taken to hospital where his foot with the amputated toes was treated. Hudson, who had suffered from a breakdown on Elephant Island, elected to go back to England quickly and alone. The sailors went next, and the others toured Chile in a gesture of thanks to the country.

Shackleton received decorations and made speeches of grateful thanks. On 3 October they left Chile by train for Argentina, to Buenos Aires, where Shackleton gave a public lecture. Then Shackleton and Worsley left for New Zealand, while the remainder of the party sailed for Britain. They reached home, and another uncertain future in the war, on 5 November 1916, after an absence of two and a quarter years.

The only pressing problem now, for an otherwise relaxed Shackleton, was his Ross Sea party.

The *Yelcho* returns with the rescued explorers. Huge welcomes awaited them at every port they touched at in Chile and Argentina.
Dulwich College

CHAPTER 10

New Zealand with Shackleton

Joseph Russell (John) Stenhouse, chief officer of the second Imperial Trans-Antarctic Expedition vessel *Aurora*. The vessel was swept away from moorings in the Ross Sea and had to return to New Zealand, leaving 10 men marooned on Ross Island. Stenhouse and Frank Worsley became close friends in New Zealand when Shackleton was trying to get back to rescue them. Stenhouse died at sea during World War 2.
Mantell family

After the joy of the rescue and the enthusiastic South American reception, especially that in Chile, Shackleton, who had by then learned of the drama in the Ross Sea, had to re-focus on the rescue of his men on the other side of Antarctica, the 10 from the *Aurora* left on the ice two years earlier.

Captain of the *Aurora*, and leader of the party, was Aeneas Mackintosh, who had been second mate with Shackleton on the *Nimrod* in 1908. Chief officer of the *Aurora* was Joseph Russell (John) Stenhouse, usually known as 'Sten' or 'Stennie'.

The Ross Sea party, unlike the men from the *Endurance*, at least landed on the continent, and a good part of their assignment was achieved. 'The depot that was the main object of the expedition was laid in the spot that I had indicated, and if the trans-continental party had been fortunate enough to have crossed they would have found the assistance, in the shape of stores, that would have been vital to the success of their undertaking,' Shackleton wrote later in *South*.

The *Aurora* sailed from Hobart for the Ross Sea on 24 December 1914, about two months after the *Endurance* left England, and made fast to sea ice near Hut Point a month later. Three separate parties, two with dog teams and the third with a motor-tractor which soon failed, were landed and ultimately reached the huts left from earlier expeditions. Ten men ashore set about the business of wintering on the ice; they were then to strike south and lay the required depots, the last of them at the Beardmore Glacier.

Stenhouse, on the *Aurora* with 18 men, had moved the ship to Cape Evans, where he was to have made her secure, to be used as the main base during the winter. But one night in May 1915, the wind rose swiftly to gale force. 'The ship broke away from the fast ice in blizzards, and then we went dodging about the [McMurdo] sound from the Ross Island side to the western pack, avoiding and clearing floes and growlers in heavy drift when we could see nothing, our compasses unreliable, and the ship short-handed,' Stenhouse later recorded. 'Here we are drifting, with all plans upset, when we ought to be lying in winter quarters.'

By late May the *Aurora*, like the *Endurance* a continent away, was beset in the ice, drifting helplessly. Stenhouse wrote of his concerns for the men ashore, because a lot of equipment, including warm clothing for the sledging further south, was still on board.

'I see little prospect of getting back to Cape Evans or anywhere in the sound. We are short of coal and held firmly in the ice. I hope she drifts quickly to the north-east. Then we can endeavour to push through the pack and make for New Zealand, coal and return…we must get back to aid the depot-laying next season.'

It was not until February 1916 that the *Aurora*, badly crushed and leaking, and with her rudder smashed, set some sail and moved slowly and erratically northward through the diminishing heavy ice pack.

By mid-March a makeshift rudder was in place and the *Aurora* cleared the last belt of the pack. Stenhouse started the struggle northwards to New Zealand against the wind and head seas, having to use his dwindling supply of coal for the engines. Shackleton later praised him for 'fine seamanship and dogged perseverance. He accomplished successfully one of the most difficult voyages on record in an ocean area notoriously stormy and treacherous.'

On 23 March, Stenhouse established radio communication with Bluff Station, New Zealand, for the first time since the *Aurora* had reached the ice. And for the first time it became known that men were still stranded there.

At the request of the Prime Minister, William Massey, the Otago Harbour Board's tug *Dunedin* met the *Aurora*, now almost helpless with the jury rudder partially carried away, and towed her into Port Chalmers. One other vessel could have done the job faster, Worsley's old ship *Amokura*. The vessel was away at Port Ross, in the Auckland Islands, on a training cruise, but she did not then have wireless communications installed.

Ten men had been left on the ice. Were they still alive? They had been there for two years; nothing had been heard from them. The final task for the expedition's

A montage of photographs taken during the towing of the *Aurora* from south of New Zealand to the port of Port Chalmers. The *Aurora* was under jury rig and, as the photo bottom right shows, had her second jury rudder. Shackleton was full of praise for Chief Officer John Stenhouse's seamanship in saving the vessel.

Alexander Turnbull Library, No G-12190-1/2

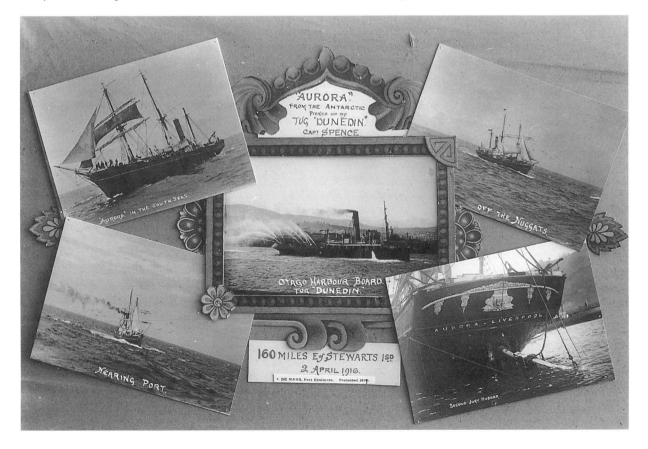

leader was to rescue those who might have survived, or at least to discover their fate.

So, in the midst of a horrendous world war, governments were being asked to make considerable efforts to save the lives of a few explorers, when on the other side of the world thousands of servicemen were being slaughtered daily. It is a tribute to the personality of Shackleton that such an effort was even contemplated, let alone activated. And Shackleton was determined to be present for this last act of his trans-continental drama.

He assumed that he would take command of the *Aurora*; after all, he owned the ship and was expedition leader. He decided to take Worsley to New Zealand with him, both because he thought he owed his captain a trip to his homeland after the *Endurance* adventure, and in case he needed another sailing master.

There were huge complications. The governments of New Zealand, Australia and Britain had already agreed to organise and finance the rescue solely on humanitarian grounds, putting up about 20,000 pounds. But the Australian authorities, influenced mainly by the Australian polar explorer, Douglas (later Sir Douglas) Mawson, who still nursed a grudge against Shackleton over publication of scientific papers from the 1907 *Nimrod* expedition, wanted Shackleton to be excluded.

The Australians were also responsible, with the support of New Zealand and Britain, for the appointment of John King Davis as captain of the *Aurora*, even though Stenhouse was still on board the ship at Port Chalmers and was Shackleton's choice as skipper. Stenhouse was particularly bitter: he first heard of Davis's appointment in the Dunedin newspaper, the *Otago Daily Times*.

Shackleton and Worsley sailed up the Pacific coast from Valparaiso, Chile, then through the Panama Canal to New Orleans where they caught a train to San Francisco to embark on the steamer *Moana*. They reached Wellington on 2 December and were met by Shackleton's lawyer friend, Leonard Tripp.

Tripp had befriended Shackleton in 1903 and had visited the explorer in England. Shackleton told him that he would have Davis removed; the impetuous Worsley even suggested seizing the *Aurora*. These ugly thoughts and subsequent machinations were suppressed by Shackleton from all public record of the expedition. He even excluded the pivotal role played by his friend Tripp, and Worsley did not even rate a mention in this part of the published record.

Stenhouse came north to Wellington to join Shackleton and report personally to his leader. He met Worsley for the first time, and the two sailors soon became the best of friends, an association that lasted 25 years, into the next world war.

It was Tripp who introduced Shackleton to the man who ultimately resolved the issue, the Minister for Marine, Dr Robert McNab. The minister explained to Shackleton that New Zealand had had little say in the appointment of Davis: the Australian Government had acted first, after consultation with the Admiralty.

The Australian Government had set up a supervising committee headed by Rear Admiral Sir William Creswell, who had invited Davis to take command. It was this committee that decided not to allow Stenhouse to remain in charge.

New Zealand, which was paying the smallest part of the rescue costs, was then asked to approve that to which the other parties had already agreed.

When he heard that Shackleton was coming and expected to take command of the *Aurora*, Davis anticipated an unpleasant confrontation, and decided to resign. He sent his resignation to Admiral Creswell, who refused to accept it. Creswell's committee then confirmed that the claws were out for Shackleton by insisting that Davis, and not Shackleton, would lead the rescue.

McNab also bluntly told Shackleton that when the arrangement was made, Shackleton was 'not in existence', and that he was not to go to the Ross Sea in charge of the rescue.

In a letter dated 6 December, to a friend in London, R. J. S. Neville, a British member of Parliament, seeking a grant to help Shackleton meet his mounting expenses, Tripp pointed out that the explorer had turned down a deal worth 15,000 pounds for 78 lectures in the United States because he wanted to rescue the lost men of his Ross Sea party. That money would have cleared Shackleton's debts, and more. Tripp also said Shackleton 'desired to stay loyal to Stenhouse, who was loyal to him, and also to another man he has brought here with him, who has been loyal to him [Worsley].'

Davis, who had previously commanded the *Aurora* for Mawson, was apparently disturbed by the battered and worn condition of the vessel. Much time would have to be devoted to refitting and refurbishing. He also questioned Stenhouse's wisdom in trying to secure a winter anchorage at Cape Evans.

Worsley and Stenhouse met McNab, without Shackleton being present. Tripp recorded that the minister told them of the 'awkward position' of Shackleton, who was prepared to sink his own position, but not at the cost of being disloyal to his two captains. McNab then asked Worsley and Stenhouse to 'voluntarily

Below left: Leonard Owen Howard Tripp, the Wellington lawyer who befriended Sir Ernest Shackleton and succeeded in settling his financial problems associated with the *Aurora*. Tripp also helped resolve the dispute over whether Shackleton should be allowed to sail in the *Aurora* for the Ross Sea rescue attempt.
Earle Andrew Collection, Alexander Turnbull Library, No. F-43288-1/2

Below right: Robert McNab, the New Zealand Minister for Marine, who intervened in the row over the *Aurora* command. Although Shackleton owned the vessel, he finally sailed in her as a supernumerary at one shilling a month to bring the issue to a close.
Earle Andrew Collection, Alexander Turnbull Library, No. G-14360-1/2

Sir Ernest Shackleton was feted by the local people while he rested in Wellington, New Zealand, pending resolution of the row over command of the *Aurora*. This 1916 picture shows him with Harold S. Hislop (right), with whom he was staying. The lady is Mrs C. Gray and the man in uniform is Captain Chaplain Mullineux. The picture was taken during a drive over the Rimutaka Range, near Wellington.

G.T. Grant Collection, Alexander Turnbull Library, No. F-29480-1/2

offer' not to go down, as Davis already had his crew ready to sail.

'I believe that they are going to agree to that, and so relieve Shackleton entirely, and that the Government will arrange for Davis to take Shackleton down. Although Davis will be in supreme command, Shackleton will be able to advise and take charge of any shore party,' Tripp told Neville.

McNab arranged for Davis to come to Wellington to talk with Shackleton. They had had no contact since Shackleton had tried to recruit Davis as captain of the *Endurance* in 1914. Davis told Shackleton, among other things, that the Australian Government in 1914 had not wanted to help the *Aurora* expedition, but was bullied into backing the operation because the trans-continental party was counting on the depots being laid by the Ross Sea party.

There was also a high degree of incompetence, arising from poor funding of the Ross Sea operation which was a 'bankrupt enterprise' that now had to be revived from its desperate state in the face of much more important events.

With Worsley and Stenhouse placated, and Shackleton accepting his unaccustomed subordinate role, the way seemed clear for the rescue to proceed. But there arose a fear that Davis, operating a secret agenda from Australia, would sail without notice – and without Shackleton. This fear was featured in a letter to McNab from Tripp, dated 8 December, following a cable message from Dunedin saying that the *Aurora* was to sail on 15 December. Shackleton had already suggested a sailing date between Christmas and New Year, and believed this had been agreed to. 'I want to see that, unknown to you, the ship does not get away without your consent, and without Shackleton,' Tripp wrote.

He also told McNab: 'A friend told me that Shackleton, Stenhouse and Worsley have made a great impression here, and that if moneys were wanted to equip the ship, and we mentioned the fact, he is quite satisfied that they would soon be forthcoming. I hope it will not be necessary to take any proceedings to prove that Shackleton is entitled to the ship, and that everything will be settled in a satisfactory manner.'

Shackleton by then had charmed McNab to such a degree that the minister did not want to see the great explorer 'humbled' by having to sign on under Davis on his own vessel.

In a reference that excluded all but the Australian committee, Tripp recorded: 'There is no question that influences were working against Shackleton, and McNab said someone wanted to humble him, which was the work of narrow-minded men whoever they are. Shackleton has always said that it was not the big men of the Admiralty who were against him.' Nor was it to be found in the New Zealand connection.

Shackleton left Wellington for Port Chalmers on 18 December, and the *Aurora* sailed on the 20th. Worsley and Stenhouse were there to see him off in his supernumerary officer's position, as was McNab. The explorer and ship's owner had signed on at a salary of one shilling a month. He had told Tripp he 'did not care whether I am being humbled or otherwise'.

As for Worsley and Stenhouse, Tripp said in a letter to Ernest Perris of the *Daily Chronicle*, London, writing a full account of events at Shackleton's request, 'The public generally consider that Shackleton, Stenhouse and Worsley are bigger men than ever, Stenhouse and Worsley for saying to the minister that they would make a sacrifice so that Shackleton could be free to go and not have to go into litigation to get his ship. The New Zealand Government has also agreed that Stenhouse and Worsley be given passages to England…there is no doubt that both are bigger men today than if they had gone down.'

Two days before the *Aurora* sailed, McNab wrote to Shackleton advising him that the New Zealand Government would make no claim against him for repayment of any moneys it had spent in connection with the relief expedition. The Australian Government had decided 'to the same effect' as far as its contribution was concerned. As for the British Government's contribution, should any claim be made on Shackleton in connection with it, 'the New Zealand Government will provide at its own expense for any defence which you may set up, whether in New Zealand or in any other place, so as to ensure that your legal position will not be prejudiced.'

New Zealand would also pay to Stenhouse and the men of the *Aurora* who were not taken on by Davis their wages up to the date of sailing, and steamer passages to their homes. Britain did agree to the New Zealand proposal, and this final act of official generosity cleared the way for Shackleton later to sell the *Aurora* and clear all debts in New Zealand and Australia.

When he returned to New Zealand, Shackleton still needed 5000 pounds to pay off the men of the Weddell Sea party, honouring his promise on the ice in the dramatic near-mutiny incited by the carpenter McNeish railing against the orders of Worsley. Tripp and his brother put up 500 pounds each, and within a week the whole sum had been banked from New Zealand friends.

Typical of comments which accompanied contributions was a letter to Tripp from Sir Walter Buchanan, a wealthy farming industry pioneer, with a cheque for 100 pounds, 'showing that there are some New Zealanders who can and do appreciate a man of true grit and character when they come in contact with him'.

Shackleton sold the *Aurora* for 10,000 pounds and immediately returned the 5000 pounds, with interest, to the lending syndicate, and 1500 pounds to the New Zealand Government which had been loaned without interest to pay off the Ross Sea party. Another of the syndicate, G. Moore, returned the interest, writing to Tripp that it was 'a little help to a brave man who has had cruel bad luck and has set us all a bright example'.

It was always said of Shackleton that he brought all his men home safely; that certainly applied to the men directly under his personal command, such as the 28 from the Weddell Sea party. Sadly, it excludes the men from the Ross Sea group, who were under the direct command of another. Three men, including the leader, Mackintosh, perished in the ordeal that for the seven survivors lasted more than two years. The others who died were Victor Hayward, who perished with Mackintosh, and the padre, the Rev. Arnold Spencer-Smith, who succumbed to scurvy. The bodies of Mackintosh and Hayward were never found. Mackintosh's diary was lost with him.

In *South*, Shackleton recorded briefly that the seven survivors were 'all well, though they showed traces of the ordeal which they had passed'.

Davis's account of the condition of men was more vivid: 'They were just about the wildest-looking gang of men I had seen in my life. Their hair was matted and uncut, their beards impregnated with soot and grease. Their speech was jerky, at times semi-hysterical, almost unintelligible. Their eyes had a strained harassed look – and no wonder! Events had rendered these hapless individuals as unlike ordinary human beings as any I have ever met. The Antarctic had given them the full treatment.'

And back in the small wardroom of the *Aurora*, where the rescuers were anxious to be hospitable, Davis said the space was 'too poorly ventilated to be bearable for those whose nostrils were accustomed only to the odours of the more civilised world'.

Huntford wrote: 'Shackleton was profoundly shocked by what he saw. These men were in an even worse state than those had been on Elephant Island. They too were filthy, ragged and unkempt. Bloodshot eyes stared out from pallid faces...a wandering expression on their faces, and their unmodulated speech, hinted at the lurking mental strain.'

Shackleton took the party from the *Aurora* ashore to meet the survivors at Cape Evans. As a means of sending a message to Davis on the ship, three of the *Aurora* party then lay down on the ice, to indicate that three of the original party were missing.

One of the survivors, an Australian crewman, Irvine Gaze, in an interview taped when he was 87, still had vivid memories of the occasion. He spoke of the agony of seeing the *Aurora* disappear. 'It was all guesswork as to whether she would be coming back.' The stores that had been landed to that point were not enough for the stranded men; without stores found in the huts at Cape Evans and Cape Royds, supplemented by seals and penguins, they could never have lasted so long.

Shackleton had been expected to appear from the south, at the end of the trans-continental march, made possible by the splendid work of the Ross Sea

Shackleton's second ship, the *Aurora*, is pictured homeward bound for New Zealand after rescuing the seven survivors of a party of 10 left on the Ross Sea side of the continent. Shackleton sailed on the *Aurora* for the rescue after a huge row over his status, even though he owned the vessel. Worsley and Stenhouse (former chief officer of the *Aurora*) were banned from sailing in her.

men in placing the required depots on his route. But after the *Aurora* was sighted returning to the Ross Sea, and a party came ashore, the seven men finally realised that the original plan, laid so long before, had come to nothing, because 'as they came towards us, we recognised Shackleton,' Gaze said. The full story followed.

'All that remained to be done was to make a final search for the two bodies,' Shackleton wrote in *South*. There was no possibility of either man being alive: they had been without appropriate equipment when a blizzard broke the ice they were crossing eight months earlier.

On 9 February 1917 the *Aurora* berthed at Wellington. Much of the conniving had by then become public property, and for the New Zealand public Shackleton was seen to have been hard done by. Davis was singled out for the villain's role, and the mayor of Wellington, J.P. (later Sir John) Luke, was even moved to exclude him from a civic reception for the explorer. However, Shackleton had by then totally charmed Davis back into their natural pecking order, and responded by demanding that all or none of his men would attend, with Davis on the mayor's left hand and Shackleton on his right. And that is how it proceeded.

With Tripp having resolved his local financial problems, Shackleton decided that money from his lectures should all go to charity, and he gave one lecture to start a trust fund for Mackintosh's near-destitute widow. His final act before heading back to England, via the United States and a month of lectures, was to visit Australia. He demanded a private meeting with the local *Aurora* relief committee to face his most bitter critics.

Shackleton had also renewed his association with the New Zealand journalist Edward Saunders, at the insistence of Tripp, who was concerned that he might go off to fight in the war and be killed before the story of the Trans-Antarctic Expedition would be told. It was Saunders who helped Shackleton write the explorer's earlier book, *The Heart of the Antarctic*. The two men had met while Saunders was a reporter on the *Lyttelton Times* in Christchurch, in March 1909.

Shackleton faced his Australian judges with Saunders present, acting as his secretary. In a letter to Tripp, Saunders said, 'I received the impression that some members of the committee had been strongly prejudiced against Shackleton, and that personal contact was forcing them to revise their estimate of the man.' Shackleton, in a cable to Tripp, was more blunt: 'Have had committee on carpet. Now feel better and buried hatchet.'

What did Shackleton say to the Australians? There was no verbatim record kept of the private meeting, but Shackleton clearly disarmed them individually and collectively by not appearing to want to continue the quarrel. Worsley said Shackleton 'gave me an illuminating account of this interview and I remember being much amused at the way in which he got his own back'.

CHAPTER 11

1917: The Submarine

After seeing Shackleton off at Port Chalmers, Worsley and Stenhouse went to Christchurch and rested there at the Worsley family home, Ringloes, in Fendalton. In a letter dated 30 January 1917 to Tripp in Wellington, in which he also mentioned writing to McNab about getting a passage back to England and the Great War, Worsley referred to a recently completed three-day holiday at Otira Gorge, near Arthur's Pass in the Southern Alps. 'I camped out with two pals and had a ripping time,' he said. 'The scenery of the gorge is magnificent, but most of the scenery on this side is much less interesting.' One of the 'pals' was probably Stenhouse, his house-guest.

Worsley and Stenhouse were back in Wellington on 9 February 1917, when the *Aurora* returned and Shackleton was once more firmly the man of the moment, the Antarctic hero. By then his two captains, Worsley and Stenhouse, had established a friendship that led to their frequently joining each other in sea-going enterprises.

Worsley and Stenhouse left New Zealand in late February, sailing on the RMS *Makura*. With them was John Lachlan Cope, who had been on the *Aurora* as surgeon, though in fact he was no more than a student of science and medicine.

They arrived at Liverpool on 9 April, ready to face the dangers of a war the Shackleton expedition had expected to last six months when the *Endurance* had left in late 1914. Had Worsley, as an RNR officer, known that hostilities would have lasted so long, he would probably never have sailed with Shackleton.

The danger he was now to face was coming from under the sea in a type of warfare he could never have anticipated three years earlier, but one which was now threatening the very outcome of the war: Germany had let loose the U-boat.

At the time Worsley and his friends were crossing the Atlantic in 1917 there were two important developments: the United States had entered the war and losses of ships to the U-boat predators and the loss of supplies to maintain the war effort were becoming so huge that the Allies were being brought to their knees. One ship in every four that left a British port was being sunk before it could return. There were too few new ships being built, and neutral countries which had been persuaded to supply vessels were backing off. If such losses continued it was possible that the war would be lost.

With the Germans trying to put more and more U-boats to sea there had to be a change of tactics: it was no longer sensible to send ships to sea on their own. In mid-1917 the convoy system was officially adopted, after being resisted by the Admiralty as unnecessary, and it was immediately successful. But the sheer number of U-boats in action ensured that shipping losses continued to be high. At any one time, there were about 150 U-boats prowling the Atlantic Ocean, the North Sea, the Irish and English Channels, and the Mediterranean.

One weapon against the submarines was what were called Q-ships, or P-boats and PC-boats. Q-ships were usually coasters or colliers, innocent-looking boats of a kind seen every day in the seas around Great Britain.

They posed as unarmed vessels, but were crewed by navy men, increasingly men of the Royal Naval Reserve like Worsley and Stenhouse. They had guns concealed from outside view, often disguised by false hatches or dummy lifeboats, and the crew was also in disguise.

Torpedoes were still an inexact method of destruction, and a helpless ship could more easily and accurately be destroyed by surface fire. The Q-ship tactics were to send a 'panic party' away in lifeboats at the first hint of a submarine attack, often a failed torpedo attempt.

The submarine would become vulnerable when, having scouted around the ship, scanning it by periscope, deciding it was unarmed, surfaced and prepared to fire. At that moment the remaining crew concealed on board would discard their disguises and open fire, usually with 4-inch guns. These tactics were often effective, causing the Germans to seek a counter with better torpedo-guidance systems, thus avoiding having to surface to get a 'kill'.

Depth-charges were in use, but were still crude devices. The only other method of sinking a submarine was to ram it and tear open the hull, a tactic that depended as much on luck as anything else.

The P-boats, or patrol boats, were purpose-built, designed to supplement the work of destroyers in convoy-escort duties as well as in anti-submarine operations. Most P-boats had sharp bows, cut-away funnels built into the superstructure, and sterns that sloped almost to the water's edge, making them look like large submarines on the surface. They were not as fast or as heavily armed as destroyers, and so were cheaper and quicker to build. They had a light draught, which gave them some protection against torpedo attack, and could reach speeds of at least 22 knots. They had a 4-inch gun, two 14-inch torpedo tubes, and also carried depth-charges.

The P-boat lines soon became familiar to U-boat commanders, who learned to avoid them, leading to a development that was to benefit Worsley as he entered the Great War in its last and most desperate stages. Ten of the last P-boats to be built were given a somewhat different silhouette, making them more like merchant ships. These were known as PC or PQ-boats.

The day after Worsley and Stenhouse arrived in Liverpool they were in London looking for work. They were given three days to get kitted out with uniforms and were appointed to the shore station, HMS *Pembroke*, at Chatham for three months to learn about fighting U-boats.

While at Chatham, Worsley was appointed to command PQ61. Stenhouse was to be his first officer. PQ61 was then fitting out in Belfast. They were told to 'provide yourself with plain clothes suitable to be worn on board ship whilst she is in commission'.

Their ship was commissioned on 31 July, and was constructed to look like a small coastal steamer. Her main armament was a semi-automatic 4-in gun which was hidden by a tarpaulin stretched over what appeared to be two cargo derricks above a big case. The tarpaulin could be thrown clear and gun made ready for firing in less than ten seconds.

The war by now was one of attrition. The Germans were having successes on land in Europe, and at sea they were still sinking ships faster than the British, even with renewed help from neutral countries, could replace them.

About the time Worsley and PQ61 sailed into action, 120 new U-boats were under construction and 100 more were being planned, in addition to the 150 or so already at sea. There were also bigger and better U-boats with the arrival of the huge Deutschland-class, twice the size of the normal U-boat. The most successful of the war, U155, sank 19 ships on a single patrol. Decoy-boat commanders like Worsley ached to try their skills against a Deutschland.

For a man like Worsley, who sought action at every opportunity, the war quickly became boring. Worsley recorded that the shape of PQ61 was 'rather too orthodox and typical of Admiralty build' to entice a U-boat to surface and attack, although on several occasions torpedoes were fired at the ship 'when we flirted with them'. When U-boats were sighted, the best Worsley and PQ61 could do was to chase them.

Until 26 September 1917, when PQ61 met UC33, 40 miles off the south coast of Ireland… 'our one glorious day,' wrote Worsley. The official version of the action is brief:

> PQ61 at 0557 in thick misty weather, wind west 5, sea moderate, visibility $^{3}/_{4}$ of a mile, while convoying SS *San Zeferino* and after torpedoing of same by enemy, sighted submarine $^{1}/_{2}$ mile off on starboard beam, heading west at 9 knots, went full speed ahead, and at 0630, going 20 knots, struck enemy, stem on, on port side just abaft conning tower. Submarine seemed to turn over. A violent explosion took place when stern was over enemy. Sea around this spot was boiling with foam and rushes of immense bubbles coming to surface for some minutes. Oil was observed on the surface. Two men were seen struggling in the water, and one, who turned out to be the commanding officer, was saved.

Worsley's account is considerably more lively than the official version. UC33, though her prime function was to lay mines, had attacked the unarmed and lone tanker *San Zeferino*, and hit her with a torpedo under the engine room, killing three crew. The explosion was seen from PQ61, even in the misty conditions. Worsley ran his ship close by to see the damage. He wrote: 'We could see about three-quarters of a mile and I thought to myself, "If we hang around here the submarine won't come up and we shan't get a chance to bag her; then the whole war will be spoiled for me."' PQ61 moved off from the tanker and Worsley decided to try 'sound-camouflage'. This meant gradually reducing the revolutions of the propellor to convince the Germans, who were no doubt listening on the submarine's hydrophone that PQ61 was abandoning the tanker. The decreasing beat of the propellors would enhance the impression that the intruder was well clear of the submarine, and getting further away by the minute. Such a ploy might lure the Germans to the surface.

Four miles out, and Worsley turned PQ61 to return to the tanker from another direction, using the damaged vessel to conceal the approach of the British ship from where he thought the U-boat would surface. 'As we swung around her stern Stenhouse spotted a faint blur on the horizon.' The captain of UC33 had ordered his submarine to the surface to finish off the tanker by gunfire.

Worsley ordered 'hard a-port and full speed ahead', and at 24 knots PQ61 raced towards the submarine. His timing was perfect. The German crew was by then on deck, preparing their gun for the easy task of shelling the *San Zeferino*. Worsley reckoned that if he delayed long enough to turn to bear his own 4-in gun on the submarine, the time wasted would enable the enemy to submerge and escape. He decided to drive his 600-ton craft straight at the 1000-ton submarine and ram it.

He recorded that the first intimation they would have had of the approach of the British ship through the mist must have been the sight of a great bow-wave. 'The submarine was now travelling across our bows at eight knots…we were bearing down on her beam at 24 knots. We certainly must have looked like the Angel of Death to those unfortunate Germans. I gave the order "prepare to ram" and the crew flattened themselves on the deck.'

All the skill of an Antarctic skipper was now called into play. Worsley had done this sort of manoeuvre hundreds of times when driving the *Endurance* through the ice of the Weddell Sea, though at far slower speed. It was a question of timing: full power had to be stopped at exactly the right moment.

The stem of PQ61 was reinforced with a small ram made of solid steel, in much the same way as the *Endurance*'s bow had been strengthened. PQ61, however, had a draught of only seven feet forward, and at full speed the stern settled down and the bows lifted until the stem was only four feet in the water. To strike the heavier submarine in that position would mean turning the tables: instead of sinking the enemy, the bottom of Worsley's ship would probably be ripped out and he would become the defeated.

> The moment before the impact the engines were stopped and our bows settled down in the water just as I had timed that they should. As the bows fell, the ram caught the submarine amidships, tearing her sides open and rolling her beneath us. We felt a terrific shock and at the same time heard the unearthly rasp of tearing steel. She sank rapidly beneath us and immediately afterwards we were shaken by a tremendous explosion.
>
> For a moment I thought that another submarine had got us with a torpedo, but it was either the chamber of the rammed vessel bursting open or her mines exploding. Stenhouse sang out down the tube to the engineer to ask if our engines were all right, and on receiving the reply "yes" we went full speed ahead again.

The sea was boiling up in huge bubbles and foam. Oil started to spread. The UC33 was finished, with almost her entire crew. Among the oil and debris two figures were spotted and life-buoys were thrown to them. One man, an officer, secured his and calmly awaited rescue; the other man panicked and sank from sight, one of the 24 crew who died.

It was most satisfying. UC33 was a mine-laying submarine, a type that could wreak much damage to unarmed coastal vessels. She was one of only six sunk in the Irish Channel during the war, and was the 88th submarine casualty of the conflict. The July–September quarter of 1917 was one of the most successful periods against submarines, with 20 confirmed sinkings and 45 possibles.

Another account of Worsley's brilliant action comes from the book *Endless Story*, a record of the work of destroyers, flotilla-leaders, torpedo boats and patrol boats in the Great War by the notable British writer of naval affairs known as Taffrail (a pseudonym for Captain Taprell Dorling, DSO, RN).

He singles out Worsley's attack as a text-book example of the work of which P-boats were capable. It differs in one respect, stating that Worsley's crew managed to get away some shots from a 12-pounder gun as PQ61 worked up to full speed, one shell hitting the submarine near the conning tower.

The sole survivor, the commander, had been the last man to get below before the UC33 submerged to escape the advancing decoy-ship. Before being sent below under guard on PQ61 – and motivated no doubt by self-preservation after one narrow escape from death – he volunteered to Worsley the information that three of his 'pals' were in the area.

So there still was danger. However, Worsley had to care for the disabled tanker, and the task of securing the much larger tanker for towing he left to Stenhouse while he scanned the sea for a fresh enemy. He gave full praise for his first lieutenant's 'splendid seamanship' in making a cable fast in now-heavy seas for a 600-ton ship, not fitted for towing, to drag a damaged 7000-ton tanker 80 miles to the safety of Milford Haven.

To help take care of any new attack, Worsley called in other ships and several stood by to chase off vengeful U-boats. Two enemy submarines were spotted as the small convoy approached the south-west corner of Wales, but they submerged immediately they were challenged.

The tow took 12 hours, and Worsley said he feared being picked off in the bright moonlight, so he kept very close to the coast; so close, in fact, that the captain of the *San Zeferino* later confessed that he was more afraid of being wrecked than torpedoed, as the ships at times were no more than 100 feet from cliffs. He did not appreciate then that he was being guided by one of the great navigators of the day.

That night, after anchoring, Worsley recorded that he and Stenhouse were dead-tired from a day packed with thrills and excitement, but they were 'jolly as schoolboys'. Next morning they had breakfast with the German captain, Ober-Leutnant Alfred Arnold, who reckoned that he would have submerged and escaped in another three seconds. Then he invited Worsley to come to Germany and stay with him as a guest when the war was over.

In another gesture, Arnold wrote to Worsley thanking him for saving his life and expressed his pleasure in sending to the New Zealander his silver whistle 'as a small present and expression of my thanks'.

Frank Worsley's mystery ship, PQ61, towing the damaged oil tanker, *San Zeferino* to safety after it had been torpedoed by a German U-boat. Worsley sank the submarine, UC33, by ramming it. Only the U-boat captain was saved. Worsley received his first DSO for this encounter.
Bamford family

As a weapon of destruction, the U-boat was a success far beyond the resources involved. At most, 150 U-boats were operational at any one time during the critical years of the Great War. About 200 were destroyed in action, with the loss of 5000 officers and men. Hundreds of British warship and patrol vessels were tied up in anti-submarine work, yet by the end of the war 5700 allied ships, totalling more than 11 million tons, had been sunk by a few hundred cheap, small U-boats, most of which were manned by a crew of about 40. Hitler's Germany was to repeat the lesson in World War 2.

Clearly then the destruction of a U-boat was welcomed by the Admiralty, whose propaganda estimated that one sunk enemy submarine was worth five million pounds sterling to England. A bounty was paid on 'kills' – one thousand pounds sterling. Worsley later wryly confessed that in his imagination he stood ready to make a lot of money simply by ramming submarines, which in the right conditions didn't seem too difficult. 'My estimated wealth was colossal,' he wrote.

The letter which the U-boat commander, Alfred Arnold, presented to Frank Worsley. The letter said, *inter alia*, 'I have much pleasure in sending you my silver whistle as a small present and expression of my thanks that you saved me from death.' The whistle is pictured top left.
Bamford family

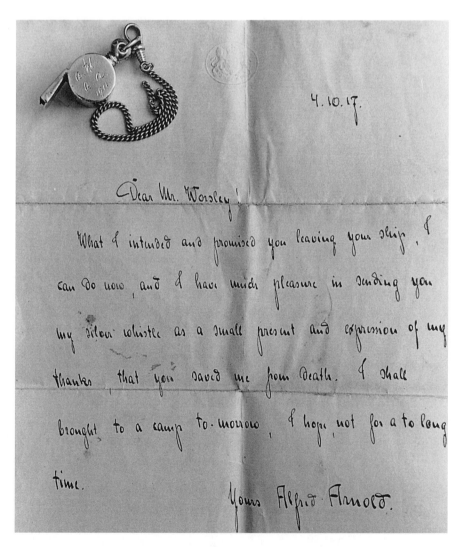

120

Above: Frank Worsley's ensign from his World War 1 mystery ship, the PQ61. The battered, tattered and torn flag is at Akaroa Museum, New Zealand. Worsley won his first DSO in action with PQ61, when he rammed a German submarine in the Irish Sea.
Akaroa Museum

Above left: Frank Worsley (right) with the captain of the German submarine (centre). The German, Alfred Arnold, has just handed Worsley a letter of thanks for saving his life.
Bamford family

Before they received the Admiralty award, Worsley and Stenhouse went to London to celebrate, had a 'really royal time' and returned minus a hundred pounds each. A little later the bounty arrived: Worsley's share was 68 pounds and Stenhouse's was 48 pounds. 'We therefore found bagging submarines an expensive amusement,' said Worsley.

For his skill and resolution in the action against UC33, Worsley was awarded his first Distinguished Service Order (DSO), while Stenhouse got a Distinguished Service Cross (DSC). Two petty officers received Distinguished Service Medals (DSMs) for good work in steering and in gun-laying. Stenhouse was further rewarded with his own command, being appointed to the Q-ship *Ianthe*.

Worsley said Shackleton's reaction to the news was a wire reading, 'Well done Skipper, Tally Ho!'

Back in action, Worsley found a grand toy to play with in depth-charges. He recognised that this was a weapon that could defeat the U-boat menace, and specialised to the point that he earned the title of 'Depth-Charge Bill'. He spent a total of 10 months at sea in PQ61.

On 16 September 1918, Worsley was appointed to take over command of the Q-ship *Pangloss*, operating in the Mediterranean, from probably the most famous of the Q-boat commanders, Captain – later Admiral – Gordon Campbell, VC, DSO and Bar. One has to attribute such an appointment as acknowledgment of the stature of the New Zealander in Admiralty eyes.

Before he left PQ61, Worsley submitted to the Admiralty a request for 'monetary reward' to his officers and crew for towing the oiler *San Zeferino* 'through a dangerous area to safe haven after she was torpedoed, disabled and the crew having taken to the boats'. However, it was ruled that there were no special circumstances, and to make no further awards than had already been paid.

Worsley's ensign from PQ61 is today in New Zealand, in the museum at his home town of Akaroa. For many years the flag was featured in the local St Peter's Church. More recently it was renovated for display at Akaroa Museum.

CHAPTER 12

Russia

Worsley never got to the Mediterranean and command of the glamour Q-ship *Pangloss*: Shackleton, and the fear that in the final stages of the war there might be no U-boats left to fight, got in the way.

In a letter to Leonard Tripp in Wellington, dated 26 October 1918, Worsley explained that a month after his appointment, while on his way through London to Gibraltar to join *Pangloss*, he had met Shackleton, who was then preparing to go to northern Russia to be attached to the hastily organised North Russia Expeditionary Force.

'Of course I wanted to join him, especially as we anticipated some really good fighting,' wrote Worsley from the ship *Ella* steaming north bound Murmansk. He added that recent developments 'look as though there will be little or no fighting submarines from now on in the Mediterranean'.

Shackleton had successfully applied to the Admiralty to have Worsley transferred to the expeditionary force, while still retaining his naval rank of lieutenant-commander.

Although Shackleton's own work with the force was no more than staff officer in charge of Arctic equipment at Murmansk, with the army rank of major, he already had several of his old companions assigned to him. Frank Wild was in Russia ahead of them all, and he was followed by Dr James McIlroy, second surgeon on the *Endurance*. Dr Alexander Macklin, the chief surgeon, was also part of the expeditionary force, code-named Syren for the Murmansk detachment and Elope for a party based at Archangel.

Leonard Hussey, the *Endurance* meteorologist, was also with Shackleton in London when Worsley met the Boss and, as Worsley told Tripp, 'of course nothing would do me until I got my old pal Stennie [Stenhouse] with us, and Sir E applied for him, and here we are together again, and happy as sandboys'. He said of the journey to Murmansk, 'We four go everywhere together and had great fun at Newcastle, Edinburgh (2 days) and Kirkwall in the Orkneys. We expect to land in Lapland tomorrow night.'

Worsley described the journey as 'fine and uneventful since the evening after we left Newcastle, when our escort sank a submarine that was endeavouring to attack our convoy. I enjoyed seeing somebody else, for a change, dropping depth charges and blowing the sub to the Devil.'

Worsley told Tripp that while he could not say anything of what they were going to do in Russia, what he would like 'would be for us to finish up each driving a dog-team over the snow into Berlin' at the time the 'victorious British,

New Zealanders, Yanks and French troops burst in from the Western Front'. And with typical Worsley ebullience, 'We are going now to the Murman coast – no mermaids'.

Worsley also wrote: 'There was plenty of ice and snow to remind us of old times, and it was just as though we had never separated at all…the old gang was on the warpath!'

The North Russia Expeditionary Force was brought about by the Bolshevik revolution of November 1917, and the growing threat of a Russian desertion of the Allied cause against Germany in what was becoming the hour of greatest need on the Western Front: resisting the final German offensive that brought the enemy to within 60 miles of Paris, and turning the Germans back to their own country.

The prospect of the new leaders of Russia making a separate peace with Germany while consolidating the revolution at home, thus freeing another German army for action in the west, was a major fear. Another was to stop the Germans from occupying permanently ice-free Murmansk and using it as a submarine base from which U-boats could be used to attack the ships bringing United States troops to Europe.

The 'Workers and Peasants' Government' of Russia, born of the socialist revolution and dominated by the Bolsheviks, in January 1918 proclaimed the country to be a Republic of Soviets of Workers, Soldiers and Peasants' Deputies, founded on the basis of a free union of free nations: a federation of Soviet national republics. It aspired to no great foreign policy apart from the expectation that workers in capitalist countries would take heart from the events in Russia, and would perhaps make the revolution international.

While the imperial powers were appalled at what was happening, the Bolsheviks were endangered more from within than from without. Peace with Germany was a priority to free the small 'Workers and Peasants' Red Army' to protect the revolution.

In February peace negotiations opened at Brest-Litovsk in German-occupied Ukraine. The Bolshevik leaders were forced to accept shameful terms, including abandonment of the Ukraine, and the peace treaty was signed on 3 March, bringing to a halt the final German advance into Russia.

The danger of Murmansk falling into German hands was now over, but there was still the need to try to keep some German forces occupied in the east by boosting Russian units remaining loyal to the allied cause. The month the Treaty of Brest-Litovsk was signed, the British occupied Murmansk. In April, Japan landed troops at the other side of Russia, at Vladivostok, reinforced two months later by British and United States detachments. In July, British, French and United States troops occupied Archangel, on the White Sea south of Murmansk.

The allies hoped that by re-opening the Eastern Front, pressure on their armies in the west would be eased. The expectation that the war in North Russia would last at least another winter convinced the authorities they needed somebody to organise transport and equipment in polar conditions. Shackleton was chosen for the job: a winter-only contract. However, two weeks after Shackleton, Worsley and friends landed at Murmansk, on 11 November the Armistice was signed and the war with Germany was over.

But still there was fighting as forces loyal to the former Imperial Russian rulers, with nowhere else to go, shaped up to the new and growing Soviet peasant army in a civil war. The west by now had interpreted the revolution as an assault on the whole capitalist system and feared that it was primed for export, so for political reasons the Allied forces in Russia, while made up of unfit or war-weary units considered inadequate for service elsewhere, remained to assist Tsarist (White) units undermine the Bolshevik (Red) consolidation. The Bolsheviks slipped easily into the role of enemy, though no war as such was ever declared.

As 1919 began, the Allied troops started to display their lack of enthusiasm for conflict. Many of the soldiers also developed a measure of sympathy for the workers' government. In April, there was a mutiny in French naval vessels at Odessa, on the Black Sea. Similar problems were headed off at Murmansk and Archangel with a progressive withdrawal of Allied troops. But the hostile intentions of the western capitalist states remained, and the withdrawal of troops was compensated by an increased flow of military supplies and military missions attached to any force willing to line up against the Bolsheviks.

One of the areas where support was openly extended was around Murmansk and Archangel, where an independent North Russian government was centred. It was planned that the British mission there would help train a local army and give the regime some capacity to survive against the Reds.

Worsley did not remain with Shackleton for long. General Edmund Ironside, one of the British commanders in the North Russia campaign, was on the Archangel front, and he wanted somebody there to carry out the same duties as Shackleton at Murmansk – director of Arctic equipment and transport. Worsley was chosen.

He quickly devoted himself to assessing the winter conditions and their effect on the various units living in the Dvina River area. In early December he reported that he had visited 'blockhouses and billets', addressing the soldiers on the dangers of frostbite and how to exist in the extreme cold. He found the soldiers 'a little stale' with too few officers. He urged that the solders be relieved in batches for two weeks' rest every two months.

Worsley found much of the equipment inadequate, particularly gloves and footwear, and warned that frostbite could disable the entire column. He suggested that until soft leather mittens were available, native coarse flax gloves should be bought. Boots should have felt insoles, leather straps and sennegrass lining, like the best Antarctic equipment.

The 'natives' should be induced to sell cattle to the force, with the army then selling back the hides to recover some of the cost. The American unit had the best iron stoves, and Worsley said more should be bought immediately and distributed. WCs in use should be covered around the base 'to prevent uprush of cold air chilling the men', and pigs should be kept both for food and to help get rid of refuse. Fresh meat should be available two days a week, with a daily issue of oatmeal and potatoes or onions to prevent scurvy.

Of the Vaga River column, on which Worsley reported at the end of December, he again praised the conditions established for the American soldiers, in particular their diet of fresh beef, potatoes and onions each day. In another report on the Vaga force, in January 1919, he said he had instructed some American officers on the use of skis, while a Canadian sergeant taught them to use snowshoes.

Being at the front on these missions, Worsley got his first taste of the conflict. 'During this time there were several alarms and mine attacks by the Bolsheviks. The spirit and eagerness held by A Company of the 339th – the best of the Americans – was very marked,' he said. When Russian troops replaced the Commonwealth force, artillery accuracy showed a marked decrease, 'though this will probably improve'.

Of his lectures, he said he spoke to about 2000 troops, 'British, US and a few odd Ruskies who came in for a sleep'. Frostbite was the constant danger, and Worsley emphasised this in relation to his Antarctic experience, 'until everybody said either I was a liar, or it was better to be in Russia than in Antarctica, which was just what I was trying to drive into them.'

Away from the fronts at the end of January, Worsley was resting with his comrades when the Bolsheviks made big advances and all but captured the Dvina and Vaga River forces. All available men were sent back into the danger areas, and with the rivers frozen over to preclude action on water, Worsley attached himself to any active unit on the Vaga front.

'I'd ride as a trooper with a Cossack patrol, go hay-raiding with the Kings Liverpools, crawl through the forest with the Royal Scots and Americans driving the Bolos back, or go up the road with Canadian artillery officers surveying and taking angles for indirect fire etc,' he wrote home to Christchurch in a letter.

'All units are short of officers, and twice I took command of Liverpools and Royal Scots platoons, and once a company of Russians. That was great fun. They were game to go anywhere, as long as they were led by an "Angleskee offitzer".'

At the end of April, when ice on the river started to move, Worsley was posted back to Archangel, where he sought and was given command of the gunboat HMS *Cricket*.

'My knowledge of ice stood me in good stead…the commodore allowed us to be the first gunboat to work through the broken ice up the Dvina River, and the first to engage the Bolsheviks. I had two happy months of fighting in her: that is, we'd have two hours' fighting every other day,' he said. 'We shelled "Bolo" gunboats, land batteries, villages and troops and assist in the re-capture of some 10 miles of ground lost in the autumn and winter.'

Worsley, who had no difficulty in viewing the Bolsheviks as 'the enemy', did not share the commonly held view that the western forces were fighting a disorganised rabble. 'The "Bolo" isn't half the fool a lot of our people try to make out he is,' he wrote.

In order to get further up the river, *Cricket* had to be lightened, and Worsley took his vessel back to Archangel to have the work done. It was also planned to mount longer-range guns on her. While this work was progressing, Royal Navy officers arrived from Britain to replace the RNR officers like Worsley, something he took 'a bit hard, as there was now a good chance of a general advance'. However, in June he was appointed to HMS *Fox* for duty in fitting out gun-barges for work up the river, and in the following month he was appointed to command HMS *M24*, a monitor and tender to HMS *Fox*.

But clearly the main thrust of action was to come on land, and Worsley did not want to miss out. In August, he had himself attached to a unit of the Hampshires, commanded by General Grogan, VC, on the Pinega River, west of the Dvina and south-west of Archangel.

On one 'cheery evening' in the mess, Worsley was asked if he wanted to take part in a 'bit of fun' – a secret raid across the river and through the Bolshevik front line to capture some men and get information about a suspected 'Bolo' offensive. It involved 25 men from the Hampshires, with three horses. They planned to be away two days, and Worsley was advised not to tell his commander that he was taking part.

Worsley, on horseback, was headed for the startline across the Pinega when he came across General Grogan's car stuck in soft sand on the riverbank, the general and his staff trying to push it clear. Worsley felt obliged to help, and the general, wondering why he was out riding with full action kit, asked bluntly: 'Where are you going, Worsley?' Worsley professed not to hear while he struggled to push the car from the sand, and General Grogan soon grasped the situation.

'Look here, Worsley, you are not going on that raid,' he said, to which Worsley replied, 'Sir, it's a very fine day for it.'

The Royal Navy vessel HMS *M24*, which Frank Worsley commanded when the North Russian winter was over and river operations against the Bolsheviks were possible in 1919.
Bamford family

General Grogan: 'You are not supposed to be mixed up in this raid.'

Worsley, giving the car the final push that started it: 'Good-bye sir.'

General Grogan: 'Well, good luck to you!'

Early next day the raiding party trekked through about 20 miles of forest to the Bolshevik front, camped for the night, and early next day crossed the Pocha River on logs and gained shelter in forest within the 'Bolo' lines. About eight miles in they came across a road with telegraph wires. One of the party, a telephone operator, tapped the line and noted a lot of valuable information, some of it messages from the Bolshevik stronghold of Petrograd.

One message referred to a Bolshevik convoy coming their way. The raiders set a trap and opened fire on the horse-and-cart convoy, killing some drivers and guards. Others escaped into the forest.

The raiders grabbed what looked like valuable papers, and scurried into the forest with the carts and all the horses, dismantling the carts and releasing all but the six best horses.

'We knew that the countryside would be buzzing like a hive of bees after us, but as they could not know for a time in which direction we had gone, they would have some trouble striking our trail or intercepting us. We made for a different part of the [Pocha] river from that which we had crossed,' wrote Worsley.

The raiders found three boats that had been hauled up into the forest about 100 yards from the river, and these were grabbed and used to get across, with the horses swimming. They were seen by local peasants, and knew there would be a chase. Worsley the navigator, using the same compass he had on in the crossing of South Georgia, became the guide through the forest. The raiders by now had no food and had been in the field for two and a half days with little rest.

Frank Worsley in army uniform in North Russia, where he was posted as an advisor on Arctic equipment and transport. When the rivers froze over and naval operations were not possible, the restless Worsley turned to land-based adventures with British army units stationed there. One of them led to him receiving a bar to his DSO, following an operation behind the Bolshevik lines in 1919.

Bamford family

On the afternoon of the third day the condition of the men's feet in the rough going was giving concern. In an opening in the forest the officer in charge, Captain McFee, ordered a rest. A sentry spotted a group of Bolshevik soldiers approaching and McFee split his force, taking command of one section on one side of the clearing with Worsley the other.

The Bolsheviks did not know how close they were to their quarry, and the raiders opened fire on them and then charged with fixed bayonets, Worsley yelling his trademark 'Yoicks! Tally-ho!', which he said was 'echoed by our party with great heartiness and seemed to strike terror into them'.

The British soldiers grabbed more papers from the dead and dived back into the shelter of the forest, pursued now by more than 200 'Bolos'.

McFee felt out of his depth and told Worsley: 'You are much more experienced in tramping this sort of country…will you take charge of the march?' Worsley arranged for the men whose feet were worst affected to ride double-banked on the horses, and paced the march to 20 minutes at a time with two-minute breaks. 'I remembered our experience in South Georgia, when we found how valuable had been the two minutes' rest at each halt when crossing the mountains,' he wrote. 'It also enabled the men to get a meal of berries each hour. Yes, undoubtedly it took me back to old times!'

Late that day they had to ford several difficult streams and at dusk, a dangerous-looking marsh. The small Russian ponies almost submerged and had to be man-handled through the swamp. When they all got through, it was 'dark, misty and piercingly cold'. They dared not light a fire. 'At my suggestion, we snuggled up together for warmth, just as we had done in the boats when we escaped from the pack-ice and were making for Elephant Island,' Worsley wrote. Next afternoon, all 25 men were back safely at their starting point.

For what Worsley called a 'small part in this little adventure', General Grogan and Captain McFee recommended him for a Distinguished Service Order (DSO) to go with his earlier DSO.

Why they thought it so deserving 'I have never found out…nevertheless I am deeply grateful to them for obtaining for me an honour which I greatly prize,' Worsley wrote later.

The citation to the award, dated 17 October 1919, was clear:

In recognition of the gallantry displayed by him at Pocka, in North Russia between the 2nd and the 5th of August, 1919. This officer formed one of a large patrol which, in circumstances of great danger and difficulty, penetrated many miles behind the enemy lines, and by his unfailing cheery leadership he kept up the spirits of all under trying conditions. By his assistance in bridging an unfordable river between the enemy lines, he greatly helped the success of the enterprise.

In addition to the bar to his DSO, Worsley was also awarded a Russian decoration for his work for the cause, the Order of St Stanislaus.

Worsley's coolness at times of great danger is evidenced in one instance during the withdrawal to safety of the raiding party. At a rest point he is reported to have produced a pack of cards and organised a game of bridge. He claimed he and his partner were about to win the rubber when the game was interrupted by a 'Bolo' alert.

Shackleton, meanwhile, had been trying to get close to those potentially with power in the North Russia government, should it survive. He had entrepreneurial plans for the development of Murmansk, and for exploitation of natural resources and hydro power; those elusive riches were beckoning again.

But he was disappointed once more. Likely financial backers were not impressed, and by the end of 1919 the Allies withdrew from Murmansk and Archangel just before both towns fell to the victorious Bolshevik forces.

Stenhouse, who was at first stationed at Murmansk and won a DSO while in command of a lake flotilla of gunboats, joined Worsley in Archangel and they had 'a few more adventures and skirmishes which afforded us plenty of fun with our cheery friends in the army'.

With the evacuation of North Russia, they returned to London. Shackleton was already home, his own Russia adventure lasting just five months, while Worsley and Stenhouse spent a full year there.

One of the first things Worsley did in England was to renew acquaintance with an old and dear friend, and to introduce Stenhouse to her: the gallant and battered little *James Caird*.

At South Georgia three years earlier, after the excitement of the boat journey, all attention was on rescuing the men from Elephant Island; Shackleton and his men from the *James Caird* had little time to ponder a future for the lifeboat. But the Norwegian whalers there had tremendous respect for the *James Caird*, and they took care of her and later shipped her to England.

Worsley and Stenhouse went to Liverpool, where the ship *Woodville* arrived on 5 December from South Georgia with the *James Caird* as deck cargo. They supervised the loading of the boat on to an open rail wagon and escorted her to London.

CHAPTER 13

The Annie *and the* Quest

Worsley was demobilised on 2 January 1920. He was a month short of 48 years of age. In the previous five years he had survived the full *Endurance* experience and more than two and a half years of war, winning medals for gallantry both at sea and on land, a 'mentioned in dispatches' and a Russian award. A letter from the Admiralty dated 12 January stated that he was now on the retired list of the RNR, from his date of demobilisation, and at liberty to assume the rank and title of retired commander from that date.

The new challenge was how to make a living. The time he had spent in Russia, while exciting and food for Worsley's desire for adventure, meant that merchant navy jobs at sea befitting his rank and experience had long been taken up by other demobilised officers.

His bank account, at least, was in credit. The Admiralty had granted him a special subsistence allowance of one pound a day in respect of his service in North Russia. Worsley had had to draw on that for much of his time on active service, and with final adjustments he was left with a credit of 396 pounds for the period 1 October 1918 to 31 October 1919. Also included were 'climate pay and field allowance'.

And he had one more important appointment in relation to his erstwhile service career: an investiture at Buckingham Palace. He was ordered to report there on 12 May 1920 and receive from King George V the Order of the British Empire (OBE) for his services to Great Britain.

One casualty during these years of high adventure, danger and achievement was Worsley's marriage. Theodora Blackden – Mrs Frank Worsley – had quite literally disappeared. Worsley did not appear to be distressed by the development: he had more pressing needs, such as how an unemployed, albeit distinguished, sea captain approaching middle-age was to survive in a hard new world.

He saw Shackleton frequently in London, and the explorer's hopes of getting another expedition together were discussed. Worsley was certain of a post, but there was nothing on the immediate horizon. He had to find work.

With Stenhouse, who was in the same position, and some army friends from North Russia, Worsley formed a company with the intention of buying a ship and trading with the new republics of the Baltic. The company had five directors who held five DSOs between them. It was named Stenhouse Worsley & Co., the precedence being decided by a game of billiards which Worsley clearly lost.

Given Worsley's dismal financial history to date, it might have been just as well that Stenhouse should have nominal control: he at least came from a family with some business acumen. His family business was in shipbuilding, a Scottish firm, Birrell Stenhouse & Co. of Dumbarton, famous in its day as a builder of clipper ships.

Stenhouse's daughter, Patricia Mantell, years later recalled that Worsley and her father had 'a very hard time when they returned from Russia – almost right until the Second World War'. They had to take what work was offering. But both men were consistently cheerful: 'carefree – a bit irresponsible,' she said. Stenhouse in 1924 finally earned a billet as nautical adviser to the *Discovery* Research Committee, responsible for rigging and equipping Captain Robert Scott's famous old vessel. He commanded the *Discovery* for five years, the longest period of employment he had between the wars.

Stenhouse Worsley & Co. bought a small schooner, the *Annie*, with a capacity to carry 150 tons of cargo. She had only sails; there was no auxiliary engine. While fitting out proceeded, the Baltic freight market collapsed, and the first commercial ventures were around the British coast; there was no profit.

In early November, 1920, Worsley and Stenhouse sailed the *Annie* with a cargo from Leith in Scotland to Reykjavik in Iceland. It was an exhilarating journey before a gale from the south from which the regular steamer on the route had to run for shelter, while the *Annie* carried on.

Worsley said his big fear was that the strong current would drive them danger-ously close inshore in the dark, but his navigation was again perfect and dawn broke before they sighted land. They were already in Reykjavik by the time the steamer arrived, which greatly pleased the sailors.

Finding a return cargo proved difficult, and Stenhouse, who had been offered a position in an exploration party crossing Brazil, left the *Annie* and returned to England by the steamer. Worsley, still seeking a cargo and fast running out of money, paid off the crew. He spent months in Reykjavik, and while he found Icelanders most hospitable, he developed a dislike for the port which he later referred to as 'a drunken, dissolute prohibition town'.

When he finally got the promise of a cargo, it was at Bildudalur, a small settlement 320 miles away, at the end of a fiord on Iceland's north-western coast. He loaded scrap iron as ballast, and also some provisions for the local fishermen. His cargo was to be 120 tons of salt fish for Kirkwall, in the Orkney Islands, and then for a final destination in Britain.

Experienced Icelanders knew that such a journey in a small vessel without an engine in the middle of winter was foolhardy. Worsley believed he had no choice but to back his experience, and he hired a crew from waterfront types equally desperate for work. It was to be a huge test of his seamanship and his ability to drive men in the face of great danger; it was a test worthy of the Boss himself.

He estimated that the voyage, with luck, could be done in 32 hours. 'Actually the gales were so bad that it took me as many days,' he wrote later. Easterly gales lasted for three weeks, driving the *Annie* into the Denmark Strait close to Green-land. Worsley boldly struck northwards across the Arctic Circle, in the hope of getting a change of wind. They were driven so far they were almost caught in the

Arctic pack-ice. But the wind did change direction, and after three more days the *Annie* was within 40 miles of the Iceland north coast.

Worsley's scratch crew by now was so 'scratchy' he was careful not to bring the *Annie* windward of land, for fear that they would lower the lifeboat and desert schooner and skipper. 'I also deemed it prudent to sleep with my revolver under my pillow,' he wrote. The ship's provisions were so sparse the captain and crew broke open the cargo they were carrying for the residents of the fiord, something that was permissible under maritime law.

For three days Worsley drove the crew hard, tacking and working the ship to windward until she was close to land near the entrance to Arnarfjord, and only a few miles from port. But every time the *Annie* was nosed into the fiord the wind that was funnelled out of it 'would leap up at us with a force an suddenness almost comparable with gunfire...we lost sail after sail and were driven back time after time. After each unsuccessful attempt we repaired our sails and then gradually drew up again close to the shelter of the mountains. There was considerable danger of our being blown bodily out to sea.'

After three days of this, with the crew now desperate and hungry and the *Annie* nearly out of control through loss of sails, on the 31st day of the terrible voyage, a battered and rusty old trawler – British – hove into sight. Worsley was not too proud to hoist a flag of distress, and the trawler crew secured the *Annie* and towed her to port.

Some of the crew promptly deserted, and Worsley paid off the rest, then hired some real sailors, four young seamen and a mate for the voyage to Kirkwall.

Worsley wrote to a new friend, a young Scottish woman he had met in London, Maggie Jane Cumming, known as Jean. 'I have been having a rotten time. I've been captain, mate and crew...every damn thing, I wish this blasted Iceland had been a thousand fathoms deep before I was fool enough to think of bringing a sailing vessel to it in winter. I've had every sort of cursed trouble except bad health.'

Just before sailing, the shipper of the cargo brought Worsley an Icelandic newspaper carrying a report about Shackleton and a new expedition, this time to the Arctic. It mentioned that he was trying to contact Worsley. 'I immediately despatched a cable saying that I would be with him before the end of April.'

Worsley sailed from Bildudalur late in February 1921, and there were more problems to test his navigation and seamanship. He headed the *Annie* south to catch westerly gales that would carry the vessel towards the Orkney Islands. After three days the barometer started to drop. 'Never anywhere in the world have I seen a barometer so low. It was an uncanny sight to watch it falling, as though it would never stop,' he said.

Soon after, the hurricane it presaged struck, blowing more sails, smashing bulwarks and testing the rigging so hard it showed signs of parting. 'There followed a truly hellish week during which we worked incessantly to prevent the schooner from foundering.'

Worsley agreed to turn back to Reykjavik if the wind became fair, but in truth he had no intention, with the promise of a fresh adventure with Shackleton, of delaying his return to England; more so, since running the *Annie* would clearly not secure him a fortune. When a new gale with a wind favourable for Reykjavik arrived, he charted the ship's position 60 miles east of the true position to deceive the crew, and did not turn back.

Close to the Faroe Islands, Worsley decided that much of the rigging was so weak after the hurricane that the mast needed to be secured. The crew literally bound the *Annie* by passing heavy cable on each side of the vessel and drawing it up and securing it abreast of the foremast, and then stabilising the mast itself. Had the mast been carried away, the vessel would have been driven on to one of many rocky island coasts.

Four days later they reached Kirkwall. Fresh orders told Worsley to take his cargo to Grimsby. He exchanged telegrams with Shackleton and promised to join him as soon as possible.

It was at Kirkwall that Worsley began his lecture career. In recognition of the kindness of the local tradespeople, who knew he was virtually penniless and often refused to present bills for goods and services, he gave one lecture on the *Endurance* drama free, and another for the ship.

Also at Kirkwall he heard about an old and very ill sea captain in the town, and went to visit him, finding none other than Captain Jock Sutherland, his skipper on an early voyage on the *Piako*. 'Why, if it isn't little Worsley,' Sutherland said. 'To think that it was one of my lads that went south with Shackleton!'

Worsley still had some outstanding debts on the ship, and a mortgage as well, so after unloading his cargo at Grimsby he hurried to London and explained his problem to Shackleton. 'I must have you on the *Quest*,' Shackleton told him, writing two cheques, one to pay off the crew and return them to Iceland, the

The *Annie*, the small sailing vessel bought by Stenhouse Worsley & Co. to trade with the newly formed Balkan states. That venture failed, and the *Annie*'s one voyage was a near-disastrous journey from Scotland to Iceland. Frank Worsley is the man with the hat in the right-hand photograph.
Bamford family

The *Quest*, Sir Ernest Shackleton's somewhat inadequate vessel for the Shackleton–Rowlett Expedition in 1921. Frank Worsley was sailing master and hydrographer.
Scott Polar Research Institute, No. P53/18/4

other to clear the mortgage on the *Annie*. 'It's worth it to have you free from anxiety and to take that glum look off your old face,' he said. The other good news was that some of the old *Endurance* men were signed on for the *Quest*'s Arctic voyage: Wild, again as second-in-command; Macklin, McIlroy, Hussey, Kerr, McLeod and the cook, Green.

On the other hand, the *Quest* herself was a worry. Worsley's first inspection revealed a Norwegian sealer only 111 feet long, of less than 200 tons, and with a straight stem that made her unsuitable for work in the ice. She was only a little larger than the *Annie*, but she did have an engine, though not a very powerful one. Some modifications were made to the rigging at Worsley's suggestion, and a deckhouse was added for extra accommodation.

While this work was progressing, Shackleton learned that promised financial support from the Canadian Government was not to eventuate. This killed the plan of going to the Arctic, where he had hoped to discover new lands north of the Beaufort Sea.

Another financial backer of the new expedition was an old school friend from Dulwich College, John Quiller Rowlett, a wealthy man in the liquor trade. Shackleton persuaded Rowlett to take on the full expense, and it became the Shackleton–Rowlett Expedition.

But it was by then too late for the Arctic, and Shackleton could not wait around for months for the next season. He decided to go south again for the Antarctic summer, proposing a circumnavigation of the continent, among other things, without getting too close to the ice in the straight-stemmed *Quest*. He would also look for lost sub-antarctic islands, and finally he planned to spend the southern winter relaxing in the warm Pacific, where the old dream of finding one of Worsley's pearl lagoons might be realised.

The crew of the *Quest* in London before departure in 1921. Sir Ernest Shackleton is seated wearing a hat and Frank Worsley is standing on the left smoking a cigarette. Frank Wild is seated to the right of Shackleton.

Scott Polar Research Institute, No. P53/18/20

Worsley's special job was sailing master of the *Quest* and hydrographer to the expedition. He was to carry out deep-sea soundings, magnetic work, and to chart or complete the charts of out-of-the-way places that might be visited, something that interested him as, he said, while he was no scientist, 'I was interested in all forms of life beneath the waters.'

There was much scientific and sounding equipment on board, and the Admiralty also lent the expedition a naval wireless set, which meant receiving correct Greenwich mean time for checking chronometers frequently and ensuring that longitudes observed were accurate.

The *Quest* left London on 18 September 1921, with vessels lining the banks of the Thames and dipping ensigns and blowing whistles. 'It was a great send-off, and Shackleton, who took a boyish delight in being made a fuss of, was highly delighted,' Worsley wrote.

He noted also how well the Empire was represented, with New Zealanders,

The *Quest* passes the Tower of London on 18 September 1921. Her defects soon became apparent, and the expedition all but collapsed with the death of Sir Ernest Shackleton at South Georgia early the following year.
Dulwich College

Australians and Canadians among the 20 men on board. The other New Zealander was Major C. R. (Roderick, or Roddy) Carr, DFC, from Feilding, whom Worsley had met in North Russia. Carr had a distinguished wartime flying record and was to take charge of a seaplane which, it was planned, the *Quest* would carry. This was the Avro 554 Antarctic Baby (see Appendix 4).

Another interesting member of the crew was an 18-year-old boy scout, James Marr, put there by special arrangement through the *Daily Mail* newspaper. The youngster later went on to a distinguished career in exploration and diplomacy, and joined Worsley a few years after the *Quest* voyage for a journey to the Arctic.

The expedition did not go smoothly. Worsley reported a near-accident at the very start, when bascules of Tower Bridge had not been lifted as arranged. The *Quest* came swiftly on a flood tide, and the bascules finally rose as the mast seemed about to touch them. 'Although we had little space to spare, we swept through,' he said.

Every account of the *Quest* voyage from people who knew the old Shackleton commented on how ill he appeared, and how physically spent. Worsley said he learned that the Boss had had one bad spell of pain before leaving London which, in the light of later knowledge, must have been a heart attack. 'The one subject that seemed to interest him these days and to take his mind off the worries which quickly came upon him, was my pearl lagoon.'

The ship sailed badly and the weather exacerbated her defects. There was engine trouble and she had to put in at Madeira for repairs for a week.

In mid-Atlantic, close to the Equator, the *Quest* stopped at St Paul's Rocks, a group of tiny islets 'white with guano and without vegetation'. While a shore party explored and fished, Worsley took the *Quest* around the rocks, taking soundings. At the same time he charted their outline and measured the height of each rock. The chart he made was later handed to the Admiralty, together with

Roderick Carr and Sir Ernest Shackleton (both wearing white trousers) at Rio de Janeiro, Brazil, in December 1921. They were presented with the Diploma of Brazilian Aviators. The only other holders of the diploma were the King of Belgium, one Brazilian and the Prince of Savoy.

L.D.H. Tripp Collection, Alexander Turnbull Library, No. F- 98532-1/2

one he made of Gough Island in the South Atlantic Ocean.

The engine continued to give trouble, the ship leaked and Shackleton, though eager to get to Antarctica, had to put into Rio de Janeiro on 21 November. The *Quest* was laid up there for a month. At some stage – either at Madeira or Rio, though no report of the expedition makes it clear – the Avro 554 was off-loaded from the *Quest* and sent on with some other stores to Cape Town. The original plan was to visit Tristan da Cunha and then Cape Town, picking up the aircraft and making the South African port the base.

While at Rio, Shackleton and Carr were honoured by the Brazilian Government for services to aviation, both men receiving the Diploma of Brazilian Aviators.

But the delay in Rio, in Worsley's words 'sorely tried Shackleton's nerves and was a source of constant worry to him'. He was afraid he would miss part of the brief Antarctic summer. Just before leaving Rio, Shackleton had a massive heart attack, and to Dr Macklin, at least, it was obvious that he was suffering from heart disease.

Instead of sailing to Cape Town, where the Avro 554 was to have been picked up and assembled for the first flights over Antarctica, Shackleton pressed on to South Georgia instead.

The *Quest* sailed from Rio on 18 December. Worsley recorded more trouble – a crack in the boiler; a leaking water tank; new leaks in the hull. But these problems, curiously, now seemed to rouse Shackleton: or was it the impending return to South Georgia, scene of one of his greatest triumphs?

At any rate, Worsley said that for the first time on that voyage 'I saw his shoulders hunched in the old aggressive way and his jaw thrust forward. To me this was a wonderful, heartening sight, for it brought back a thousand memories of Shackleton's gallantry, his coolness and his power.' However, he recorded the Boss' disgust at having to keep a watch again. It was 'almost comic and he would warn

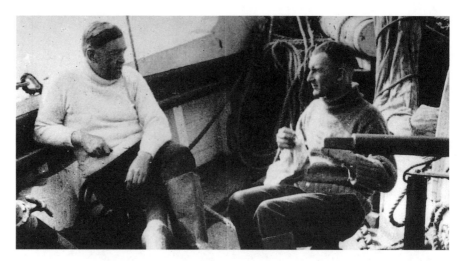

Sir Ernest Shackleton and Frank Worsley yarn on the deck of the *Quest* during the journey to South Georgia in late 1921. Worsley recalled their pleasure at seeing the island, which they had crossed in 1916, and in pointing out features to the rest of the crew.

Scott Polar Research Institute, No. P53/18/24

me every time he turned out at night of the evils of skylarking'. In a letter dated 28 December 1921 to Jean, he wrote: 'I had been driving the *Quest* as hard as I dared all night, with the ship half under water, until 7am when Shackleton came up and said: "None of your games, Wuzzles – heave her to," which we did.'

As the mountains of South Georgia came into sight. Shackleton and Worsley were both excited and happy, with Shackleton calling Worsley out at 6am as they approached land. The skipper said: 'Sir E and I like a pair of excited kids rushing around showing everyone where we first came over the mountains.' Shackleton was continually pointing out spots where he, Worsley and Crean had been six years earlier.

He would call Worsley down from the bridge, saying: 'Skipper, show the boys where we slid down.' Worsley recorded that 'the dear old Boss was quite prepared for me to let the ship wander along on her own'.

The *Quest* arrived at Grytviken on 4 January 1922, and Worsley said Shackleton displayed all his old energy when going ashore to arrange details of work. That night he came back on board for dinner while the others went ashore, leaving him alone with Worsley.

Shackleton was eager to talk, Worsley recorded, and he offered the New Zealander the chance to land on Antarctica with sledges and four or five men to make his own exploration, and to have anything he discovered recorded in his own name. 'I was greatly moved by this generosity,' Worsley said. 'Most men who had endured all that Shackleton had been through would have felt entitled to take the credit of discoveries made by any of their party.'

The old companions chatted about the real prospect of landing at a Pacific pearl lagoon after the scientific work off Antarctica, and Worsley recorded how Shackleton, in a sudden mood swing, then said in a tone full of doubt, 'I wonder whether I shall ever see the Skipper's lagoon?' Then suddenly he was back on the subject of the size of the pearls.

It grew late and Worsley went to his own cabin next door. He thought he heard Shackleton calling him, so he returned to the Boss' cabin, but did not stay.

'I glanced at him as I closed the cabin door, but nothing warned me that this was the last time that I should see him alive.' The rest of the crew returned late, and Worsley heard Wild and Shackleton talk briefly before he slept.

A few hours later, in the early morning, Shackleton woke and summoned Macklin, who was then on watch. Shackleton told the doctor that he had had one spasm of pain, apparently in his back, and was suffering badly from another.

Worsley recorded that Shackleton requested 'in his usual imperious way' that Macklin get him medicine to alleviate the pain. Macklin went away to get the medicine, and on his return found Shackleton very bad, but notwithstanding this, the Boss asked, 'You are always telling me to give up things, Mac; what am I to give up now?'

Shackleton tried to take the medicine, but vomited and Macklin, fearing a fatal seizure called the other doctor, McIlroy. Shackleton died as McIlroy arrived at his cabin at 2.50am on 5 January 1922.

Macklin called Frank Wild, who then asked that Worsley be woken. Wild broke the painful news and Worsley noted that Shackleton had often said a fortune-teller told him he would be dead at 48. He died within 41 days of attaining that age.

Worsley told Jean Cumming how he felt: 'It is a terribly sad blow. I have lost a dear pal, one of the whitest men, in spite of his faults, that ever lived.'

Shackleton's body, escorted by Hussey, was on its way back to England when Lady Shackleton intervened and decided that her husband should be buried on South Georgia, where he had always been at his most indomitable. Hussey returned to South Georgia with the body on 27 February, and a week later the funeral service was held and the coffin was buried in the little cemetery on a hill overlooking Grytviken.

While this was happening the *Quest* expedition resumed, with Wild in command. Nothing startling appears to have been achieved, though Worsley, according to his diary (22 January), had one narrow escape when there was 'a slight difference between Wuzzles and the staysail sheet block'. The result was severe concussion that put the skipper out of action for two weeks.

The diary also glossed over a much more serious incident. It is covered more fully in *The Seventh Continent*, by Arthur Scholes. On a fine day, though a long broad swell continued to run from the westward, Wild decided to take his chance and swing out the port lifeboat, to have her more ready to lower away and to give space on the bridge deck. The boat contained a quantity of emergency stores and was very heavy.

> The *Quest* rolled considerably and during the operation a guy parted and the boat, swinging forward, pinned Worsley against the after bulkhead of the bridge-house, almost crushing him to death. For two or three days the surgeon had doubts of the captain's recovery but once over the shock he rapidly regained his health.

In a letter to Jean, Worsley admitted how close he had come to death. 'The boat had half a ton of stores, and swung in with a violent rush, pinning me against the afterside of the bridge. Fortunately Thorneycroft [the ship's builders] had not built the bridge as strong as they might and it smashed in a good deal with me,

Frank Worsley (smoking) and Roderick Carr, the other New Zealander on the *Quest*. Carr, who had a distinguished flying record in World War 1, and went on to an even greater career in World War 2, missed out on being the first person to fly in Antarctica, as the seaplane carried on the *Quest* was never used.
Bamford family

saving my life. Thank the Lord I'm tough…I was laid up only four days.'

And the scout James Marr, in his book on the *Quest* voyage, *Into the Frozen South*, said that when the lifeboat swung back 'there was a cry, the splintering of wood and the awful snap of human bones as Worsley's ribs gave in'. He had broken ribs and crushed muscles, and 'but for the smashing of the wheelhouse, he must inevitably been killed outright'.

Worsley had little good to say about the performance of the *Quest*. One diary note records:

> Slowly onward we go, the sport of the ocean, the plaything of the winds, buffeted to and fro like a shuttlecock by the seas, reeling and staggering; a dissolute drunken derelict on the face of the waters she lurches to starboard and the Cape pigeons chatter shrilly in ridicule; she falls to port and the lordly albatross poises a moment in amazement; she pitches, trips, spins, pirouettes, then falls down and picks herself up again to the loud laughter of the gods, and the derision of all the little fishes.

To her 'unfortunate inhabitants', the *Quest* was 'a harlot, a strumpet, a bawdy, a randy thing'. These were 'the politest epithets, accompanied by suggestions of impropriety about her parentage, and enough about her Norwegian ancestry to cause another war'.

One day the *Quest* out-lurched herself in Worsley's estimation when 'the antics and gyrations of this contortionist craft' sent Query, the ship's dog, overboard. 'The poor chap probably was rolled over by a sea and drowned in a very few minutes…he is very much missed as he was very playful, a most pally dog and of the gentlest disposition.'

Wild later wrote a book on the expedition, *Shackleton's Last Voyage*. Among the dry minutia is a reference to Roddy Carr, who never got to try his flying skills over Antarctica as Shackleton had missed out Cape Town on the way south after sending the aircraft there. But Carr fitted in well on the *Quest*, doing routine work and helping with meteorological work. Worsley recorded that at one stage he a spent a week stoking the engine, and was as cheery as ever in spite of sea-sickness. His versatility was also shown in carpentry work – cupboards and shelves – after which he was known as Roddy Carr-penter.

In mid-March the *Quest* was beset for a week in young ice in the northern part of the Weddell Sea, and Worsley, lamenting the absence of the aircraft, said, 'We could have sent Carr up and I feel he would have seen land in an hour's flight.'

On 28 March the *Quest* was at Elephant Island. The veterans of the *Endurance*, Hussey recorded, 'gazed with binoculars picking out and recognising old familar spots…few thought when we left it last that it would ever be our fate to see it again.'

On 6 April the *Quest* returned to South Georgia, and Hussey, who had returned with Shackleton's body, reported to Wild. A few weeks later a site was selected for a memorial cairn at the north head of King Edward Cove. Worsley's diary records: 'May 6: all hands except one officer, one seaman and one stoker ashore building cairn to memory of Sir Ernest Shackleton, and making cross for a surmount.'

In a letter to Jean he wrote: 'We have just finished erecting a stone cairn 9 feet high, with a cross of plain oak. Wild and I and Macklin and McIlroy decided on the wording, my own contribution being "explorer" and "erected by his comrades". The full wording read:

> Sir Ernest Shackleton
> Explorer
> Died here January 5, 1922
> Erected by
> his comrades.

The original cairn in honour of Sir Ernest Shackleton at South Georgia, erected by his comrades in May 1922. Frank Worsley is standing on the extreme left, next to Dr Macklin.
Bamford family

On 9 May, the *Quest* sailed for Tristan da Cunha, where Worsley surveyed the island and verified the position of important features. At St Helena, the party lunched with the governor and visited Napoleon's tomb. Worsley also noted that New Zealand flax was being cultivated all over the fertile areas of the island. The *Quest* touched at Cape Town, then returned to Britain.

While the irrepressible Worsley was to go on seeking adventure at sea, the *Quest* voyage was the last made by Frank Wild. The Yorkshireman reputed to be a descendant of Captain James Cook had an unrivalled record of polar exploration, having been on five expeditions, starting as a seaman with Scott in 1901. From the first, he showed gifts of leadership. He was with Shackleton in 1907, and with the Australian Douglas Mawson in 1911. Wild was with Shackleton again through the *Endurance* drama, and finally with the *Quest*. He got the call for that journey while trying cotton-growing in Central Africa, and it was back to Africa that he went to settle in late 1922, on a property he called Quest Estate in Northern Zululand. He had married a woman he met in Russia, a widow whose husband had been a tea-planter in Borneo.

Wild's great weakness was for liquor, and by now he may have been alcoholic: on the *Quest*, after Shackleton's death, he drank steadily, something he had never before done at sea. The farming venture failed, and for a time he worked as a barman in a country town until, through the efforts of friends, he was rescued from impoverishment with a civil list pension of 170 pounds a year. Wild died at Klerksdorp in the Transvaal in August 1939, from pneumonia.

After the *Quest* adventure, Worsley was once more beached. At least his romance with Jean Cumming was prospering, but he needed work. One trade flourished at this time: the North American run, with cargoes of crude spirits destined for the illicit liquor business in the prohibitionist United States.

In May 1923, Worsley had command of a ship, the *George Cochran*, crossing the Atlantic for the Canadian port of Montreal. Anxious to maintain his schedule, he entered the St Lawrence Seaway in thick fog, and proceeded against advice without a pilot. Ever confident in his ability to navigate a ship, Worsley nudged his way ahead through a river system notorious for its canals, fierce eddying currents, and thousands of islands and rocks. At Montreal, he was deemed to be quite mad by those who knew the waterway better, but once more his skill had conquered circumstance.

The *George Cochran*, a freighter which Frank Worsley commanded on a voyage from Europe up the St Lawrence Seaway to Montreal. He was fortunate to negotiate the tricky passage in fog without a pilot, but once again his instinctive navigation saved him.
Bamford family

CHAPTER 14

Arctic Exploration

A 1923 portrait of Frank Worsley
taken at Montreal, Canada.
Bamford family

There was much about Grettir Algarsson that must have appealed to Frank Worsley. They met in 1924 when the young Canadian was fitting out a small boat for a modest voyage of exploration to the Arctic. Worsley was committed to other work, but he gave Algarsson some advice about sheathing the bows of his vessel for sailing in the ice. Worsley liked his engaging personality and his talent for organisation; he may have seen something of a young Shackleton in the 23-year-old.

At that time, Worsley was captain of a four-masted schooner called the *Kathleen Annie*. Late in 1924, he was sailing her from Bremen to Newfoundland, Canada, with a cargo of 20,000 cases of crude spirits, when he put into Kirkwall in the Orkney Islands for repairs. The *Kathleen Annie* then sailed, but was soon caught in a raging south-easterly gale and was driven ashore in the Orkneys.

A newspaper account of the incident said it was apparent that the ship must soon break up. What happened next was described as 'a thrilling story of the sea…how the entire crew was saved by the daring and resource of the skipper, Commander Frank Worsley, DSO, and the bravery of a sailor who swam ashore with a rope'. The newspaper rather breathlessly called it a story 'that will rank among the great epics of the sea'. Worsley may not have seen it in the same sensational light: he never recorded the event in print, though he did keep some newspaper clippings.

In the drama, with the gale at its worst and the vessel practically unmanageable, one man swam ashore with a line that was hitched to the bowsprit. 'Commander Worsley then, without a moment's hesitation, swung himself out on to the bowsprit and, watching his opportunity, aided the crew, one by one, to leap into the sea, seize the rope, and swing to shore.' When all were off the doomed ship, he performed the operation for himself.

The men had to jump with the incoming waves, as with the backward surge of the breakers it was impossible for them to hold on to the rope. It was a three-hour operation in which all the crew escaped, but the ship was wrecked. Another report said it was Worsley himself who took the rope ashore to effect the rescue of the crew.

Algarsson was born in British Columbia, Canada, of Icelandic parents. He was adopted at birth and was brought up by a Scottish family. His 1924 voyage was short-lived, his ship, the *Beltai*, being damaged in a collision with floating wreckage in the North Sea. The following year he asked Worsley to command another ship. The plan for this new expedition had a madcap quality that probably further attracted Worsley to Algarsson.

142

The race to fly to the North Pole was the exploration issue of the day. The Norwegian Roald Amundsen, conqueror of the South Pole, and the American Richard Byrd were prominent in testing the limits of polar aviation. Algarsson was another starter for North Pole honours. He needed an air base in Spitzbergen, far to the north of Norway in the Arctic Circle, and Worsley to command the ship that would take his aircraft and pilot to the island, part of the archipelago known as Svalbard, which is today under Norwegian sovereignty. Algarsson would then fly 600 miles to the North Pole, where he would crash-land the small aircraft. He and the pilot, with supplies for 100 days, would sledge back to civilisation.

Worsley was willing. His restless spirit was ready for more adventure. He had never been far to the north though the original plan for the *Quest* expedition would have taken him there with Shackleton. The challenge, in the company of an enthusiastic young man, was irresistible.

The Algarsson North Polar Expedition, as it was to be known, was soon in familar waters: there were problems over finance. Algarsson had his boat, the brigantine *Lady of Avenel*, which he renamed the *Island*. Worsley called her 'a fine specimen of the old-time shipwright's handicraft, built of British oak in the days when swelling canvas broke the horizon and dominated the Seven Seas'. She was 51 years old, 99 feet long and 114 tons and had been around Cape Horn – 'glory of glories for a small windjammer'. No wonder Worsley felt comfortable, despite the *Island* 'being profaned in 1920 by a semi-diesel engine with a two-bladed propellor'. He dismissively reported that this was capable of driving her at six knots 'when all was well'.

But the cost of finding a suitable aircraft stripped the available funds to the point where not only was the flight plan postponed, but also all those crewing the *Island* could not expect to be paid. But still there was enthusiasm to sail north, and Worsley and Algarsson decided to make the voyage and carry out the charting and hydrological work that was Worsley's responsibility, and the zoological and geological studies that were also in the plan. The North Pole crash flight would have to wait another year.

In the event, Algarsson's flight never took place. In 1926, with plans well advanced for another voyage north to be concluded by the flight to the Pole, the General Strike intervened. Work on the aircraft was delayed, and during the strike Amundsen and Byrd 'did the job', in Worsley's words.

There was also a crisis of sorts over the leadership. In a letter to Jean Cumming, Worsley said, 'I've been asked to take sole command and leadership of this expedition and I have written fully on it to Algarsson, asking him to come up to discuss it. I think for his own sake he'll be forced to do it to avoid coming a crash. He is coming up from London tonight to discuss the matter with me.' The result of their discussion was agreement on joint leadership, but the title of the expedition would continue to feature Algarsson's name.

Worsley gave these as the amended aims and objectives of the *Island* expedition:

> To go as far north of Spitsbergen as possible for meteorological and upper-air current data for Algarsson's proposed flight polewards the next year, for which we carried a

The *Island*, the small vessel owned by the young Canadian, Grettir Algarsson, who wanted Frank Worsley to take the ship far into the Arctic region to enable him to fly an aircraft to the North Pole. The expedition went ahead in 1925, despite having to drop the North Pole flight idea. Worsley called it 'the last great exploration in the region under sail'.
Bamford family

flight balloon; correct the charts of the north-east coast of Spitsbergen where they are in error; search for rocks and dangers on the coast of North East Land; search for Gillis Land, reported north-east of Spitsbergen in 1707; sound between Spitsbergen and Franz Josef Land to the limits of the continental shelf to settle the question of a submarine plain between these two lands; observe magnetic variations of the compass, correcting discrepancies on Admiralty charts; make deep-sea dredgings; carry out geological and zoological work; establish a farthest-north record in navigation; keep a continuous meteorological record and mark the limits of the pack-ice from Franz Josef Land to south of Greenland.

Notable in the 15-man party of unpaid volunteers were two others from the *Quest*, J.C. Bee-Mason, as a cinematographer, and James Marr, the boy scout sponsored on that voyage by a British newspaper. Marr, now with MA and BSc degrees from Aberdeen, sailed in the *Island* as biologist, naturalist and seaman.

A second New Zealander, the engineer, Gordon Burt, 26, was said by Worsley to be the handiest man on board: 'no engine ever seen on the ocean could defeat him'. Burt, from Dunedin, interrupted engineering studies at Liverpool University to make the journey. (See Appendix 3.)

Worsley described himself in crew data as 'Skipper, 5 feet 7 inches, thick-built and dark, born and bred in New Zealand of which he was proud.' He had commanded 20 vessels, four of them warships, and three lifeboats making ocean voyages.

The *Island* sailed from Liverpool on 21 June 1925, to Belfast, leaving there on

Grettir Algarsson and Frank Worsley (raising the flag), on the *Island*. The expedition came under their joint leadership during the voyage, which attracted speculation from the British press.
Bamford family

27 June. She sailed out of the North Atlantic Ocean and into the Norwegian Sea, separating Greenland and Spitsbergen, in which shipping usually found the maximum southern limit of drift ice.

The small vessel was soon in it, and she moved slowly north along the west coast of Spitsbergen towards the high latitude of 80 degrees, inside of which, between Spitsbergen and Franz Josef Land, Worsley hoped to find the mysterious feature of Gillis Land, which was still marked on charts at that time despite not being confirmed since a sighting in 1707.

In pack-ice, heading north-west towards the likely site of Gillis Land, an accident occurred as Worsley turned the *Island* to avoid a heavy floe. The bows struck another floe, which threw her quarter against a deep, heavy mass of ice. The tip of one blade of the propellor struck the hard ice, snapping the blade off at the boss.

'The shock was felt throughout the ship, and the heavy vibration that followed told what had happened,' Worsley wrote. 'Full of misgivings, I told Burt to try her ahead again at very slow speed, but at only one knot the vibration was so heavy that it made her leak aft through the stern-gland…for practical purposes our engine was out of commission until we could replace the propellor. The idea of forcing our way to Gillis Land was at present out of the question.'

When ice barred the way, soundings were taken and this exploration of the ocean floor proved the existence of a submarine plain between Spitsbergen and Franz Josef Land. The scientists also brought up 'strange and beautiful, as well as very ugly, creatures from the depths'.

The engineer Burt 'refused to go on the dole', Worsley reported, and raced aloft with the seamen, but the names that Burt gave to the ropes and gear aloft 'were appalling to a seaman's ears, or a parson's for that matter'.

The tracks of polar bears were often seen on the floes, and the first bear they saw was a huge creature on top of an iceberg. Algarsson shot it, and fresh bear steaks were on the menu. Worsley, with the knowledge that Shackleton had long taught about the value of fresh meat to combat scurvy, that scourge of seamen up to recent times, and the bugbear of polar explorers, said it was largely owing to the constant supply of bear meat that the party returned fit.

On 30 July, a steamer came close to the *Island*: it was the *Quest*, Worsley's old command. Worsley, Marr and Bee-Mason all went on board. The vessel was now Norwegian-owned, and was carrying a party of Italian noblemen looking for sport.

After surveying the northern coast of Spitsbergen, in Liefde Bay, 'we made down the coast and discovered a harbour suitable for small vessels of 15 foot draught.' Worsley said they took soundings and bearings as the *Island* entered, and he made a rough survey of the anchorage.

'After tossing for it, Algarsson christened it Worsley Harbour…no other navigator had mentioned the anchorage,' Worsley recorded. He also noted new positions on the chart for Great Island, on the east coast.

Before he could set the *Island* north again for the elusive Gillis Land, the ship became beset in the ice, with growing damage to the rudder. In a small natural ice harbour, Worsley cut a dock, forcing the vessel astern into the dock to give access to the rudder, which Burt strengthened while the ship drifted south for 13 days.

On the fourteenth day, the ice opened to the south and the east and as the wind freshened, Worsley worried about damage from the floes. He decided that he had to risk using diesel power to help get the *Island* clear of the ice.

Burt started his beloved engine, and half an hour later the ship had edged clear when there was a heavy jar: the last blade of the propellor had gone. 'Poor Burt was quite upset that he could no longer use the engine he had looked after so well and so fondly,' Worsley wrote.

But the sailor was at last in his true element: the *Island* was once more a sailing

brigantine, and in Worsley she had a master worthy of the challenge of setting new standards of achievement under sail in northern waters. He was later to call it 'sail's last unaided battle with the polar pack; the swansong of square sails driving the ship through the floes, handled by British seamen…by the 1000-year-old skill of seamanship'.

Danger soon loomed to test the *Island* and the crew's prowess under sail. It came in the form of a 50,000-ton iceberg straight ahead, with a narrow and closing passage to leeward – the sole visible way out of the pack. Worsley wrote:

> We raced for the passage…like a steamboat we rushed through, our hissing wash breaking off pieces of ice on both sides. We were so close to the floe to leeward that our bulwarks plumbed it as we heeled to the breeze, while our weather-side was less than 2 foot clear of the berg. The passage was 3 feet wider than the ship…nothing but long practice could have justified the risk.

Free of the pack, the *Island* sailed north-east for Franz Josef Land 200 miles away. This is a group of islands discovered in 1873 by an Austrian expedition, and named after the Austrian emperor. The islands are just inside the 80 degree latitude, and with neighbouring Spitsbergen, they are close to the limit of the permanent ice pack surrounding the North Pole.

The *Island* beset in the Arctic ice. The ship's engine became useless after the propellor was broken. Frank Worsley enjoyed the challenge of taking her well to the north under sail only.
Hocken Library, Dunedin

147

Late in August, off Cape Barents on one of the southern islands of the group, the *Island* had another narrow escape when the ship was carried by strong tidal currents into a passage between two icebergs.

The passage was about 300 metres long and 30 metres wide, and Worsley moved the *Island* through stern first, backing and filling the sails before the wind and the current. At the narrowest part of the passage the ship cleared the bergs by less than 2 metres in a nerve-wracking 20 minutes of frantic manoeuvring. That night the two bergs came together with a mighty thud.

Worsley's skills were acknowledged later by Burt in an article in the *Otago Witness*, the Dunedin (New Zealand) newspaper, of 12 January 1926, which stated that Worsley 'seems to have acomplished something quite wonderful in the way of navigation, and to have fortified his reputation of being one of the most skilled commanders of sailing craft in the world today'.

Burt wrote:

> The way he manoeuvred the vessel was absolutely marvellous. With the ice and bergs all over the place, he would pick his way just as though we were propelled by steam. We would come right up to an iceberg, the square sails would be adjusted and the bowsprit would just clear the berg and away we would go in another direction. At times he would even make the ship go astern. Everyone on board felt they would be ready to follow the skipper to the ends of the world.
>
> We got into several violent storms, and on one occasion we heeled over so far that our lifeboats were in the water…

Worsley and some crew landed at Cape Barents, where he and Burt claimed to be the first New Zealanders to set foot on the archipelago. He raised the Union Jack, and commented later, 'I trust this does not annoy those simple, sensitive souls, the Bolsheviks, for I understand they have claimed the group.' The Soviets had the last word, however: the islands were annexed by the Soviet Union a few years later, in 1928.

The *Island* sailed on northwards, with Worsley determined to take a sailing ship where no steam vessel had ever managed to go: through Franz Josef Land to Gillis Land, and then south-west back to Spitsbergen. But huge icebergs abounded as the permanent ice-pack loomed. The way ahead was now impassable to steam or sail.

The most terrifying event of the voyage came on 1 September, with the *Island* back south of Cape Barents and preparing to try once more to sail north, this time between Franz Josef Land and Spitsbergen, to find Gillis Land.

Once more the plaything of strong currents, the *Island* was drifting down on a big stranded iceberg Worsley estimated at nearly half a mile long. 'We set sail after sail till there were no more to set,' he wrote, but the vessel continued to drift in a strong current steadily down on the berg.

'The berg was too long to clear by a sternboard and there was the ever-present danger of the swell under-cutting it until it calved, when thousands of tons might have fallen on us, or the berg might have capsized,' he said. 'I gave a fearful yell of "all hands on deck to save the ship".'

The port lifeboat was lowered and manned to try to tow the *Island* ahead and to starboard. The swell lifted the ship and threw her almost under the berg's overhanging crest. The fatal blow seemed imminent.

Suddenly the berg front calved, and a mighty mass of ice slid into the sea 40yds astern. The wave rushed forward and swept the ship and the lifeboat along. 'We cleared the corner by about 2ft,' Worsley wrote. 'The men in the boat felt positive that our yards struck under the overhanging cornice; I am not sure that we did not strike the berg somewhere. It was a noble sight to see the little ship surge clear of the great gleaming masses of blue-veined marble by a hairsbreadth margin.'

Later at breakfast Worsley found the consensus was that his terrible language 'so shocked the purity of the berg that it calved forthwith. This was a libel called forth by envy of a certain seamanlike fluency and precision of language that I acquire in moments of stress.'

Marr, interviewed after the voyage, speaking from experience in both the Antarctic and the Arctic, had no doubt that the skipper saved the ship. 'Hundreds, perhaps thousands, of tons of ice showered down,' he said. 'But for the captain's wonderfully cool and skilful handling of the situation, and his timely lowering of the boat, we should most certainly have been crushed to pulp.'

Worsley continued to work the *Island* north, hopefully towards Gillis Land. Early on 13 September pack-ice was sighted in the direction he was now scanning all day. Tacking north in the early light, the temperature fell and the weather became bright and clear with excellent refraction.

'The delicate colouring and exquisite beauty of the morning, typical of the Antarctic rather than the Arctic, beggared description. It would have driven an artist to despair to reproduce; its sheer beauty would have made the whole futurist school sick,' he wrote.

Refraction – a ray of light deflecting at a certain angle when it enters obliquely from another medium of different intensity – also played tricks with a nearby iceberg: 'Its shape altered every few minutes; it drew itself up into a high-gabled house shape, leaned over one way, then the other, and then squatted flat along the horizon. It assumed such a wonderful variety of shapes that when we looked elsewhere for half a minute, we could never be sure for a while that we were looking at the same berg.'

Algarsson and Worsley were photographed saluting the British ensign; it was also the day the expedition changed its name, something that newspapers later picked up as indicating some sort of coup to replace Algarsson as leader. The *Otago Witness* article stated that the party had encountered many difficulties, and there had been allegations of 'grave irregularities', adding that Algarsson was deposed by Worsley.

But there was nothing in Burt's report to the paper, which emanated from London, to support this sensational development, which seems to have been based only on the fact that the expedition had been re-christened with Algarsson and Worsley as joint leaders, as earlier agreed.

Worsley later explained, in a telegram from Granton, Scotland, and released to newspapers, how the joint leadership was achieved. He said all members of the expedition were annoyed by 'unauthorised and exaggerated' statements. The facts were that with its amended programme, without the polar flight, Algarsson had asked Worsley to command the ship, and offered joint leadership. With the work of the ship becoming the principal part of the expedition, Worsley, as an experienced ice-master and navigator, was given control, 'with a few reservations', by Algarsson.

All members of the expedition, being volunteers, had a voice in decision-making of this nature, and with unanimous approval the name of the expedition was changed to 'The British Arctic Expedition' under joint leadership. The letter containing this explanation was signed by all on the *Island*. Worsley commented: 'It is unusual on a polar expedition to be so democratic, but it was solely owing to our members being unpaid volunteers that the expedition had been run so cheaply, or that it had sailed.'

Worsley and Burt also hoisted the New Zealand flag, the same ensign that had been given to Worsley for Shackleton's *Quest* expedition by the New Zealand High Commissioner in London. Worsley called the picture: 'New Zealanders at the pole', adding that he meant the flag-pole, not the North Pole. 'Burt was bursting with beef and pride at upholding our Dominion's ensign so far from home,' he said.

But there was no sign of Gillis Land, which Worsley reckoned should have been just 60 miles away. 'We had neither proved nor disproved its existence. From the look of the ice, I was afraid it was hopeless for us to sail farther north-east so late in the season, with the sea freezing around us.'

Then on the dawn of 14 September a 'strong appearance' of land appeared against the glow of the approaching sunrise. 'We saw it for three hours without alteration of bearing or shape, though the clouds in that direction had been moving steadily before the wind. There is some probability that it was Gillis Land, the elusive, not seen by man for over two centuries and now revealed by that magician, the mirage, aided by the sun's rays behind the land.'

At midnight the crew saw the same dark appearance on the same bearing with the same shape. Worsley concluded: 'It seems certain that it is Gillis Land, but west of the position given on the chart.'

By 19 September the *Island* had completed a circumnavigation of North-East Land, the northernmost part of the Svalbard archipelago, of which Spitsbergen is the largest section, and next morning the ship reached its farthest north: 81° 15′ N. 'We hoisted the Blue Ensign, while Burt sleepily waved my New Zealand flag,' Worsley wrote. He said the *Island* was the first sailing ship ever to have done a circumnavigation of North-West Land in that direction.

They continued sailing west, then south down the coast of Spitsbergen where by 1 October it was at the entrance to Ice Fiord. Houses around a coal mine in Green Harbour, their destination, were sighted. But a gale blasting out of the fiord kept the little sailing ship outside; it blew without relief, and in seven days the *Island* had moved only 10 miles.

'I was forced to do what a seaman should not do – take risks,' said Worsley. Desperate to make progress to the harbour, he tacked the ship and used the anchor to swing her to a new tack when there was no room to move any other way so close to the rocky shore. He tried every trick, backing and filling the sails, when she bumped on a rock shoal. The skipper thought he had lost his ship, and was apologising to Algarsson, when she lurched free. The lifeboats had already been lowered, and one reported deeper water 200 metres away.

In his temporary anchorage, Worsley said he snatched some sleep, still fearing that he had put his ship in a position from which he could not extract her. At dawn, the position looked hopeless. 'The sea around us was covered with the foam of at least 100 breakers and shoal-heads,' he said. From one of the lifeboats, a possible way out was marked with buoys of wood, but the crew had to spend another night in 'Hell's kitchen'. Worsley said they all slept dressed and ready.

Just after dawn the moment he had been waiting for came – a lull in the gale. The crew set all sails on the starboard tack in four minutes, and the vessel gathered speed as she raced for the passage marked by the buoys, 'walking the waters like a thing of life'.

'We scraped past the sunken rocks and headed for the outer ring of breakers,' Worsley said. He steered for the leeside of the foaming area 60 metres short of the outer reef, 'our ears almost deafened by its clamour as we cut through its

The New Zealand flag flies at its farthest north in 1925. The flag is being held by the engineer on the *Island*, Gordon Burt, the second New Zealander on the expedition. Frank Worsley is on the right saluting the flag.
Hocken Library

151

backwash'. The helm was put hard-a-starboard and the mainsheets were let fly. The *Island* swung off the wind and swept towards the open sea. 'We were clear of the damnable reefs.'

Two more days of fighting to get the brigantine back into Ice Fiord followed before the entrance was breached. It had been a huge effort and all hands were exhausted. When a powerful motor-boat came to greet the *Island*, Worsley had no hesitation in accepting the offer of a tow to safety in Green Harbour – so called because the Gulf Stream flows into it and it is consequently clear of ice until well into the winter.

The population at Green Harbour was primarily Dutch, working for the Dutch Coal Mining Company, even though Spitzbergen had by then been taken over by Norway.

The crew got mail, Burt receiving news that his father in New Zealand had died. The engineer had been curing a polar bear skin for his father; it now seemed a worthless trophy. Next morning both the British and the New Zealand flags were half-masted as a mark of respect 'for our ship-mate's sorrow'.

Worsley learned that there had been reports about the *Island* being lost. One said the ship had sunk and the crew rescued from lifeboats; another had the *Quest* reporting the *Island* as being disabled in pack-ice and planning to winter there. A cable was sent to British newspapers telling of the ship's safe arrival.

The *Island* could not be repaired before the station at Green Harbour closed for the winter. Poor tides made it almost impossible to careen the brigantine sufficiently to replace the propellor: the alternative to being towed away from Spitzbergen was to be frozen in for the winter. In these circumstances, three of the crew left: Burt, with no engines to attend, for New Zealand and his grieving family; the cinematographer Bee-Mason for England to develop films that might otherwise deteriorate; and the surgeon, Dr A. Wallace Sinclair, to take up a new post that needed swift acceptance. They boarded the steamer *Ameland*, which was heading for Holland via Tromso, Norway.

The co-leaders accepted the offer of a tow to Tromso by the *Ameland*, a 600-mile, five-day voyage that Worsley said was itself a feat of merit by both crews, a 6000-ton boat towing a sailing vessel of 114 tons through rough seas at more than nine knots. 'It required a high standard of attention by the helmsmen,' he commented. 'Everyone was ordered to keep off the port side as much as possible, for if anything had parted the tow-rope might have killed any man on that side of the deck.'

The door to Worsley's cabin was on the port side, with the coir tow-rope pressed against it. 'I went to my cabin as seldom as possible, and had to force myself through the narrow gap as swiftly as I could.'

Apart from interesting finds by the zoologist Marr, and Charles Bisset the geologist, who made their own reports, what did the expedition accomplish? Worsley said:

> A little – not so much as we had hoped, but we had pushed forward the frontiers of knowledge. This is how knowledge comes and discovery proceeds: little by little.

Sometimes great or fortunate men make a phenomenal advance, but progress is generally made a bit at a time, by ordinary men such as we were. We had proved that the submarine plain extended 200 miles father to the north, had rectified the easternmost coast of Spitsbergen and corrected the variation of the compass between Spitsbergen and Franz Josef Land...without engines, we "sailed where no ship had ever sailed" (Tennyson) in what was probably the final triumph of British seamanship under square sail in the pack-ice – the seamanship of splendid volunteers and amateurs.

He was unable to state definitely that Gillis Land existed, 'but on two occasions we saw – in a position slightly west of that given on the chart – the appearance of land'. No other navigator was ever to confirm the existence of Gillis Land, which is no longer marked on maps.

Algarsson's preface to Worsley's book on the *Island* adventure, *Under Sail in the Frozen North*, summed up the feelings of those who shared the voyage: 'To captain a half-disabled ship is a stiff-enough task; but when pack-ice is added to the mix-up, the elements of a nice mess are all present. The average reader of this book will rightly think that it was very fine work indeed; but only we who were his shipmates can appreciate it at its true worth.' Hardly the words of a disgruntled deposed expedition-leader.

In the *Otago Witness* article, it was stated that in any story that might be told of the expedition by Commander Worsley, there would be a notable omission. 'That omission will be the remarkable part played by Worsley himself,' it said.

It is perhaps natural that Mr Burt should have returned full of hero-worship, but a more experienced traveller in the person of Mr Bee Mason, the photographer who was with Shackleton in his last expedition, wants to call his film [of the *Island* adventure] 'Worsley's Triumph'. An AB [able-bodied seaman] on board made the remark that Commander Worsley could manoeuvre his sailing ship with as much dexterity among the ice-floes and icebergs as another man could a steamer.

CHAPTER 15

London Life

If Worsley was a spectacular failure in his lifetime in finding the riches which he chased so enthusiastically, he was brilliantly successful when it came to friends. His ebullient nature ensured that he attracted attention. This quality led him to Shackleton in the first instance; it also led him directly to the woman who became his second wife, who adored him and who was adored by him without reservation; the real love of his life.

Worsley's 1907 marriage with Theodora Blackden did not survive the strains put upon it by, one can speculate, his frequent and long absences. There were no children and the first Mrs Worsley had dropped from sight by the time Worsley returned from war service and was demobilised in early 1920. Neither he nor any of his contemporaries referred to her in their writings.

The easy-going mariner had also acquired a public image from publication in 1919 of *South*, the official account of the Imperial Trans-Antarctic Expedition, under Shackleton's name. That story, and his wartime adventures such as ramming and sinking a German submarine, gave him a glamour that ensured the attention of the powerful national press. In the light of the times, his was a household name, and he was often referred to as 'Polar Hero' or 'Famous DSO'.

Like many other New Zealanders in London without a permanent address, Worsley used New Zealand House, the office of the high commissioner, as a mail centre. He would call there from time to time to collect letters. It was on one of those visits, some time in 1920, that he met Jean Cumming.

One account of their meeting has Worsley entering the foyer of the office as Jean, an employee, was walking upstairs. The sailor's larrikin streak got the better of him and his very audible comment, that 'there goes a fine pair of legs', echoed around the floor. It was an arresting moment that changed both their lives, as it led to a formal introduction and immediate and enduring mutual attraction.

Jean Cumming – christened Maggie Jane, and described in a newspaper report as 'a cheery Aberdonian' – was barely out of her teen years and was living at home in Aberdeen, Scotland, when World War 1 broke out in 1914, and Worsley, then aged 42, was sailing off on his great adventure with the nation's hero, Shackleton.

During the war almost every eligible man was called up for active duty, leaving open thousands of jobs for young women to fill. Like many other young women from the north, Jean headed to London to work for the war effort. Her first job was as a nanny, and later she applied for and secured a post advertised by the New Zealand High Commission in The Strand. She was considered a 'smart girl' who did her work so efficiently that she was made a member of the permanent staff after the war ended. The mature sailor and the young Scottish woman were soon inseparable, apart from those periods when Worsley found work at sea.

About this time Worsley met another person who was to greatly influence and assist him through the remainder of his life: Eric Bamford, an Oxford-educated civil servant in the Treasury who fought as a soldier in the war and was badly wounded in the Battle of the Somme. Bamford, later to be knighted three times over for his public services, grew to be one of the country's most influential civil servants during and after World War 2.

Worsley probably met the Bamfords – Eric and his wife, Alice – while boarding in London. They were to form the nucleus of a group that grew to include Stenhouse and his wife, which Worsley years later referred to as 'the old gang' in London. Stenhouse after the war had visited Gladys Mackintosh, widow of his former skipper on the *Aurora*, Aeneas Mackintosh. Their friendship developed, and they married in 1923.

Jean Cumming and Worsley wished to marry, but the first Mrs Worsley was not easily to be found. It was several years before the former Theodora Blackden could be traced and a divorce obtained. Then, in August 1926 at a West End, London, registry office, Frank Worsley married for the second time. He was aged 54, more than 20 years older than Jean.

The Aberdeen newspaper the *People's Journal*, on 14 August 1926, reported the marriage of local girl Jean 'to a man whose name is a household word, and who is a man's man in every sense of the phrase'.

Jean Worsley, to all who knew her, was attractive, lively, and modern; in every way a very special person, which she had to be to survive the difficulties of marriage to a middle-aged and out-of-work sailor through the troubled years of depression between the world wars. Fortunately Jean shared his passion for the sea and sailed with him on every possible occasion.

A man of Worsley's age and seniority had great difficulty finding work at sea, but in the adventurous life he had led found another means of making a living, in writing and lecturing. He wrote his first book, *Shackleton's Boat Journey and Crossing South Georgia*, in 1924. It was well reviewed, and enhanced the reputation he was developing as a lecturer worth listening to.

Worsley had the confidence to speak up in any company, and he told a good tale; he also had some good tales to tell. He was greatly respected for his achievements, and in the pre-television days when notable people could entertain the public with their adventures, and make it pay, a lecture season was common.

Worsley gave his first public lecture at Kirkwall, in 1921, at the end of the *Annie* debacle, to pay debts. It registered with him as a way of making money, and between voyages through the 1920s and the 1930s, right up to the start of World War II in 1939, he returned to the lecture trail when possible. It was a means of paying the bills, providing the Worsleys with some measure of comfort, but never giving them the security a couple of their age must have wished for.

He also secured occasional work on behalf of British business interests. In a note to Leonard Tripp in Wellington in 1925, written from Finse, Norway, Worsley

Commander Frank Worsley, in 1925. Hocken Library

said he was assisting in a trial of a British tractor for polar work. 'Most successful,' he said, reminding Tripp that Shackleton and Orde-Lees had been at the same venue 11 years earlier, 'trying his motors' to be taken south on the *Endurance*.

Worsley became serious about lecturing in 1923, while living at Cricklewood, London. In February that year he planned to lecture on the life of Shackleton, and he wrote to Dr Mill, Shackleton's biographer, saying Lady Shackleton had recommended they meet. Lady Shackleton had lent Worsley a large number of the Boss' slides. She was anxious that Worsley's enterprise should not conflict with Mill's book, not yet published.

'I should like to think your book was published about the time I start lecturing,' he told Mill. 'Although Lady S has lent me the photos, I think I will require your permission to use some of them.'

The Worsleys lived at several London addresses from which the sailor scouted for any type of work, and for lecture bookings, through the 1920s and the 1930s, the period being interrupted by the Arctic expedition on the *Island*, which led to another book *Under Sail in the Frozen North*, in 1927.

But there were times when Frank and Jean Worsley were in nearly desperate circumstances during the depression years. It was then that they had to turn to their oldest friends, the Stenhouses and the Bamfords. Eric and Alice Bamford, in particular, were to provide the Worsleys with a lifetime billet at their lovely family home at Claygate, Surrey, whenever and for as long as required. Worsley was soon cheerfully and grandly referring to the home, called Linksfield, as 'my country estate'.

Eric Bamford was then rising rapidly in the public service: at one stage he was private secretary to Stanley Baldwin when Baldwin was Finance Secretary to the Treasury. Baldwin was also British Prime Minister on two occasions in the 1920s and 1930s.

Patrick Bamford, one of the sons of the house, recalled meeting the Worsleys when his father first brought them to Linksfield. He was then five years old. 'The whole family instantly fell under his charm; he was always welcome.' Worsley was soon 'Uncle Wuz' to the Bamfords' three children, and Jean was 'Auntie Jean'. But Patrick Bamford was also aware in later years of the darker side of the Worsleys' life: the times when they did not come to Linksfield for relief when they probably did not have the rail fare, and when Frank Worsley, on more than one occasion, took temporary employment selling Walls' ice cream in the street from a tricycle.

The Bamford children, John, Pat and Ann, knew when the Worsleys were about to arrive at Linksfield: across the fields between the railway station and the house would come the stentorian cry: 'Yoiks Tally-Ho', and everyone knew that 'Uncle Wuz' was approaching on foot. This was an occasion of great joy to the youngsters as well as their parents, for the Worsleys, who had no children of their own, loved to play with the young Bamfords.

For lectures, Worsley found schools a good touch: he related very easily to young people. There was also, from time to time, a London 'season' or lecture tour, for which he had an agent.

Worsley would ask for dates at schools, giving his price-list: 12 guineas for a large school distant from London, 10 guineas for smaller schools, or 8 guineas each for two lectures at close dates in the same neighbourhood. 'If accommodation is included, the price may reduce to 5 guineas if there are three lectures.'

Worsley lectured with either 80 slides, or 50 slides and 200 feet of cine film, for 70–100 minutes. 'If the film is required as well as the slides, I add 1 guinea to the fee.'

Soliciting letters to boys' schools ended: 'I find that boys are always thrilled by the Shackleton lecture, in particular.' And to girls' schools: 'The lectures are keenly appreciated by girls as well as boys.' This was during 1932–33, when he was giving lectures both on the Shackleton adventures ('With Shackleton in the Antarctic') and on a more personal note, 'My Polar Adventures'.

Undated portrait of Frank Worsley, probably 1930s.
Bamford family

He later added to his repertoire with 'Under Sail in the Frozen North' and 'Voyages in Clipper Ships', and in the late 1930s, after the Cocos Island affair, 'Treasure Hunting in Cocos Island'. For the last named, in a season at The Pavilion, Torquay, admission was one, two or three shillings, with special terms for schools.

He approached Tre-Arddur House, a school for boys in Anglesey, in February 1936, on the recommendation of a friend, Mrs Irving Bell, after learning that the school had formed an Antarctic Society. The school accepted, and Worsley received, in addition to his fee, a set of cuff-links which he promised, in a letter of thanks and appreciation of hospitality, to wear. Dr and Mrs Irving Bell, who lived at Bristol, were mentors of Frank Worsley, and helped Jean Worsley handle her affairs apropos Worsley's books after his death.

Worsley lectured at public venues up and down Britain, and on cruises. Stenhouse, who was also on occasion a host to the impecunious Worsleys, in a letter to Leonard Tripp, referred to Worsley's absence from Stenhouse's wedding, where he should have been the best man, because he was away lecturing. Worsley simply could not afford to miss a lecture engagement, even on such an occasion involving the man he considered one of his best friends. He was also at that time (November 1923) negotiating to lecture on a 'cinema cruise'.

Worsley's lectures appeared to be well received. The *Streatham News* in 1927 described one of his lectures on Shackleton 'an absorbing evening…Commander Worsley told some gripping stories of the expedition'. The *Balham News*: 'Deeply interesting and instructive lectures on Antarctic adventures before large audiences.' Two audiences of more than 2200 people crowded into the Wesleyan Central Hall at Southfields: 'The great audiences followed with enthusiasm the story.'

The occasion that pushed Worsley further into the limelight was the film *South*, billed as 'the late Sir Ernest Shackleton's thrilling screen epic of the Antarctic'. This was the cine film, supplemented by slides, taken by the Australian Frank Hurley on the *Endurance*, now dressed up for the age of talking motion pictures with a commentary written and delivered by Worsley. It was released in London and the Polytechnic Theatre near Oxford Circus in 1933, showing twice daily and three times on Saturdays.

The national press reviewed the film, with Worsley highly praised for his commentary. The *Morning Post* said, 'Commander Worsley talks just like what he is – a keen, efficient "Captain Courageous" – with a never-failing sense of humour.' The *Daily Telegraph* said, 'A wealth of racy comments on the most insurmountable difficulties he and his hardy fellow-explorers successfully overcame.' The *Daily Express* praised the 'marvellous ice pictures', and *The Times* was moved to comment, 'The photography is excellent and the accompanying comments always interesting.'

The film opens with a most dapper and suited Worsley showing a young man some of the *Endurance* artefacts that survived the great journey. He presents as something of an English gentleman, with no trace of a colonial accent as he recounts to his young friend the Antarctic adventure. Jean Worsley, in a letter to her friend Dorothy Irving Bell in 1952, commented, 'Do you remember Wuz giving a yarn at the beginning, looking quite film-starish?'

The film *South* was later re-issued with extracts added from *Southward on The Quest*, under the title *Endurance*, still with Worsley's commentary.

For the launch of *South*, he was keen to get a veteran's opinion of the film and his commentary, and he invited the respected Albert Armitage to view the film. It was Armitage who interviewed Shackleton for the Scott expedition in 1901, and recommended him, launching Shackleton's remarkable Antarctic career.

Armitage was navigator and second in command of the *Discovery*, under Scott as master. He had earlier been on the Jackson–Harmsworth expedition, again as second in command, in 1894, and had been awarded the Royal Geographical Society's Murchison Award for his scientific observations. Armitage was in all respects capable of judging the quality of the film and the performance of its players.

His conclusion, in a letter to Worsley (7 March 1933), was that while the pictures were marvellous and the film was produced wonderfully well, 'you are too modest in regard to yourself'. The complete letter reads:

> Dear Worsley,
> I received your letter and card of invitation to lunch when I returned…Thank you most heartily for kindly asking me to a most enjoyable lunch, and still more for giving me the opportunity to see *Endurance*. You asked me to criticise the film. The only criticism I have to make is in regard to your commentary, which is, in the main, so excellent.
>
> The pictures are marvellous and produced wonderfully well. But you are too modest in regard to yourself.
>
> I had a great personal affection for Shackleton, and much admired his qualities. I knew him well: it was due to my report about him that he joined the *Discovery* in 1901.
>
> At the same time I cannot help knowing that he had neither the experience nor the practice, nor, indeed, that love of the sea which one must have to become a great seaman.
>
> I have been blown off the land by a howling gale and blizzard in a whale-boat. Six of us, of whom only two were sailors. For three days and nights…nothing to eat or drink, the sea freezing as it came a'board.
>
> So I say that you were too modest, for I know that Worsley was the seaman, the sailor-man, who made that boat journey from Elephant Island possible. By your

commentary, the ordinary audience cannot realise that such was the case.

Anyhow, I salute you!

All the best and again, many thanks.

Yours very sincerely,

Albert Armitage

The magazine *The Blue Peter* serialised Worsley's book *Shackleton's Boat Journey* between May and July 1924, and the segment *Crossing South Georgia* between August and October the same year. The book *Endurance* was serialised by the *Sunday Chronicle* newspaper in 1930, with a front-page teaser written by Earl Jellicoe, who said the book was the story 'of a few supermen who pitted their own endurance against the perils of ice, blizzards, solitude and starvation'. It would be, he said 'one of the most sensational books of recent years.'

Worsley also wrote magazine articles such as 'A Million Ton Iceberg', and 'Dog', in the *Cherwell* magazine in 1927, the latter being an appreciation of the huskies taken south, used rarely and finally executed. 'There was no room for our loyal friends – it was their lives or ours – they had to go. We could not leave them to die a miserable or lingering death: we had to shoot them.'

'The Last Pipe' was a revealing article (*The Yacht Owner*, 1924) about one of the Elephant Island men he called Mac who, when he ran out of tobacco, smashed one of his two rank pipes into small pieces and boiled the bits with sennegrass, a Norwegian meadow grass dried and used for stuffing in their boots as protection against frostbite. In time the boiling process allowed the sennegrass to be impregnated with the full, rich flavour of his old pipe. After drying the grass before a fire, Mac chopped and shredded some of his treasure, stuffed it in his remaining pipe and lit up. He generously offered some to his colleagues and they all enjoyed his 'genuine Elephant Island Mixture'. Orde-Lees reported on the same incident, and he identified the dedicated smoker as the aptly-named Canadian seaman, William Bakewell.

Patrick Bamford recalls Jean Worsley wryly commenting on her husband's pleasure at the sale of another article. He usually wrote one when the bills were mounting and there was a real need for money in the house. Worsley, however, having sold an article and collected payment, invariably found the occasion worthy of celebration, and often returned home beaming with delight and carrying a bottle of champagne under his arm. The bills sometimes just had to wait.

Worsley secured a contract in connection with a hunt for pirate treasure on Cocos in 1934, taking a party of treasure hunters and their equipment to the Pacific island in an adventure that lasted two years; again Jean shared the occasion. Stenhouse was also associated with the venture for the first stage.

In 1936 a British Empire Photographic Expedition to Antarctica was being considered, and negotiations began for the purchase of Scott's old ship, the *Discovery*, which had been rigged and equipped under the direction of Stenhouse for whaling research work 10 years earlier. The objective was to explore 3500 miles of coastline, from Princess Elizabeth Land to the Banzare Coast in the east of the continent. Worsley was selected to skipper the *Discovery*. But the project collapsed.

Frank and Jean Worsley. The picture was probably taken on the sailing vessel *Westward* in 1938. Worsley and his friend John Stenhouse were in charge of the vessel, the owner of which wanted to make sailing ship tours with wealthy guests. The coming of World War 2 in 1939 finished the idea.
Bamford family

For many years Worsley had been recording reminiscences from his upbringing at Akaroa, New Zealand, and the maturing experience of his first voyage under sail in 1888. It was published in England in 1938, under the title *First Voyage in a Square Rigged Ship*, and was praised as a beautifully crafted description of, in the first instance, pioneer life in the young colony, and then of the impact on a very young man of sailing around Cape Horn to England in a wool clipper.

Stenhouse and Worsley were together again in 1938, when they briefly re-lived their glory days under full sail. On this occasion Stenhouse was captain and Worsley was his first officer. The venture involved the four-masted schooner, the *Westward*, which had started life as a Scandinavian sailing freighter just after World War 1. In 1925 she was converted into a luxury yacht intended to take a wealthy group on a world cruise, but the venture never developed and she lay at berths at Southampton and the Isle of Wight, her hull gradually rusting. In 1937 her owner decided that the cruise under sail was an idea whose time had come, and the *Westward* was brought into prime condition to get the first passenger-carrying certificate for a modern British sailing ship.

The first cruise, with the old firm of Stenhouse and Worsley in charge, sailed in April 1938 from Southend Pier, London, with 72 passengers, assisted by a tug. Out in the English Channel, a journalist on board thrilled as the 'great mainsails were set and the *Westward* felt the urge of freedom…in a spanking breeze, she swept down the channel, a relic of a fashion which only old sailors can remember in its full glory'. Her commanding officers were certainly two of those who could relive the experience, even though it lasted only 48 hours to Plymouth.

There is no record stating how many voyages the *Westward* made, but with another world war looming, far more dangerous and demanding work was facing the ageing warriors at the helm.

Through the 1930s, Worsley was also a director of a ship and yacht delivery business, Imray Laurie Norie and Wilson Ltd, of St Ives, Huntingdonshire. The company in a 1937 brochure said, 'All deliveries are under the personal supervision of Cdr Worsley, supported by a few selected pilots.' The firm said more than 50 yachts had been handled that year 'to the owners' satisfaction'.

Worsley's longest delivery was of a 1200-ton steamer, the SS *Harelda*, from Manchester to Hong Kong between November 1938 and February 1939. Jean sailed with him. Earlier deliveries included yachts to Europe along the canal system, and to the Mediterranean. Jean also sailed with her husband on many of these occasions. She was on one yacht that was delivered to Germany with perhaps a little undeclared cargo: a photograph shows her with Worsley and another man, with the caption, 'After rum-running at Kiel.'

In a letter of reference from the company, written in November 1939 two months after the outbreak of World War 2, when clearly the firm's operation had to be closed, Worsley is glibly described as 'practically a teetotaller and a most careful living man in every way. He is tactful, with a special charm of manner, and has more energy than most men of his age. We have much pleasure in strongly recommending him for a position to suit his undoubted capabilities and wide experience.' It was probably an attempt to enhance his prospects of getting back into active service.

In 1929, the Antarctic Club was established by a Scott Terra Nova expedition veteran, Commander John Mather. Worsley was a member from its inception, and in 1937–38 was president. Alfred Stephenson, who joined the club after an expedition to Graham Land in 1937, recalled attending the club's annual dinner that year at the Cafe Royal, London. Stephenson became secretary of the club in 1956 and retired from the position in 1995.

Above left: Frank Worsley in formal dress, with medals at a London function. The figure on the left is not identified.
Bamford family

Above right: Through the 1930s Frank Worsley was a director of a ship and yacht delivery firm. He often delivered yachts to European centres, travelling via the canal system. This picture has the caption 'After rum-running at Kiel'. Frank and Jean Worsley are on the left.
Bamford family

He admitted a 'hero-worship' for Worsley and regretted that he did not get to know him as well as he did some others from the *Endurance* days, 'but I got an interesting insight into him at the dinner'. He said:

It was our custom to indicate when a toast was about to be made, and on the menu card it indicated that at 'three bells' for example, the toast to absent friends would be proposed. The original ship's bell (I think from the *Terra Nova*) was mislaid, and as Frank Worsley happened to have one, he brought it to the dinner.

After the formal proceedings a few of us went down to the Basement Bar. Much to my astonishment, when we needed a second round of drinks Frank beckoned the waiter by ringing the bell. This was accepted the first time, but he continued to ring it – and it was a large and loud bell.

The waiter came up with a message from the manager: 'It may be eight bells, but all's not well!', and he would like the bell until we went home. I was living in Wimbledon and offered to drop Frank near Hammersmith. As we proceeded down Regent Street and the Strand, I realised that Frank was ringing the bell outside his door: we proceeded at great speed through the West End, with everybody getting out of our way.

Stephenson said this was his only experience with the man he held in great respect 'and awe at times'.

CHAPTER 16

Treasure Island

Nothing more exemplifies the physical toughness and mental alertness of Worsley at age 62 than the events that started in 1934 and lasted two years, during which he took part in what was probably his most pleasurable activity after guiding a ship under sail through a bad storm: treasure-hunting.

Like Shackleton, Worsley was always short of money, and he was vulnerable to get-rich-quick schemes; indeed, he was responsible for some, and in this regard he had a ready audience in the Boss. The pair of them indulged in dreams of instant wealth from pearl lagoons on a once-lost Pacific island. The pearl lagoon treasure was a Worsley picture readily painted for their excitement in moments of relaxation or when seeking diversion. They did this regularly on the *Endurance* voyage, and later. While others sharing that experience might have gone along with the myths just to relieve boredom, albeit briefly, there is no doubt Worsley and Shackleton believed in such treasures and in their destiny to find at least one.

Worsley was the instigator, because he reckoned he had once found a pearl lagoon in the Pacific when he sailed on New Zealand Government vessels at the turn of the century. In times of stress, Shackleton often reminded Worsley about this, and the New Zealander had to repeat this tale, and others, of his days in the Pacific. In particular, Shackleton liked the story of the lost island of Tuanaki, and in his mind associated the island with a pearl lagoon that would bring him riches and an end to constant financial niggles.

Worsley would recount how, as skipper of the government schooner *Countess of Ranfurly*, he was sailing in the South Pacific and first heard about Tuanaki. He had tried to reconstruct events surrounding Tuanaki from the tales of natives and missionaries in the Cook Islands.

He believed Tuanaki lay 200 miles south-east of Rarotonga and was once 'inhabited by Kanakas'. It was hilly and well-wooded, with plenty of fresh water. The island probably had a harbour – 'at all events, it was said to have been visited by whalers.' How the island disappeared was never recorded, but apparently a whaler one day set out to visit Tuanaki and could not find it: it had simply vanished.

Worsley later studied the chart and believed he knew where the island had been, in an area where the sea bottom shelved from roughly 2000 fathoms to about 60 fathoms. He certainly fired up the Boss: Shackleton was so keen on searching for Tuanaki, he made it part of his scientific programme for the *Quest* expedition of 1921–22, after the planned exploration of a major part of the coastline of Antarctica.

Shackleton was so determined on this that he made inquiries about Tuanaki with the London Missionary Society and received what Worsley recorded as 'some confirmation' of the legend of the vanished island. That and the prospect of finding Worsley's pearl lagoon decided Shackleton to spend the southern summer of 1921 along Antarctica in the *Quest*, and the winter studying oceanography – and pearl lagoons – in the warm Pacific.

But this dream was never fulfilled, even though the dreaming continued right to the final hours of Shackleton's life. On the *Quest*, on the night of 4 January 1922, Shackleton and Worsley yarned in the Boss's tiny cabin when the topic that 'invariably seemed to divert him' came up. Worsley recorded the conversation in his book *Endurance*:

> 'Now, about that old lagoon, Skipper,' Shackleton said. Eagerly we discussed the South Pacific and the fabulous size of pearls that had been found there.
>
> 'Do you think we could get anything like the Southern Cross?' he asked, referring to the wonderful cluster that was brought up by a diver off the coast of north-western Australia.
>
> 'It was sold for six thousand pounds I think,' was my reply.
>
> 'Yes,' commented Shackleton, 'but was resold for double.'
>
> Then a curious thing happened. For upwards of three months he had always spoken of our journey to the lagoon as a certainty, and as though there remained only the details to be settled. Now suddenly his mood changed. It seemed as if he had forgotten for a moment that I was there, sitting beside him, for he mused aloud, in a tone full of doubt: 'I wonder whether I shall ever see the Skipper's lagoon?'

A few hours later, in the early hours of 5 January, Shackleton died.

Worsley never returned to the South Pacific to explore for Tuanaki, or his pearl lagoon, but he eagerly accepted the opportunity to hunt for lost Inca gold on the Costa Rican island of Cocos, a few hundred miles north of the Equator, in 1934.

He was as keen as ever on becoming rich, as quickly as possible. He was physically fit and mentally tough, capable as always to face the rigours of the sea and, on uninhabited Cocos, an equatorial jungle.

In London he made a precarious living from his books, public lectures on the adventures with Shackleton and in the Arctic, talks to schools around the country, and occasional special projects for the government such as testing cold-weather equipment. Nothing would satisfy him more than a treasure hunt at the end of another sea journey, particularly for a prize as glamorous as pirate gold looted from Spanish galleons and buried in an original pirate lair. It was his opportunity to live the action of Stevenson's *Treasure Island*, and his great regret was the absence of his old friend Shackleton, who would surely have revelled in the occasion.

Worsley received the applications for the trip and chose the crew. He told of one application from the hundreds received: 'The young man wrote "I s'pose you are not wanting a feller like me. I can work hard and shoot straight. I was eight years old at Christmas. I send you a photo so you can see the sort of man I am, and if you are wanting more help, please send for me". Worsley sent the youngster a 'good letter regretting that we had no vacancy for a fine young man like he was'.

This is the story that lured Worsley (from Foreign Office handbooks):

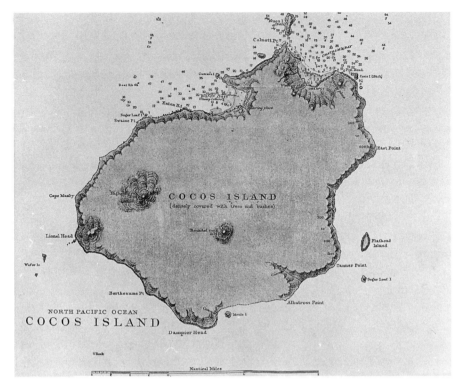

A map of Cocos Island, an acknowledged location of pirate buried treasure. Frank Worsley spent two years assisting a British company, Treasure Recovery Ltd, to establish a camp on this small island off the coast of Costa Rica. Worsley twice sailed yachts there from Britain, with men and supplies, and supervised landing them in small boats through heavy surf.
Bamford family

The existence of treasure concealed in the island is well established. In the 17th century and later, Cocos Island came to be the favourite resort of privateers and fillibusters. The island, after visits from Lieutenants Colnett and Vancouver [George Vancouver, English navigator who accompanied Captain James Cook on his second and third voyages, and later charted much of the west coast of North America] appears to have lapsed into a period of oblivion. Advantage of this was taken in 1818 by a notorious pirate known as Bonito, alias Bennett Grahame, to secrete there a vast plunder he had obtained by rifling certain churches in Peru.

Incas valued gold only as ornaments and as a symbol for their sun god: it was too plentiful to use for anything else. Spaniard invaders looted the New World treasure and shipped thousands of tons back to Spain. But then galleons heavy with cargoes of gold began to fall prey to the swift vessels of pirates, and much of the loot found its way to Cocos, which had then become the pirate base.

The first pirate to use Cocos as headquarters was Davis Dampier Wafer, after whom the only reasonable landing place on the island – Wafer Bay – was named. He is said to have deposited there 130 tons of silver dollars, and 733 bars and seven kegs of gold. In 1818, Benito Bonito – 'Bonito of the Bloody Sword', as he was known – is supposed to have buried 350 tons of bullion as his hoard.

Three years later Bolivar the Liberator marched on Lima and the Spaniards loaded the great wealth of the city and its churches on the British brig *Mary Dier*. The day after the treasure was secured on the ship the master, a Scot called William Thomson and his crew slaughtered the Spanish escort and sailed to Cocos, where the treasure was buried.

Thomson in fact was serving under Bonito. He is said to have added $12 million worth of gold coins, jewels and silver ingots to the island's pirate bank. The *Mary Dier*, Thomson, and his crew were later captured and the crew were all shot. Thomson, however, escaped, but died a few years later while fitting out a ship in Newfoundland in an effort to get back to Cocos Island to recover the treasure.

Worsley estimated that about 20 expeditions before his own had failed to find the Cocos loot. One of these included Britain's world speed record holder Sir Malcolm Campbell, who spent four days on Cocos treasure-hunting, but left empty-handed and complaining of ghosts. 'They never disturbed me while I slept, but the chaps say that no decent ghost would dream of disturbing me,' Worsley commented.

In 1934 the treasure was estimated by the Foreign Office to be worth five million pounds sterling; other estimates ran as high as 25 million pounds. 'Enough to go round if we can only find it,' Worsley said.

The New Zealander was asked to join the Treasure Recovery Ltd (TRL) expedition sailing in the vessel *Queen of Scots* from London. John Stenhouse was another of the team of 'field executives' commanding the splendid 600-ton yacht chartered for the expedition. Jean Worsley accompanied her husband, whose main task was to supervise the landing of stores in small boats through the tricky surf of the island. There were 18 men in the party, and their ship carried stores, huts and equipment for what was considered at the time a sophisticated search. They had enough supplies to establish a village at Wafer Bay, the pirates' lair.

In a script for a series of lectures Worsley later delivered in London, appropriately entitled Treasure Island, he told how he found the surf at Wafer Bay too heavy the day of arrival. 'I've made thousands of landings on Pacific and New

The Treasure Recovery Ltd prospectus. Frank Worsley and Jean sailed in the luxury yacht, which soon proved too large and expensive for the operation.
Bamford family

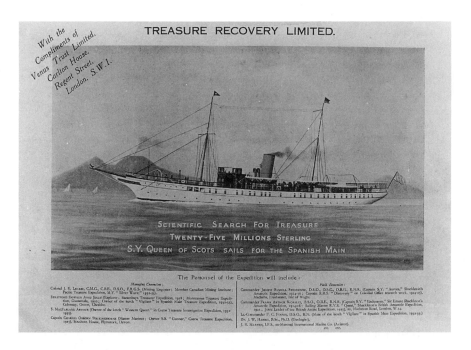

Zealand coasts and once got promoted through an officer and three seamen being drowned after capsizing in a heavy surf,' he said.

Next day, in a small boat he used a 14 foot oar to steer through the surf to Wafer Bay, and men and stores were landed. Prefabricated huts were erected, a dynamo was bedded in for power and lights, and wireless links with Britain were established. The kitchen was set up; it had a refrigerator packed with meat and butter from New Zealand, via Britain. Later the refrigerator stored wild pork and fresh fish. Even a vegetable garden was established.

In a cable to his principals in London, dated 9 October 1934, Worsley reported: 'We landed everything successfully on Cocos. Huts built and everything going well.'

In a letter to his god-daughter, Madeline Meares (later Denham), in New Zealand, he said that just around a point of land, out of view of the suspected site of the planted treasure, was the old village, 'where the pirates kept their wenches so that they could not know where the treasure was buried; they said they couldn't trust women.'

The biggest problem in finding the treasure was the state of the land. 'There have been so many landslides and earthquakes since it was buried – some of it three centuries ago – and so many hundreds of pits have been sunk by different parties searching.'

He described the bush on Cocos as dark and hard to penetrate, but with a 'strange, wild beauty'. Great trees ran to 200 feet with huge vines with stems as thick as a man's body creeping up them. There were many ferns, 'but not nearly as fine as New Zealand tree ferns'.

Undergrowth creepers and jungle grass 7 feet high, which cut like a fine saw, made the boulder-strewn slopes difficult to cross. Precipices, pits and gullies made parts of the island impassable, even to wild pigs.

> Many parts have been overrun by a vine with a beautiful purple convolvulus flower. But the vines are deadly to the trees, strangling them so that there were dozens of great green ghostly shapes and columns where there had been formerly fine forest trees.
>
> The vines cover the ground and treacherously cover the bluffs and precipices. We have to be very careful...once I suddenly fell through a mass of vines and saved my life by grabbing a great armful of them until I very cautiously worked myself into safety.

He was enthusiastic about some fine mahogany trees, and beautiful waterfalls shooting out from the forest over cliffs and 400 feet into the sea. He also wrote about 'the most graceful bird in the world', the frigate bird. Thousands of them flew high overhead. One 'lady bird' took a fancy to him when he was steering his surfboat. 'I waved my arm; she floated down. I beckoned again – she swept closer. I held my arm up – she swooped and seized my finger in her long hooked bill. Finding it rather tough and tarry, she gave it a friendly nip and let go.'

Worsley's enthusiasm for his surroundings may not have exceeded his lust for finding treasure, but at an age when most men had retired from labour of any

Above: One of the beautiful waterfalls on Cocos. This one splashed into a pool which was used for bathing. Both Frank and Jean Worsley enjoyed the beauty of the island, but found the organisation of the expedition left something to be desired.
Bamford family

Above right: The camp at Wafer Bay, Cocos Island. The bay had been the site of a pirate village, near which the treasure was supposely buried.
Bamford family

kind he was taking great pleasure in hard work and in recording the beauty of the island and the seas around it for a young woman far away in New Zealand.

> The average temperature is 82deg, but you can have 20deg more without extra charge. The sea averages 84deg, so bathing would be good if the bays weren't so stiff with sharks that you can hardly haul a fish up before a blackguard of a mouth almighty snaps him off. We never let go anchor without braining a pair of 'em…yesterday we saw a great manta 12 feet across. Mantas are giant rays or skates, and the only way to tackle them is with a rifle or a harpoon. One has been known to leap up and crash down on a boat, completely blanketing it and four men.
>
> Rowing at night you notice the sea is dotted with round green lights that follow you – the eyes of a few score hungry sharks…we have been catching plenty of red schnapper and today at low tide we put our hands under rocks in the pools and pulled out two dozen crayfish in five minutes. They are jolly good eating for a change.

He explained that the island was 333 miles north of the Equator and 540 miles west of Panama. It was 5 miles long by 3 miles wide and 'as rugged as any part of New Zealand, and buried in evergreen forest'. There were no harbours and 'we are the only inhabitants, except birds, wild pigs, two goats, four cats and four deer that we brought here to breed'. The stag gored the Costa Rican cook and then turned on Worsley. 'I seized his antlers and as he drove at me, forced his antlers into the ground. Then I gave him a cowboy's side-twist which he didn't like, so when I let him go he didn't ask for any more. Now we're good friends and he takes bread out of my hand.'

The cook, he wrote, tried to feed them on rice and beans, and what he called bread 'so we go to the orange tree where the wild pig congregate, and shoot pig for dinner, else we fish in the bay and also gather coconuts, oranges, limes and pawpaws at the back of the camp'.

Two of the crew were 'comedians', so they were called Laurel and Hardy. They shared a hut apart from the rest. One day there were revolver shots heard from their hut. 'We rushed over to stop murder and found the large one standing with a grim look and a smoking revolver. The small one was kneeling on the sand, saying: "I can't find a bit of him!" We retired in disgust: they'd been shooting spiders.'

The expedition planned to use modern techniques centred on a metal-detecting instrument. The aim was to run 1000 feet of insulated wire around a selected area. The square patch was then electrified by the dynamo.

A wire from the dynamo ending in a metal spike was carried across the patch, the spike being prodded into the ground every three yards by an operator wearing earphones connected to the wire. If he heard a humming sound there was no metal about; if there was silence he was over metal. Silent ground was then pegged out and closely examined with another instrument. This had an arrow which pointed to anything conductive below. The likely area was then narrowed to smaller limits, and drilling followed. However, Worsley commented later, 'The electrico-conductive instruments appeared quite as sensitive to water as to metal – and there was a lot of water underground.'

While this work was progressing, Worsley was to sail the *Queen of Scots* back to Panama, en route to England, to secure a smaller vessel and return with fresh supplies and communications: the company found the *Queen of Scots* too expensive to lease and too large for its needs. But at Panama Worsley heard that Costa Rica was about to send troops to evict the British treasure-hunters. He cabled an objection to the Costa Rican president, who then dropped his 'hostile attitude'. However, the president did order that two men of the Cocos party should proceed to Costa Rica to explain their presence; in the meantime, the rest of the party would be left alone to work.

'Unfortunately, just as we were getting quite chummy, the president dropped a spanner in the works,' Worsley said in his lecture notes. 'A statement was published that the Union Jack had been hoisted on this tree, annexing Cocos to Britain, and that Costa Rica dared to haul it down. The report was exaggerated, but the Costa Rica Government got fed up with us and decided to take the whole party off.'

The plight of the treasure-hunters made international news, particularly through the presence of Worsley, who was still a popular public figure in Britain. British newspapers reported the events and the news was also featured in New Zealand papers.

However, the geography of the Pacific became somewhat confused, with cable reports talking about the polar hero being likely to be thrown into jail by Chile. 'They meant Costa Rica,' Worsley wrote in his letter to Madeline. 'And anyway, they haven't done so yet.' Journalists were probably confusing the Costa Rican port of Puntarenas with the Chilean port of Punta Arenas.

He also explained to her, 'People mix this island up with Cocos-Keeling Islands in the Indian Ocean. The owner of those islands has been sued for income tax – I wish that this could happen to us in 1936!' He called Cocos 'the treasure island that boys dream of'.

The shore party, before the interruption by political games, was getting reactions from the metal-divining instrument 'that seemed to prove we were on the right track'. There were boulders under the surface that appeared to have been rolled there to cover something, and the treasure-hunters were rigging gear to lift the boulders when they heard that Costa Rican troops were coming, so they stopped the operation. Costa Rica sent 90 soldiers to the island and removed the whole party to Panama.

The early results were good enough for Treasure Recovery Ltd to persevere, and this time the principals went about it with some tact: the last thing they wanted was more intervention by the Costa Rican Government, officials of which would surely be waiting for the next expedition.

The parties negotiated and TRL was granted a concession, the terms of which stated that Costa Rica would take one-third of any treasure recovered, in return for its assistance.

While Worsley shaped a good story for his lectures, Jean was keeping a personal diary, and that gave a somewhat different account, recording as it did some of the tensions and bungling that dogged the expedition, starting with an incident at Tenerife where two of the crew were arrested after a drunken brawl with locals, and one crewman was charged with attempted murder. He was released two days later.

But nothing was to spoil the favourable impression Jean had at her first view of Cocos: 'Such a beautiful looking green island…it looks just as a treasure island should look.' The small boats were launched at Wafer Bay and Worsley 'looked so happy at the stern oar' as he guided them through the surf.

Worsley told Madeline,

> You would have laughed to see us landing stores and machinery from the yacht. My surfboat had been built by a pirate we had with us called Captain Polkinghorne, but known to us as Polkie. My strike oarsman was Andy, a stalwart Scot. My rivals in the other boat were Finny [Lt-Cdr F.C.Finnis], a retired naval officer, and Drew, another amateur pirate.
>
> Our rig was moth-eaten bathing trunks, battered Panama hats and cheerful grins. Whenever Jean could stop laughing at us, she cheered us on from the yacht. It was great to be alive and working hard. The rainy-roasting season was on: 50-50 drowned in a cloud-burst or frizzled to death by the sun. There was great rivalry between the boat crews…it was a glorious sight to see the two boats racing through the roaring surf, their crews yelling and the boat-steerers straddle-legged, grasping the steering oars, and exhorting the crews to 'pull you——darlings'.

Jean recorded that during the confrontation with Costa Rica, the principals of TRL still with the *Queen of Scots* left the yacht, which was being held under a bond of 600 pounds sterling at Christobal, in Panama, and sailed for England. 'Everything is very worrying: I wish Wuz was out of the whole show,' she wrote.

Local papers reported the landing of Costa Rican troops on Cocos, closing down the treasure-hunters' radio link and confiscating their gear before shipping them to Puntarenas. These actions left the expedition in the hands of the 'field executives', headed by Stenhouse and Worsley.

Seventeen men had been left on Cocos and were now in Costa Rican custody. Worsley was concerned to ensure that in the event of the operation being closed down permanently, they were not be abandoned, as had happened with previous expeditions. In a message to the company in London, Worsley also said he was using his own money to feed the crew, stripping the small reserve he had kept in case Jean had to be repatriated.

The British consul negotiated a cash settlement to bring the party from Costa Rica to Christobal. 'A great relief,' wrote Jean. But when the party arrived they 'all looked very weary and seemed very bitter. I do not look forward to the trip home and wish it was over.'

TRL in London then cabled Worsley, appointing him controller, and demanding immediate resumption of work. The company was 'relying on the expedition's loyal co-operation'. Jean said this was greeted with hoots of laughter as 'there is nothing to control.' Worsley's reply declined the offer 'unless 1000 pounds cabled for expenses for those remaining'. It wasn't.

Another cable from TRL demanded 'elimination of dissatisfied elements' and ordered the vessel to St Lucia, Barbados, where Stenhouse, acting on a new instruction, sacked everybody, giving them a month's notice. The *Queen of Scots* then sailed back to England.

Worsley made his peace with TRL, and early in 1935 he took command of the *Veracity*, a much smaller yacht of 83 tons. Jean Worsley and the wife of the yacht's owner were on board. Jean again kept a diary, and recorded (13 February): 'Ship looks so nice I believe it will not be so bad.'

But they sailed into bad weather and the *Veracity* was damaged in gales in the Bay of Biscay. The engines broke down and Worsley sailed the *Veracity* first to Casablanca, then Morocco, and then to Tenerife, in the Canary Islands, for repairs. But in mid-Atlantic the engines broke down completely, and the old sailor was suddenly back in his favourite element, exclusively under sail. He took the *Veracity* before the trade winds to Barbados, arriving there on 23 April after a journey of 1535 miles in 26 days, and in time to celebrate the Royal Jubilee.

TRL cabled the yacht, appointing Worsley controller of the whole operation. Jean pondered, 'I wonder how it is going to work out – I can see ructions ahead.' The engines again failed and Worsley sailed the *Veracity* first to Curacao, then to Colon and through the canal to Balboa. The old problem of finance soon returned, Jean recording: 'No credits waiting for Wuz…I wish we could get home.' Ten days later: 'Food very scarce, no money and general unrest. I'm fed to the teeth with the whole show and hate the continued friction. Wuz is too good to be mixed up with this crowd.'

Next day, on 25 May, 'everything boiled up'. Worsley ordered a meeting and said he thought Finnis, who had had previous experience in treasure-hunting in the Spanish Main Expedition, was undermining his authority. Finnis denied this and, Jean recorded, they 'had it out and cleared the air a bit'.

Negotiations with the Costa Rican authorities dragged on into June, when the *Veracity* was finally cleared to sail for the treasure island, but 10 Costa Rican

Above: The *Veracity* was the second yacht used by the Cocos Island treasure-hunters. This sketch by Walter How is part of a series depicting vessels connected with Frank Worsley, held by the Bamford family at Claygate, Surrey.

Above right: Frank Worsley and his wife Jean are on the extreme left in this picture, probably taken on the *Veracity* during the voyage to Cocos in 1935.
Bamford family

soldiers were accompanying the expedition, with a Colonel Vanezuela.

After the stores were unloaded on the island, Worsley decided that Jean should not stay there. He said 'it was not good enough and he would not like to leave me even for a day'. Jean hated to leave him: 'It's miserable for both of us.'

At the Costa Rican capital, San Jose, Jean helped organise more stores and returned with them in the *Veracity*. With her was a mystery man, known initially as Paul, but who in fact was one Peter Bergmans, an adventurer who said he had been assaulted and drugged in Puntarenas in an attempt to prevent him from sailing, as he was supposed to have actually seen the treasure. She found Worsley much happier and 'looking splendid'. Everyone in the camp was in good form and working hard.

Apart from supervising the digging of areas that gave encouragement through the electrical device, Worsley spent some time with Bergmans, who said he had seen some of the pirates' loot in a cave which he thought he could recognise from the sea. Worsley twice took him sailing around the island in an effort to spot the elusive cave, without success.

Jean recorded a 'stormy meeting' with Bergmans when he went over his story again, then ranted and shouted that he had done his best. He accused TRL of not carrying out what was promised, a finer search of the beach location. Worsley disagreed and said Bergmans must show them other locations. Worsley noted that Bergmans 'was prone to go off on his own and lie about where he had been'.

Bergmans went off on his own once more, looking for his 'special place', but returned saying he had lost his way. Worsley then went with him, the two men crossing the rugged island, a 12-hour trek through heavy jungle, at times hacking a path with machetes. This was a considerable physical feat for the 60-plus Worsley,

made more arduous when Bergmans fell and injured himself. Worsley had to assist the younger man, the pair staggering along for the last couple of miles. 'A nightmare,' commented Worsley. Soon after, Jean left Cocos in the *Veracity* for the last time to wait for Worsley at Balboa. He had to be back in London by 20 October for a lecture season. He told TRL he must leave Cocos no later than September 10.

Worsley and Jean returned to England, leaving the treasure-hunters hard at work, but after three more months the concession expired. TRL extended the concession a further six months and the hunt continued, but the Worsleys did not return to Cocos.

Worsley took to the lecture trail again: he at least got something out of the business. In his lectures, he would say how he was convinced the great treasure was there and the Cocos party should find it during the coming dry season and, 'if not so quickly, I hope to have another try'.

It didn't happen, and the two-year adventure ended when TRL funds dried up and no new finance was available. 'We failed like so many before us – but I feel sure that treasure is on the island,' the optimistic old sailor said.

Frank Worsley on the *Veracity* at Cocos Island in 1935. The treasure hunt was unsuccessful, despite what was for the times a scientific search.
Bamford family

CHAPTER 17

Last Posts

The few years between the end of the Cocos affair and the start of World War 2 in 1939 continued to be uncomfortable for Worsley and his wife. They had little income and often took advantage of the open-house invitation to stay with the Bamfords at Claygate.

Worsley saw the war as his chance to revive a life of useful action, and to serve once more the cause of the Empire against Germany. The fact that he was 67 years old at the outbreak of war was no deterrent in his view. But of course there was no recall to active service from the Royal Naval Reserve, from which he had long been retired; nor was there likely to be one.

A British Expeditionary Force (BEF) was sent to France to bolster perceived unprepared French forces after war was declared in September 1939 because of German intransigence over Poland. Both Britain and France had defence agreements with Poland, though neither country had any real ability to prevent a German invasion in eastern Europe.

Germany struck at Poland and for months nothing happened in the west on the same ground on which much of the Great War of 1914–18 had been fought. Germany did not move in that direction until May 1940. The months before the invasion of Holland and Belgium became known as the 'phoney war', and it was in that period that Worsley tried desperately to attach himself to a useful service. The Red Cross was one organisation that offered a chance, and Worsley went to France and lectured to British troops stationed there. No record of just what were the subjects of his lectures exists, but his presence there is confirmed.

Another British Expeditionary Force was rushed to Norway early in 1940, almost coinciding with the invasion of that country by Germany: the British had planned to move into Norway on 8 April, despite the Norwegian desire to remain neutral, and the Germans had set 9 April for the start of their own occupation.

The German planning was far superior, and they were on the ground at several points before the BEF arrived with the objective of occupying the northern port of Narvik and some points to the south. The British aim was to control a railway link with the iron-ore fields of Sweden, another neutral state. But the Germans took Narvik first, and protected the town with a naval force.

Germany was using the rail route to Narvik, then a sea route behind the protection of offshore Norwegian islands known as the Leads, to get the iron ore to Germany's munitions factories during winter months when the more direct, safer route down the Gulf of Bothnia was frozen.

This rail link was also the most direct route to be used to assist the brave little

Finnish force that was resisting the Russian invasion of Finland in November 1939.

In a letter to a War Office official during his search for a wartime appointment, Worsley mentioned obtaining equipment for Swedish volunteers to go into Finland to assist in that struggle. But despite the strong desire to see Finland survive, there was no real chance that the country could resist the might of Russia for long. The Finns finally surrendered in March 1940.

Norway seemed to offer Worsley his best chance for active service: he knew the country well, and felt a huge debt of gratitude towards the Norwegians. He admired their independence, their sea-faring traditions, their achievements and most of all, he was forever grateful for the kindness shown to himself and the *Endurance* crew in 1914–16 by Norwegian whalers at South Georgia, and for the respect and care they lavished on his little boat, the *James Caird*.

As well as visiting the country often in his sailor days, Worsley also had been there several times to test cold-weather equipment on behalf of British business interests.

The Red Cross was planning to have a unit work in Norway in conjunction with the BEF, which also included Polish and French forces. Worsley's record of service shows that he was engaged as 'Advance Agent – Norway', between 20 May and 1 July 1940.

But the ground war was not going well for Britain. The Germans were rolling up the BEF in Norway, and about the time the Red Cross was planning to send Worsley there to prepare the way for a unit, an evacuation of the army and its air force support was being finalised. Worsley's correspondence with Jean indicates that he made one quick trip to Norway, but it was already far too dangerous for the Red Cross to be represented on the ground.

The British and Allied evacuation was also centred on Narvik, still occupied by German soldiers. The BEF had to fight its way into the town and hold it long enough for the Royal Navy to smash past the German naval presence there and evacuate the troops.

The capture of Narvik, while a gallant affair, went virtually unnoticed as more important events were building up in France where many more battered British troops were on the beaches of Dunkirk awaiting rescue. But 25,000 Allied troops were successfully taken from Norway at Narvik between the end of May and 8 June 1940. Two days later the British Prime Minister Neville Chamberlain resigned, Winston Churchill was asked to lead the War Cabinet, and the war became more resolutely engaged.

For Worsley, the Red Cross could now offer only home service, and he was appointed assistant commissioner and officer in charge of No. 1 RCSJ (Red Cross/ St John) Training Depot at Balham, London. This was a motor ambulance unit, and ironically it was closed down owing to a shortage of recruits only a few months into the period of the Battle of Britain, when Hitler ordered the German Air Force to mass-bomb the city.

The Germans had bombed London on 24 August, and when the British replied with a small-scale raid on Berlin, the German leader vowed to destroy London, switching his air force from attacks on Royal Air Force stations early in September to a massive series of attacks on the great city and its largely defenceless people.

In a letter to Jean from his Balham base in September 1940, Worsley described one German air raid, and seeing about 30 aircraft. 'Our AA [anti-aircraft] guns went quiet, so we knew our fighters were up,' he wrote. 'We heard machineguns and then bits of a Jerry came whirling down. We laughed and cheered.' In another letter he referred to an air raid being on as he wrote to her: 'There's a hell of a row from our AA guns, which is really cheering, knowing that we are knocking Jerry instead of t'other way round.' On that occasion, Worsley had sent two ambulances to Bermondsey and another two to Stepney, where they were working to ferry civilian blitz victims to safety; he had not heard from his crews for two days.

Jean was staying with her mother in Aberdeen at that time, and with the Germans occupying Norway, there was a brief invasion scare involving Scotland. Worsley said that if they did get a footing in eastern Scotland 'it would be very unpleasant, and I'd have to come up to get you out of it, or meet you in Cumberland…if things get really bad you must both go to Cumberland where I can get hold of you. We might walk towards each other!' Jean worked for some time censoring letters, and on ambulance and canteen duties.

After the Balham Red Cross depot was closed, Worsley maintained his requests for a posting, writing to the War Office complaining that his services, which he 'tabled months ago', had not been utilised. Again he offered assistance with regard to Norway. He said many Norwegian officers wanted to return to their home country, perhaps a reference to some plan to try to build up a partisan guerrilla force there.

'I can take them by steamer or sailing ship from our west coast by a relatively safe route to the north of Norway,' he wrote. He was writing after calling at the War Office and being fobbed off with the name of the officer to whom he was now directing his letters. There is no record of any reply.

He also wrote a submission on the virtues of landing a force at Spitzbergen, 340 miles north of Norway, which he knew well from his Arctic expedition in the early 1920s. 'It might be possible this summer for a daring and enterprising power to land heavy guns at Spitzbergen,' he wrote. Such a force could establish both an air base and a summer naval base. 'Submarines might even use it under the ice in winter.'

He conceded that distance from trade routes and docks might diminish the value of such a base, 'but the possibility should not be overlooked'. There was also plenty of good steaming coal to be mined and exported from Spitzbergen and Bear Island, while iron ore and whale oil, the production of which might be uneconomic in peacetime, might be useful in war.

Worsley added that Russia was interested in the islands and Britain could not tolerate any nation other than Norway occupying them. He received one quite sympathetic reply from the Admiralty, a note in which the writer said that much of what Worsley had referred to had been or was being looked at. The writer also associated himself with Worsley's age and experience, and neatly passed on the message that old war dogs like them had best understand that their time had passed. Spitzbergen today remains part of Norway.

Worsley's persistence was rewarded, though not in the form of service with the Royal Navy. He was channelled to the Merchant Navy during one of his periods of residence at the Bamford home.

He took command of a home trade vessel, the *Dalriada*, in August 1941. This 973-ton vessel was registered at Glasgow and was owned by the Overseas Towage and Salvage Co. Ltd, of Leadenhall Street, London. Worsley signed on as master on 2 August, on the then-normal half-yearly contract, listing Jean as next-of-kin and Linksfield as their address.

There was one serious defect, however, in the listing: Worsley stated that his age was 64. He was so desperate to get into action that he subtracted five years from his true age. It was a lie that was later to cost him dearly.

The *Dalriada* was based at Sheerness, at the mouth of the River Medway, east of London, and went to sea, according to the official log book, 'on Admiralty work, with freeboards of 3 feet 2 inches to 3 feet, but never less than 3 feet'. The nature of the work was not stated, but Worsley referred to it as 'wreck-busting', the objective being to keep the harbour entrance clear of wreckage by whatever means appropriate, and to salvage weapons from sunken vessels.

This included blasting flotsam with explosives, a reminder for Worsley of his days at the end of World War 1 when he used depth charges against German submarines and earned the nickname 'Depth Charge Bill'.

While preparing the *Dalriada*, before sea-going operations, Worsley lived on board, maintaining his consistent correspondence with Jean in Scotland. One letter described a German air raid on shipping near his vessel. 'It was exciting enough for a few minutes during the first attack,' he said. 'One bomber flew low towards us, so we could see him in the dusk. We gave him what-for, which he didn't seem to like and sheered off. Our men said they couldn't miss him, but they did not claim to have damaged him much.'

A letter dated 8 September 1941 hints at dangerous operations: 'We seem to have completed our first job, but when we examined the ground [the ocean bed], with a fine tooth comb, you might say, we found something else not supposed to be there; I think we will remove that tomorrow. One requires a great deal of patience.'

Other letters detail some more of the work which Worsley was doing in the *Dalriada*. On 1 October: 'We've cleared one wreck and started another, salvaging two guns, one balloon and a raft.' And, on 9 October: 'It is now 3pm and we have just come in with the final bit of the gun we have been getting from the wreck. It is a great satisfaction to me because we went out on spec in unsuitable weather and just managed to snatch it up in the only possible half-hour for a week. Now we have finished with that dirty oily job and can start again… I was also very pleased when we got a signal, "Well done".'

A more cheerful note on 12 November: 'Yesterday we popped a charge off and got about 2cwt of fine fresh fish. I had a supper of them four hours after we took them from the sea, and this morning I had a fish breakfast; very fine. Unfortunately we'll eat them all before we get back or I could have brought or sent you a pair of fine fat cod.'

The *Dalriada* log book registers eight voyages with Worsley as master, between 11 August 1941, when he took her from a Thames wharf at Deptford down the river to Sheerness, and 19 November the same year. His last entry in the log was to register on 25 November the boat and fire drills conducted the previous day, after which he was replaced as master.

This followed the revelation that he was in fact only a few months short of 70 years old, and not 64 as stated on his contract. The company's concern may have been based on the possibility that the *Dalriada* might be lost in action or even in an accident involving explosives. Word that the company was using such an aged hero in dangerous work might have led to the decision to get him out of that operation.

At any rate, Worsley was disgusted with this treatment. Although he was used again, delivering small vessels around the coast from a base at Leith, in Scotland, he was unhappy that the company had decided that he was apparently not up to the demands of his previous work simply because of his age.

He expressed his frustration in a letter from Aberdeen on 20 January 1942, to his friends in Bristol, Dr and Mrs Irving Bell, addressing them as 'my dear Squibby and Ronald':

> For the time, at all events, I have finished my wreck-busting activities. They may be resurrected for me in the spring, but I doubt it.
>
> While the Admiralty liked me well enough, the shipping company who were operating the ship and under whose control I was working did not think I was up to date in coastal ship business. So for the last seven weeks I have been taking various steamers around the coast from Leith and in between have been ruralising here and drawing reduced pay from the Merchant Navy Reserve Pool.

Perhaps in error, but perhaps out of pique, Worsley gave his birthdate when he entered the Reserve Pool as 22 February 1882: this time he was 10 years out!

Worsley was depressed about the conduct of the war, adding in his letter to the Irving Bells, 'My one hope is that we are really doing something worthy of the great past of England and are naturally compelled to keep it secret. But I see no sign whatever of it…it is absolutely incredible that we are doing nothing to avert disgraceful defeat.'

He also referred to his desire to see his books, *Shackleton's Boat Journey* and *Endurance*, in the relatively new and very popular Penguin format. He would write to his agent about this, and 'if I think you or some of your friends could be of assistance to me in the matter, and I should meet with difficulty, I know I can trespass on your good nature'. He concluded with a typical Worsley exhortation: 'God bless you and all our friends, and to hell with all our enemies.'

If the authorities thought they had seen the last of the old warrior, they were mistaken. As he passed his 70th birthday, Worsley maintained his demands for a useful posting and was given one at HMS *King Alfred*, a Royal Navy training establishment at Hove, Sussex, on 27 April 1942. *King Alfred* was where Royal Naval Volunteer Reserve applicants worked for their commissions as sub-lieutenants or

Below: Worsley's inscription to his sister, Helen, in a copy of his 1938 book, *First Voyage in a Square Rigged Ship.*
Colin Monteath

To My dear Sister
Helen Knight.
From
Frank Worsley.
29th Aug: 1938.

midshipmen. One such young officer in 1943 was Geoffrey Hattersley-Smith, a great admirer of Worsley, who called *King Alfred* 'an underground garage on the front at Brighton'.

At *King Alfred*, Worsley lectured on, among other things, charts and pilotage, but he did not stay long. Within two months he was appointed 'president additional for instructional duties' at the Royal Naval College, Greenwich, where he began on 4 June 1942.

One letter to Jean, written while Worsley was still at *King Alfred*, gave an indication of health problems arising from lifelong smoking. He confessed that he had smoked a cigar, but was abstemious with the pipe 'out of sympathy for you, with no cigarettes'. He was, he said, down to one pipe a day.

Hattersley-Smith, who attended RNC Greenwich in 1943, said the college took the 'somewhat brighter young men' from *King Alfred* on three-week courses. It was a 'polishing' operation in surroundings of great splendour, with seven-course meals served by Wrens in long white gloves. He said, 'We used to say that we left *King Alfred* as officers but not necessarily gentlemen, and were sent to Greenwich to become gents as well!'

Late in 1942, Worsley received the cruel news that his great friend John Stenhouse was missing in action in the Red Sea. Stenhouse had been on salvage duty there, conducting similar work to that which Worsley had done in the *Dalriada*, and his ship had struck a mine. There were no survivors. It was 'second time unlucky' for Commander Stenhouse: in 1940 another ship under his command had struck a mine off the English coast. On that occasion Stenhouse had been one of 12 survivors out of 23 crew.

Worsley felt his passing keenly; Stenhouse's daughter Patricia Mantell said Jean told her it was the only time she ever saw her husband cry. Worsley himself recorded that it was the greatest loss – bar his father – that he had ever experienced, 'even more than Shackleton.'

Worsley's name ranked high on the list of Greenwich officers, though on the administrative rather than the professorial staff. It is probable, however, that such a notable navigator would also have been used, at least as a shining example of the greatness that could be achieved through such skill. Hattersley-Smith said that even during his time at Greenwich, which was after Worsley's death, the great sailor's record of valour and achievement was an inspiration to the young officers.

But ill health was soon to overwhelm Worsley, a man whose tough physical condition had seemingly made him impervious to common complaints. During a period of sickness he was diagnosed in a naval hospital as suffering from lung cancer.

It was soon clear that the disease was far too advanced for anything to be done. Worsley was discharged from hospital and went to spend his last days with his beloved Jean and in the company of his loving friends, the Bamford family, at Claygate.

It was all over in a week and he died at the Bamford home – his wonderful 'country estate' – on 1 February 1943, three weeks short of his 71st birthday. He was cremated at Woking on 3 February, after which a memorial service was held

Opposite page, clockwise from top left: A representative of the New Zealand High Commission, Mr J. Balfour (centre) attended the funeral on behalf of Frank Worsley's birth country. On the right, Jean Worsley walks with Eric Bamford.
Bamford family

Other officers from the college took turns in carrying the casket, which was covered with two flags, the New Zealand Ensign and Frank Worsley's personal standard which he had carried on the *Quest* expedition and to the Arctic.
Bamford family

Captain J.C. Davies (with eyepatch), captain of the Royal Naval College, Greenwich, carries the cask containng the ashes of Frank Worsley from the college chapel. A service was held on 3 February 1943, after Worsley's body was cremated at Woking. He had died two days earlier at the home of his great friend, Eric Bamford, at Claygate, Surrey.
Bamford family

The ashes of Frank Worsley rest on a naval ship near the Nore Lightship, at the mouth of the Thames, before being scattered at sea.
Bamford family

at the chapel of the Royal Naval College, Greenwich. It was conducted by the college chaplain. Jean Worsley attended, with many friends coming to pay their respects to the gallant and cheerful warrior.

Among them, and escorting Jean, was his good friend Eric Bamford, soon to be Sir Eric, to be knighted three times (KCB, KBE and KCMG) for his public services. Bamford at the outbreak of World War 2 had gone into a new department, the Ministry of Information, and became its director-general. Later he was to be chairman of the Board of Inland Revenue.

The High Commissioner for New Zealand, William (later Sir William) Jordan was represented and the congregation included many naval officers, some of whom shared the duty of carrying the casket containing Worsley's ashes to the landing stage on the River Thames, where it was placed on a naval vessel. The cortege was lined by a guard of honour of Wrens (women sailors). The casket was covered by two flags, the flag of New Zealand and the personal standard which had been given to Worsley by the New Zealand High Commission and which he took on both the *Quest* Antarctic expedition and the *Island* Arctic journey.

The casket was taken down the Thames with its naval escort and Worsley's ashes were scattered in the sea just off the mouth of the river near the Nore Lightship, a beacon undoubtedly sighted by the young Worsley more than 50 years earlier when his sailing clipper the *Wairoa* delivered the youngster to England on his first voyage.

Worsley's death was reported in some depth by the British press, and friends from the *Endurance* adventure, the biologist Robert Clark and the geologist James Wordie, combined to write a short but fine obituary for the *Polar Record*, noting how the New Zealander was 'a splendid ship-master, with untiring energy, who made an ideal combination with his leader'. Navigation of the *James Caird* from Elephant Island to South Georgia was his 'outstanding feat', made possible by Worsley's study of the winds and currents of the South Atlantic and his knack of snapping the sun in the most adverse conditions. This 'ensured the success of the voyage and ultimately the rescue of the marooned party on Elephant Island'.

The scientists paid tribute to this 'man of action, always on the move and extremely alert, both mentally and physically. He retained this amazing vigour up to the very end and steadily refused to go into retirement.'

But they had noticed more about Worsley than this lust for life and his seamanship, and this they also generously acknowledged: 'Worsley was a keen naturalist and observer; animal life appealed to him, and he had a good working knowledge of sea birds, seals and whales.' However, it was as a navigator that Worsley had stood supreme, and 'there is nothing finer in his long sea career than his piloting of the *James Caird* to South Georgia.' they wrote.

A London newspaper gossip column, under the heading 'The Waiters Trembled', also noted the passing of Worsley:

> Commander Worsley, the Polar hero who died this week, was a man of tremendous gusto. Not long after he had sunk a U-boat with his Q-ship he told the story in a grill-room.

With the zest of the born raconteur, he recounted how the U-boat came up to look at the curious stranger, how the hatches were thrown open and the order given for full speed ahead to ram the enemy.

'We were all bellowing like bulls,' roared Worsley. 'Then as we got near the sub I shouted "all hands down!" Not one of the lads went down. It was mutiny I expect, but none of us wanted to miss the fun.'

By that time the grill was rocking in the gale and waiters were trembling.

Worsley belonged to the 16th century, but he managed to get a lot of adventure out of the 19th and 20th.

Frank Worsley's medals. The DSO with Bar is on the left, next to his OBE. His Antarctic Medal in Silver is third from right, with the Russian decoration, the Order of St Stanislaus, extreme right.
David Yelverton

This gusto was acknowledged in New Zealand in a tribute on the radio station 2YA on 5 February 1943, entitled 'Frank Worsley: an Elizabethan New Zealander'. It said he was born to enjoy life, and especially the life of action. 'The man himself might have strayed out of the Elizabethan age. He was by nature an adventurer in the old sense of the term. Not for him the routine of a sailor's job on set routes; he thirsted for work off the beaten track. He revelled in difficulties and hardships; his spirit was gay, humorous and infectious.'

The tribute, which contained much information about Worsley's period in the Pacific, may have been written by the historian James Cowan, who knew him well and had sailed with him in the Pacific. Cowan died in September the same year.

The tribute made special reference to another point of resemblance to the Elizabethans: 'he could write'. Worsley had left a good deal of the story of his career in a number of books 'which show a real literary gift'. An English critic of Worsley's book, *First Voyage*, said it was 'far above the average of its kind…this man of action must have spent as much pains in becoming a writer as modern writers sometimes spend in emulating men of action.'

Worsley was the quintessential anglophile whose wholehearted enthusiasm for the crown and the empire was, thankfully, laced with an irreverence that was pure colonial. It was this that seemed to put him off-side with those cut from a more sober cloth, like some of the scientists on the *Endurance*, even – early in the expedition, and not for long – with Shackleton himself.

Much of this emotion grew from the somewhat riotous voyage between

England and Buenos Aires, when Shackleton was not on board, as recorded, for example, in the diary of Thomas Hans Orde-Lees, who noted that Worsley ran a loose ship with too much liquor available and too little discipline.

There were episodes like this that reflected Worsley's restless spirit in periods of boredom. However, in situations demanding of his professionalism he was inspirational on an heroic scale, and those who experienced his worth at such times spoke later of the man in awe and deep respect. At those times he was 'Skipper' with the same reverence as Shackleton was 'Boss'.

New Zealand's history of heroes is not complete without acknowledging Frank Arthur Worsley.

Fittingly, Worsley is remembered in a variety of geographical features around the world: in South Georgia, the British Antarctic Territory, the Ross Dependency and Spitzbergen. These features are respectively, Mount Worsley, Cape Worsley, Worsley Icefalls and Worsley Harbour.

After his death, Jean Worsley returned to Aberdeen, where she lived with her mother, returning south again following her mother's death. She went to live with her friend Lady Alice Bamford at another home in Claygate, and when Lady Bamford died in 1976, Jean Worsley moved back to Linksfield under the care of Patrick Bamford and his wife Beryl. She died there at the age of 85, on 6 April 1978, occupying the same room where Frank Worsley, her 'Wuz', died 35 years earlier.

Jean made one lonely grand voyage before she settled down at Claygate. She sailed to New Zealand in 1956, and visited Worsley's hometown, Christchurch, where she stayed with Helen Knight (*nee* Worsley), and also the lovely little port of Akaroa, where he was born. Jean was interviewed by the *Press* in Christchurch, and during the interview she was asked whether she could recall any particularly

A painting of a ship under sail, by Frank Worsley. He enjoyed sketching, and recorded many of the sailing ships he passed during his career. Sadly his sketch books were lost in the *Endurance*. This is the one sample of his artistic skill to survive.
Bamford family

exciting adventures while travelling with her husband. She replied that being Worsley's wife was exciting enough.

After leaving New Zealand, Jean visited her sister and brother-in-law in Tanganyika, East Africa, and was there when news came through that Duncan Carse and his party had crossed South Georgia, the first men to tread the path pioneered by Shackleton, Worsley and Crean. Jean, in a letter to her friend Mrs Dorothy Irving Bell, wrote, 'Now the world will know what those three men did. I think it proves they must have been guided, don't you?'

A final irony developed years after Worsley's death. Although he and Jean were more often broke than in funds in their life together, Worsley – as one might expect from one so bold – sometimes invested in shares. Typically, he favoured high-risk mining concerns, which seemed always to fail. But he did pick a winner in Venezuela Oil – it went on to become the international company, Shell.

So Jean, in her advancing years, finally achieved financial security through Worsley's endeavours; but sadly her loving treasure-hunter was not there to share the booty.

CHAPTER 18

The Boat

After Worsley and Stenhouse escorted the *James Caird* to London by rail in early December 1919, Shackleton loaned the small boat to Middlesex Hospital for an appeal for hospital funds. The *James Caird* was by then stripped back to something like her original specifications, albeit somewhat battered and worn: in King Haakon Bay on South Georgia, her masts had been unstepped and the decking and top two planks and part of the half-deck constructed by McNeish had been removed to lighten her so the survivors of the boat journey could haul her above high-tide mark.

But the Norwegian whalers at South Georgia, with a respect for the sturdy boat that bordered on reverence, had kept her in good overall condition.

She next appeared, still untouched, on the roof of Selfridges' department store in Oxford Street in February 1920. Shackleton and Worsley were present to see the boat hoisted to the roof garden to be displayed to the public.

The *James Caird*, once back in Britain after World War I, was used as a hospital fund-raiser. The boat was also displayed at the Maritime Museum at Greenwich, London, before finding a final resting place at Dulwich College, London, Sir Ernest Shackleton's old college.
Dulwich College

The *James Caird* is hoisted to the roof of Selfridges' store in central London, where she was on public display.
Dulwich College

Shackleton was at this time thinking about his next expedition, and was finding strong support and possibly heavy backing from his Dulwich College friend John Quiller Rowlett. According to Worsley, Shackleton gave the *James Caird* to Rowlett, and the boat went to his country home in Sussex. Whether a gift or a loan at that time, when Shackleton's affairs were wound up after his death the *James Caird* became the legal property of Rowlett.

The boat was presented to Dulwich College by Rowlett as a memorial to the explorer in March 1922, though she was not delivered there until 1924, by which time a special shelter to house her had been built, mainly from funds raised by the Alleyn Club, members of which are old boys of Dulwich College. She stayed at the college for the next 20 years, apart from being loaned in 1930 to the British Polar Exhibition staged at Westminster.

In July 1944 a flying bomb exploded in the college grounds, destroying some buildings and generally causing heavy damage to others. But the *James Caird* escaped unscathed.

Another 23 years passed and new college buildings were planned for the area where the *James Caird* rested, beside the old swimming bath block; the boat had to be moved from what were by then dilapidated surroundings. She was recognised as a treasure worth preserving, and was offered on temporary loan to the Maritime Museum at Greenwich. Included were some oars, spars and sails and a sledge used by Shackleton in his attempt on the South Pole in 1908–1909. They had all been dumped in the boat, and everything was in a poor state. She was moved to Greenwich in May 1967.

The *James Caird* was put on display inside the Neptune Hall at the museum, and the next year it was decided to restore her to the state she was in for the historic journey from Elephant Island to South Georgia. At a nearby works, a shipwright repaired the hull, replaced the planks removed at South Georgia, supplied masts, yards, a boom, and a rudder. She was also given a solid timber deck in place of the original canvas one, and some old navy canvas was found to make a suit of sails.

The authorities of Dulwich College, however, were disturbed: the *James Caird* clearly belonged to the college and was only on loan to the museum. An arrangement by which the museum kept the original, and made a scale model for the college, was agreed on.

But late in 1969 the Neptune Hall had to be closed and the *James Caird* was unrigged and moved to a store, where she stayed for more than four years, reappearing in another part of the museum shorn of masts, sails and rigging.

In 1986, the museum wrote to the college explaining that due to structural alterations, it would no longer be able to display the boat. She was returned to Dulwich College where she rested in a groundsman's shed pending a decision on her future. The museum offered technical assistance and during 1989 an area in the north cloister of the college was prepared.

The *James Caird* was moved there in August, and was then rigged with masts, stays, halliards, jib, mainsail and mizzen. She was restored to as close to her state for the boat journey as was possible: a worthy monument to the college old boy who

led the desperate rescue, and to the men who sailed with him.

She has been moved just once since then: in 1994, to the Exhibition Hall at Earls Court, to coincide with the attempt by Trevor Potts and three companions to duplicate the journey from Elephant Island to South Georgia, during the annual London International Boat Show. Potts had a replica of the *James Caird* built for his successful attempt, and called her the *Sir Ernest Shackleton*.

Back at the college, and with renewed international interest being shown in the *James Caird*, it was decided that a James Caird Society should be formed to ensure that the story of Shackleton's expeditions, and in particular the epic small-boat journey, should never be forgotten.

Driving force behind the society, which is now fully launched and with members all around the world, was Harding McGregor Dunnett, the first chairman, who is also author of a fine book on the history of the *James Caird*, called *Shackleton's Boat*. (The society can be contacted through the secretary c/o Dulwich College, London SE21 7LD.)

The *James Caird* in the North Cloister at Dulwich College. She is now rigged and has been restored to close to her state at the time of the great journey. She is preserved by the James Caird Society, which operates from the college.
Dulwich College

APPENDIX 1

Edward Saunders, the shy ghost writer

A portrait of Sir Ernest Shackleton, taken in 1909 in Christchurch, New Zealand, by Hemus Sarony. Shackleton was then 35 years old, and had just returned to New Zealand with the *Nimrod* at the end of an expedition that took him close to the South Pole.

Alexander Turnbull Library, No F-18870-1/2

No account of the recording of this golden age of Antarctic exploration is complete without reference to the work of Edward Randall Cargill Saunders.

His newspaper, the *Lyttelton Times*, carried the first full account of Shackleton's 1907–1909 *Nimrod* expedition and the leader's farthest south epic, in a spread over four broadsheet pages, fleshing out the brief cables that had been sent to London from the first landfall in New Zealand on the return journey, at Stewart Island. Edward Saunders undoubtedly contributed much of the material from interviews with Shackleton and his crew.

Saunders, like so many New Zealanders – particularly those around Christchurch and Lyttelton – was very interested in the polar explorers. As a 19-year-old reporter he was among local people entertained on Robert Scott's *Discovery* at Lyttelton in 1901. There is no record of him meeting Shackleton on that occasion, but he certainly did so in 1909 to record Shackleton's triumph.

The two young men must have taken an instant liking to one another, because when Shackleton decided to hire a secretary to take dictation from him for his official account of the *Nimrod* voyage, he turned to Saunders. Three weeks after viewing the reporter's work in the *Lyttelton Times*, Shackleton contracted Saunders to prepare a manuscript for his book on the adventure that was already making him a national hero at home.

Saunders' brief was to accompany Shackleton on the journey back to England, undertaking general duties of private secretary for four months from 15 April 1909. Shackleton was to pay all travelling expenses and hotel bills, and a salary of 10 pounds a week. He was also to pay Saunders' return fare to New Zealand and expenses on the return journey. Saunders undertook to regard as confidential 'all information secured by me in the course of my secretarial work and to write for publication during the course of my engagement only subject to your approval'.

It was a brilliant collaboration, another of Shackleton's inspired selections. Shackleton was at his best as a verbal performer; Saunders was the perfect foil, taking the dictation scrupulously but at the same time being his own man, with the professionalism to question, make suggestions, edit as he thought fit, and generally buff and polish the descriptive flow. The warm friendship that quickly developed between them made this possible, with most pleasing results.

Saunders worked for 10 months on the manuscript for the two volumes of *The Heart of the Antarctic*, Shackleton's highly praised record on the voyage of the *Nimrod*. London reviews marvelled at Shackleton's work and writing, one making the comment, 'Considering that it is only a few months since the expedition returned,

188

the volumes constitute a striking monument to Mr Shackleton's literary energy and enterprise no less than to the foresight and skill with which he planned and carried out a journey of remarkable dash and brilliance.'

The *Westminster Gazette* paid tribute to 'the skill and care with which this narrative has been compiled and not less to the simplicity and modesty and truly scientific spirit in which it is conceived'.

While Saunders' part was never acknowledged publicly, this was largely at his own wish, an attitude consistent with his insistence years later when the collaboration was repeated with *South*, Shackleton's record of the *Endurance* adventure.

But Shackleton never tried to bury Saunders' obviously fine work. Before Saunders left London to return to New Zealand, Shackleton on 6 December 1909 cabled a coded message to Saunders' father, via his New Zealand agent, Joseph (later Sir Joseph) Kinsey. It read: 'Before your son returns, wish to say he was indispensable. The success of the book largely due to him. I cannot speak too highly of him in every way. This is not only my own feeling but my publishers and all he came in contact with – Shackleton.'

Saunders does not seem to have maintained anything more than a spasmodic correspondence with Shackleton, something to which the explorer alluded in a letter from Germany in November 1910 during a long lecture tour in Europe. Shackleton wrote: 'You know you are one of our nearest friends, old son, though we do not write to each other this often, hardly. There are some people that don't need letters to keep alive friendship.'

Shackleton in this letter also referred to the 'jealousy stink' that developed after Saunders left England, something that might spread to New Zealand. 'I know that under the friendly public cloak there is a bitter feeling; so it needs someone like you to watch my side. You and your father know me.'

Saunders, who in 1914 became associate editor of the *Lyttelton Times* (his father Samuel was editor from 1891 to 1914), later moved to the capital, Wellington, to the *New Zealand Times*, and in 1917 joined *The Dominion*, working in the Parliamentary Press Gallery.

When Shackleton arrived in New Zealand with Worsley in 1916 to effect the rescue of the Ross Sea party, Saunders and he got together again, encouraged by Leonard Tripp. After the *Aurora* returned with the survivors early the following year, and came on to Wellington, Saunders had an exclusive interview with Shackleton for *The Dominion*.

The occasion is described by a rival journalist, Pat Lawlor, in his book *Wellington*. Lawlor, then a junior reporter on the *New Zealand Times*, was sent out to get Shackleton's story of the rescue. Saunders would also be there, and Lawlor was warned to be on his 'tip-toes', for Saunders was 'very pally with Shackleton'. Lawlor recalled pondering about Saunders while waiting for the boat to take them out to the approaching *Aurora*. 'He was older than myself and I knew him as a serious, self-contained and brilliant reporter. I took comfort in the fact that he had kind, candid blue eyes. When he arrived he gave me a brief friendly smile.'

Ernest Shackleton as he was when he met Edward Saunders in Lyttelton, New Zealand, on the *Nimrod* at the end of his 1907–1909 expedition. Saunders reported on Shackleton's great feat in reaching closer than 100 miles to the South Pole. Shackleton was impressed with his writing, and hired the young journalist as his private secretary to help him write his book of that expedition, *The Heart of the Antarctic*.
Alexander Turnbull Library, No. F-8703-1/4

Edward Cargill Saunders, the New Zealand journalist who became Sir Ernest Shackleton's trusted friend and 'literary assistant'. Saunders was working in the Parliamentary Press Gallery in Wellington when Shackleton and Worsley arrived in 1916. Later, Shackleton left his papers and Worsley's diaries with Saunders, who shaped them into another best-selling book, *South*.
Cass family

When the welcoming party climbed aboard, Shackleton greeted Saunders 'like a long lost brother'. Shackleton told Lawlor that all he would have to say would be given to Saunders, adding that he was sure 'my friend Ed' would share with Lawlor some of the news. Saunders nodded agreement and the two friends went off together, leaving Lawlor to gather crumbs of news from the rest of the party.

Lawlor was to pick up the official story from Saunders later, and when he presented himself at the *Dominion* office that night Saunders handed him a neat carbon copy of nearly two columns, 'with one of his rare smiles'.

Saunders then turned to the task of assisting Shackleton with his official account of the *Endurance* story, first travelling with the explorer to Australia for the celebrated showdown with vociferous local critics. Saunders recorded that they were together for about three weeks, Shackleton dictating notes on the run.

Shackleton sailed back to England, leaving Saunders with some documents including Worsley's diary, which was to form the basis of the account. The reporter also interviewed Worsley, and requested of the sailor 'plans', which may have meant, among other things, Worsley's sketch of the crossing of South Georgia which was reproduced in *South*. He also wanted more 'description' from Worsley, which was delivered before Worsley sailed for England. Tripp was anxious that Worsley should fully cooperate with Saunders, as there was no doubt that the Royal Naval Reserve officer was destined to face the dangers of what remained of the Great War.

Worsley wrote to Saunders from the RMS *Makura*, thanking Saunders and his wife for their kindness to him. He also asked Saunders to credit the new material not to himself, but to Shackleton; and indeed even Worsley's signature was removed from the map of the South Georgia crossing.

Saunders took about a year to compile the manuscript for *South*. He received a typically brief cablegram from Shackleton in August 1918 acknowledging receipt of the work: 'Book splendid.' Again the book reviewers were to heap praise on the explorer for his descriptive powers.

Because of their confident rapport, Shackleton appears to have given Saunders something of a free hand to shape *South*. Hugh Robert Mill put it, 'The pen was never a favourite implement with Shackleton, but happily Mr Saunders, the congenial amanuensis who had taken down much of *The Heart of the Antarctic* from dictation, was available…' The extent of Saunders' work on *South* is further revealed in the 1957 biography, *Shackleton*, by Margery and James Fisher. The Fishers said that as Shackleton in 1917 was planning to get a war appointment, he would not be available to do much writing, 'and he gladly gave Saunders complete responsibility for putting the material together, confident that his friend knew him well enough to write it as he wanted it to be written'.

One man who knew the full extent of Saunders' brilliant reporting was Leonard Tripp. Some of the most poignant passages in *South*, such as the first reference to the presence of a 'fourth man' in the crossing of South Georgia, were dictated at Tripp's home at Heretaunga, near Wellington.

In a letter to Mill, who was at the time writing his biography of Shackleton, Tripp wrote:

> I shall never forget the occasion. I was sitting in my chair listening; Shackleton walked up and down the room, smoking a cigarette, and I was absolutely amazed at his language. He very seldom hesitated, but every now and then he would tell Saunders to make a mark because he had not got the right word, but that was only occasionally.
>
> I watched him and his whole face seemed to swell – you know what a big face he had – and you could see the man was suffering. After about half an hour he turned to me and with tears in his eyes he said: 'Tripp, you don't know what I have been through and I am going through it all again, and I can't do it.' I would say: 'But we must get it down.'
>
> He would go on for an hour and then all of a sudden would say 'I can't do it – I must go and talk to the girls or play tennis.' He walked out of the room as if he intended to go away, light a cigarette, and then in about five minutes would come back and start as if nothing had happened. The same thing happened again, after about another half-hour or so. You could see that the man was suffering.

And then he came to this mention of the fourth man, and he turned to me and said: 'Tripp, this is something I have not told you.' As far as I can remember his account of the crossing of South Georgia has practically not been altered at all since he wrote the story.

In 1922, after Shackleton's death, Tripp proposed to Saunders that he write to him about his part in the production of *The Heart of the Antarctic* and *South*. Tripp wanted then to forward the information to Mill for his biography. Tripp's motive was clearly to secure for Saunders the full credit which was his due.

The proposal displeased Saunders greatly. He told Tripp in a letter dated 10 August 1922 that he found it 'difficult to say anything that ought to be said on the subject'. The two books stood as a record of Shackleton's work in the Antarctic. 'My association with Shackleton was very intimate and to a large extent confidential,' he wrote. He told Tripp he had worked for 10 months on *The Heart of the Antarctic* and for about a year on *South*, and 'he [Shackleton] and I alone knew just how the completed narratives were produced.'

Saunders said that in 1917 Shackleton had proposed, 'with characteristic generosity', that Saunders should be named in *South* as editor of the book. Saunders did not accept the offer, telling Tripp, 'He always acknowledged my share in the making of both the books.' Had Shackleton lived, they would have worked together once more on an autobiography.

He concluded his letter to Tripp, 'The books should stand without any attempt being made now to explain just how they were produced…I do not believe he [Shackleton] would have wished me to say more or less than I have said.'

Saunders must have felt uneasy about Tripp, because he also wrote a few days later direct to Mill, enclosing with his letter a copy of his reply to the lawyer. He further emphasised that he did not want the subject of his part in producing the books to be raised in Mill's biography of Shackleton.

In this letter Saunders gives more information about how he and Shackleton worked on the *South* manuscript. In their three weeks together in New Zealand and Australia,

on boats and trains, at odd hours in the intervals of his many engagements, he told me the important parts of his new story. He left me some documents, the most important being a copy of Captain Worsley's diary. I used much material from that diary…

Shackleton's method was to tell me the story, often under conditions that made even the roughest notes difficult. Sometimes he would dictate passages where his interest was keenly stirred. But he liked questions and suggestions. I found for example that the account of the crossing of South Georgia increased in length by about one-third between the first draft and the final draft. Worsley told me some part of that story. I had to leave a gap somewhere between the loss of the ship and the start of the boat journey because I found that I had no record at all covering the period. Shackleton filled that gap after he received the manuscript.

Saunders ended his letter to Mill saying, 'Please believe that I have not the least wish to claim recognition in connection with the books. I should feel guilty of disloyalty to my friend if I made any claim.'

The following month Mill replied, telling Saunders to set his mind 'entirely at rest as to any disclosures in my life of Sir Ernest Shackleton as to his methods of preparing his books.' He was as good as his word. Apart from the 'congenial amanuensis' comment, the only other reference was to describe Saunders as a 'literary assistant' who took dictation from Shackleton.

Mill said Shackleton had submitted all the proofs of *The Heart of the Antarctic* to him in 1909, and accepted 'most of my suggestions, naturally more in the case of the scientific appendices than in the narrative'. He did not see *South* until receiving the book to review. He concluded, 'Shackleton always spoke to me of your services to him as quite exceptional, but I respect your wish not to make them more precise for the public.'

Shackleton had hoped to use money from sales of *South* to help clear his long-standing debt over the *Endurance*, but was foiled by the executors of the estate of one of the original benefactors, Sir Robert Lucas-Tooth, an Australian banker in London who had guaranteed 5000 pounds. Shackleton had used as security, among other things, future earnings from the book of the expedition. Lucas-Tooth had been dead for several years before *South* was published, but his executors demanded repayment of the loan. Shackleton settled by assigning them all rights to the book profits.

Saunders was paid for his work with money Tripp raised from the sale of chronometers brought back by the Ross Sea party. Saunders died suddenly from pneumonia in Wellington late in the same year in which his great friend Shackleton died, 1922, soon after he had resisted the opportunity to proclaim his undoubtedly fine reporting in Shackleton's cause. He was aged 40.

Emily Shackleton, who had met Saunders in London, wrote to Saunders' widow, expressing her sympathy, on the very anniversary in 1923 'at this very hour, 7 o'clock, 'that the news of her own husband's death had reached her. 'So you will realise that my heart goes out to you in very real and understanding sympathy.' She recalled 1909, when life 'seemed brimming with happiness, and your dear husband was with us'.

She said, 'My husband had a great regard for him, as had all who knew him, and he will be missed and mourned by many friends.'

T.H. Orde-Lees and Harry McNeish, Karori companions

Two of Shackleton's men from the Trans-Antarctic Expedition lie buried in New Zealand, in Wellington's Karori Cemetery. That shared adventure, and their final resting place, are about all they ever had in common.

The carpenter, Harry McNeish, and the expedition's motor expert, Thomas Hans Orde-Lees, were table-mates on the *Endurance*. Although Orde-Lees arranged that, later he deeply regretted it. He might turn in his grave if he knew they were still so close together, although the fact that he lies in the tidy and regimented ex-servicemen's section, while McNeish is at the other end of the cemetery – as far distant as physically possible and in a pauper's plot – might appease him.

McNeish, a Scot from Irvine, in Ayrshire, was the oldest man in Shackleton's party. There is confusion about his age. Shackleton believed he was more than 50 years old when the expedition started out, but the interment card at Karori Cemetery states that he was 64 years old when he died in September 1930, which would make him 48 in 1914.

At any rate, he was vastly experienced, being a veteran of Scott's 1901 National Antarctic Expedition, as were Shackleton and several others. McNeish, after a 23-year career as a carpenter in the Royal Navy, worked on the building of Scott's vessel, the *Discovery*, and then joined her as carpenter. He spent much of the trip on the *Discovery* at Hut Point. Shackleton must have had a high regard for his ability as a carpenter, and McNeish was invited to join the *Endurance*.

Orde-Lees, the son of a high-ranking police officer, was a captain in the Royal Marines in 1914. His father was chief constable of the Isle of Wight. Orde-Lees received a superb upper-class education: he went to Marlborough College, the Royal Academy, the Royal Naval School at Gosport, and to Sandhurst. He was commissioned in the Royal Marines and took part in the suppression of the Boxer Rebellion in China in 1900. He sought a position in the 1910 Scott expedition but was unsuccessful.

Shackleton wanted the Royal Navy to be represented on his expedition. Orde-Lees had already written to Shackleton applying for a position, but the navy refused him leave, saying that he would have to resign his commission. Shackleton took up the cause with Winston Churchill, then First Lord of the Admiralty, and Orde-Lees was released from duty to join the expedition, unpaid.

Orde-Lees was then superintendent of physical training at the Royal Marine Depot school. He was an enthusiastic gymnast, skier, climber, cyclist and motorist, and had experimented with motor sledges. Shackleton appreciated his diverse abilities. He took Orde-Lees to Norway to test motor-sledges, including one driven by an air-propellor. The sledges were taken on the *Endurance*, but none of them turned out to be of any great use, and they were abandoned.

His place at the mess-table was resolved by personal choice. 'I have made a point of sitting at the same table as the fourth officer, who was a sailor on Scott's expedition [probably Alfred Cheetham, who was in fact third officer], and the carpenter [McNeish], who is a perfect pig in every way…however I think it is a good thing to try to accommodate oneself to ideas and ways less refined than one's own.'

About this time Orde-Lees also took some notice of Worsley, writing in his diary: 'The captain is a remarkably nice man, a New Zealander.'

He could not leave McNeish alone. 'He is an ill-mannered brute. He sucks his teeth loudly, and picks his teeth after sharpening a match. He occasionally expectorates through the window, and at scooping up peas with a knife he is a perfect juggler.' However, Orde-Lees did concede that he felt sure 'I get on his nerves as much as he does on mine.'

Worsley and Orde-Lees sometimes hunted together after the *Endurance* was beset in the ice. Orde-Lees recorded their first attempt, armed with a revolver. 'We went on the ice to shoot a seal. However several shots only wounded the seal, which lay quietly near his "wife". ' The two men then stunned the 'wife' with a blow from an oar and cut her throat with a blunt knife – 'a disgusting piece of butchery'. Meanwhile 'Mr Seal' died and Worsley and Orde-Lees towed the corpses back to the ship.

After Orde-Lees was appointed storekeeper, he again clashed with McNeish. He found the carpenter 'unusually troublesome' on 12 February 1915 over moving some stores in the hold so that McNeish could reach the water tanks, which were part of his responsibility. 'He has an exceptionally offensive manner; it is very hard to be patient with him,' wrote Orde-Lees. A month later his opinion changed somewhat, following Shackleton's decision that the party move into new quarters in the hold of the ship as protection from the crippling cold. McNeish was 'working wonders in the main hold, the cubicles are nearly ready for us and the stove is fitted and working'.

Orde-Lees stood out in the diverse company as the tallest, probably the fittest and strongest, the most haughty, among the better educated, and the least liked. He considered himself one of the scientific staff, though on the official list of members of the expedition he ranked well below them, even below the photographer Frank Hurley and the artist George Marston, and just one step higher than the carpenter.

There was something in his manner to irritate everyone, even – or particularly – the man who hired him, Shackleton, a fellow Anglo-Irishman.

Orde-Lees recorded that once in conversation with Shackleton he asked how it was that the Boss had selected him.

'Well, you may remember that I sent you a wire telling you to come up to see me on Tuesday or Friday, whichever was the most suitable,' replied Shackleton.

'Oh yes. Of course I came up on the Tuesday,' Orde-Lees responded.

'How often have I wished since that you had postponed it to Friday,' said Shackleton.

When Shackleton needed somebody to undertake the most unattractive task, that of storekeeper, he naturally chose Orde-Lees, who had shown that he had a huge capacity to absorb abuse without reacting violently which, considering his size and strength, was a notable attribute; he could probably have whipped any man in the party.

The McNeish diary is a more personal document, and is less concerned with his companions than it is with his own feelings; he is also much kinder to Orde-Lees than the upper-class officer, who by then went under such cognomina as The Colonel, Peggie Lees, the Belly Burglar and others less generous, was with him.

Soon after the *Endurance* began meeting heavier ice than expected, the carpenter was gloomily predicting disaster: on 15 January he wrote: 'There is open water about five miles to the north-east, so we may get out before the winter sets in, but our chance is small.' A month later: 'Started to break away the ice ahead but found it getting too thick – it runs from 12ft–18ft, so we will have to wait God's will to get out.' On 8 March: 'We are drifting away from the land, so I don't think there will be any chance of a landing next spring.'

His thoughts often turned to home. On 4 March he recorded: 'This is my loved one's birthday. I trust in God she is well – also Wee Tips.' And on 28 March: 'My wee love's birthday. Hope her and my big love are well. God bless them.'

Like others, McNeish was anxious for news of the war, and the left-leaning carpenter recorded: 'We unanimously hope that the War God [the German Kaiser] has been crushed without any further loss of life and we are all sorry we have no hand in the hanging of him. We all sincerely hope the Russians will capture him, for if Briton [sic] do they will set him up in a palace for the ratepayers to keep.'

And on 9 June: 'Peggie Lees went for exercise on an old bike. A search party found him, minus the bike he left somewhere. He don't know where so he is not to leave the ship alone again. Poor fellow, he is only mad.'

The inevitable happened and the ship was abandoned. Three months later, in February 1916, McNeish's black mood is reflected in the following entry:

> There is nothing for it but get into sleeping bags and smoke away the hunger; what Lloyd George calls a luxury for working men. I wish to God he was here. I expect we will have to submit to have about two pounds ten shillings abducted from our wages after being out of the world for two years and received no benefits, and then they will say Briton is a free country. This is where him and his fellow ministers should be, for any good they ever done a working man or woman.

Orde-Lees loathed his experiences in boats, particularly small boats, and showed no interest in the business of sailing them other than working like a peasant when it was obvious that bailing out the boat he happened to be in between the ice-floe and Elephant Island was necessary to save his own life.

His companions on that journey thought poorly of his general behaviour, particularly of his failure to contribute as a rower. Nevertheless, Worsley, who commanded the *Dudley Docker,* had Orde-Lees as one of his crew and had plenty of cause to curse him, also had good words to say about the Englishman's efforts at bailing the boat when there was great danger of being swamped.

Among the many stories published about the suffering of the 22 men on Elephant Island is one that said cannibalism was considered at a time when the food supply was low, and that Orde-Lees was the unanimous choice as first offering. The story apparently grew from a comment made by the cook, Charles Green.

The first officer, Lionel Greenstreet, set the record straight in a radio interview, made in 1970 when he was 81. He said that the stranded party several times ran out of food, when the wildlife moved north in winter, 'but something always turned up – a penguin or two, or a seal.'

Greenstreet said he heard that Green told some reporters that the last food was gone by the time the rescue ship arrived, after which they were to draw lots to decide who should be eaten first. The first lot had been drawn, 'and the lot had fallen to Captain Orde-Lees, Green apparently said: 'My poor friend Orde-Lees; I should have to cook him!'

'We never thought of eating each other,' Greenstreet said. 'It was an absolute lie!'

McNeish nursed a lot of resentment towards Worsley, apparently from the time when he was unsuccessful in his challenge to the authority of the skipper to order the men to drag the small boats across the ice. When Worsley, who had the sharpest eyes in the party and usually manned look-outs, reported seeing Mt Haddington from their ice-floe on 26 February 1916, McNeish responded, 'We know him to be a liar as Mt Haddington can only be seen 80 miles off, and we are 91 miles from Snow Hill (island) and the mountain is 20 miles west of that.'

And after Shackleton finally sighted land, McNeish wrote: 'There was doubt on the skipper's part as he never saw it first after being on the lookout this last two months and reporting so many bergs as being land. He is feeling quite sick over it being seen by anyone else.'

After the rescue, both Orde-Lees and McNeish returned to Britain with most of the party. Orde-Lees, with the help of Shackleton, joined the Royal Flying Corps and interested himself in the use of parachutes.

Orde-Lees showed that while some of his companions from the Shackleton adventure thought him a coward, he did not lack courage. He made one perilous drop from Tower Bridge, in London, to demonstrate their safety, dropping from a mere 150 feet in what was probably the lowest voluntary parachute descent ever made. His Guardian Angel parachute opened only a few feet before he hit the water. British paratroops today, with vastly superior equipment, are limited to dropping from 800 feet in peacetime, and 500 feet in war.

His passion for parachuting took him to Japan after the war, where he served with the British Naval Air Mission, and taught parachuting to the Japanese Air Force. He finally settled in Japan, accepted a lectureship in English at Kobe University, and for three years was correspondent to *The Times.* He married a Japanese woman, and she travelled with him to many parts of the world.

Orde-Lees read the English news over the radio in the 20 years he lived in

The grave of Thomas Hans
Orde-Lees at Karori Cemetery,
Wellington.

Japan, and also taught English privately. He and his wife were well off and had a fine home in Tokyo, with two servants, and another property. They had a daughter, Zoe.

World War II interrupted the pleasant life. Just before Japan entered the war, Orde-Lees and his small family moved to New Zealand, abandoning their properties and assets.

The family settled in the capital, Wellington. Possibly by special arrangement with the Government, his wife was never treated as an enemy alien, most of whom were imprisoned for the duration.

Arthur Helm, of Wellington, who was secretary to the New Zealand Antarctic Society committee, got to know Orde-Lees well, and said the former officer accepted a post of office assistant for the New Zealand Correspondence School 'for want of anything better'. His duties were those of a porter and an office boy and were, said Helm, 'the least pleasant of his adventures'.

Orde-Lees became a well-recognised figure around the city. He also wrote a travel column for the children's page of the *Southern Cross* newspaper for a while, drawing on his journeys around Asia between the wars. Sometimes he escaped dull routine with gestures that attracted attention, like the time he rode his bicycle down the main steps of Parliament. He usually wore sandshoes, and often jogged around the streets of the city.

His experiences with the Shackleton expedition drew him into the organisational side of the New Zealand contribution to the 1955–1958 Commonwealth Trans-Antarctic Expedition.

'We were both on the committee in the days when we were planning our own expedition to try to do what Shackleton had failed to do – to cross the Antarctic continent,' said Helm. 'Some of the members of the committee used to get annoyed with him when he failed to turn up to a meeting, but by then he was an old man and prone to forgetfulness.'

Orde-Lees also felt that New Zealand should work to get him compensation for the lost properties in Japan, haranguing various authorities without success in a doubtless irritating manner that onetime polar colleagues would readily recognise. He died in December 1958, aged 79.

While Orde-Lees' resting place is in the servicemen's neat lawn cemetery at Karori, the funeral of the former marine officer (now a lieutenant-colonel) was not on as grand a scale as the McNeish ceremony, which would certainly have amused the old carpenter greatly.

After the rescue of the men from Elephant Island, McNeish joined the New Zealand Shipping Company, making about five trips to the then-Dominion. Finally he worked his passage on the ship *Ruapehu* and settled in Wellington, finding employment and like-minded socialist company on the waterfront.

McNeish frequently complained that the soaking ordeal of the *James Caird* journey so affected him that his bones ached permanently. At any rate, the time came when he could no longer work effectively – he also had an accident at work – and he lost his job. He was by then more than 60 years old.

Times were hard, and having no income meant that McNeish could not pay for accommodation; however, he still had good friends on the waterfront. When he needed them, he would turn up at the wharf and his mates would find a quiet and warm corner where he could sleep.

The grave of Harry McNeish at Karori Cemetery, Wellington.

Concern for his health grew and his waterfront brothers finally found a place for him in an old men's home, where he was assured of a warm bed and three meals a day. For spending money McNeish would visit the wharf most Fridays. His mates there had a weekly collection for comrades in distress, and McNeish was among those who could count on 10 shillings a week for beer and tobacco.

In fact McNeish had been entitled to a pension for years as a result of his navy service, but he had long signed this over to a sister in Scotland. It was worth two pounds seven shillings a week. When a friend asked why he did not draw it, the carpenter replied, 'Ah but my sister at home; God knows, she needs it more than I.'

When he died in September 1930, aged 64, newspaper accounts featured his Antarctic adventures, and a sympathetic member of Parliament arranged for the Government of New Zealand to pay for a plot at Karori Cemetery.

A Royal Navy ship, HMS *Dunedin*, was in port and McNeish was given a grand funeral, with the crew providing eight pall-bearers, a firing party for the former navy man and a mourning party. The New Zealand Army supplied a gun-carriage to carry the coffin.

Among the wreaths was one from the Navy League and another from HMS *Dunedin*. It was probably the most impressive funeral ever seen in the city for a man occupying a pauper's grave.

Strangly the grave was not marked at the time, and for years the whereabouts of McNeish's remains were a mystery, solved only when the New Zealand Antarctic Society searched cemetery records and erected a headstone in 1957.

McNeish always cherished the letter that Shackleton had given him at Peggotty Camp, leaving him in charge while Shackleton, Worsley and Crean marched across South Georgia. He also kept one of the two Primus stoves which were taken in the *James Caird*; Shackleton took one with the climbing party and left the other with McNeish, McCarthy and Vincent. This primus is today displayed in the Canterbury Museum, in Christchurch, New Zealand.

When McNeish clashed with Worsley on the ice, threatening a mutiny, Shackleton swore that he would not forget the incident. His revenge came at the end of the adventure, when he was able to persuade the Admiralty to award his entire party the Polar Medal, even though none of them actually set foot on Antarctica. The officers and scientists received the silver version, the other ranks the bronze.

Shackleton then excluded from receipt of the award four men whose actions he believed failed his standards: the seaman Vincent, the firemen H. Stephenson and A. Holness – and McNeish, despite the splendid services which the carpenter alone was able to perform, and which he did with distinction throughout the ordeal, save one act of madness.

Gordon Burt, a biographical note

Gordon Burt, engineer on the *Island* for Worsley's 1925 Arctic expedition, was born in Dunedin in 1899. He was the eldest of five boys and one girl, and a grandson of Thomas Burt, one of the founders of the well-known New Zealand engineering firm, of A. & T. Burt Ltd.

In 1925, when he joined the Worsley–Algarsson expedition to the Arctic as a volunteer engineer (i.e. unpaid), Gordon Burt had just completed two years' study towards an engineering degree at Liverpool University. He probably read of the planned expedition in a local newspaper, and offered his services for what must have seemed a likely adventure in the company of a famous fellow-countryman. He never completed his university studies, breaking away from the expedition to return home to New Zealand on hearing of his father's death.

On the expedition, Worsley soon developed a high regard for Burt's capabilities with engines; he himself loathed mechanical propulsion.

Burt was also an enthusiastic photographer and took many photographs on the journey. These were kept in an album, which was sold, along with other memorabilia, at auction in Melbourne in 1996 by his daughter, Jocelyn Burt.

At the time of World War 2, Burt was working as an inspector for an oil company in Singapore. When the Japanese entered the war and invasion was looming, he successfully got his wife and infant daughter out of Singapore on a refugee ship to Australia, then joined the force being mustered to defend the island against the Japanese. Burt was first with the defence force in the Singapore Volunteer Armoured Car Company. He was later awarded the OBE for his services.

When the Japanese invasion force finally landed in February 1942, Burt was chief engineer on a ship in a convoy of Royal Air Force refuelling craft, trying to get away from Singapore. The convoy was spotted from a Japanese aircraft off the island of Sumatra (in the then Dutch East Indies, now Indonesia) and was attacked.

Burt escaped by diving overboard and swimming to a nearby island, where he lived in the jungle for two days before boarding a friendly sailing junk that was attacked by a Japanese invasion barge. The New Zealander was taken prisoner and was paraded barefoot, bound and near-naked, through the town of Palembang, Sumatra, behind a Japanese soldier.

Burt at first lived at a military prisoner-of-war camp at Palembang, and was later transferred to Native Criminal Jail to be among civilian prisoners. In a diary which he maintained for two years at great personal risk, Burt described the terrible conditions that were endured, and the ways in which the prisoners endeavoured to keep their spirits high. One of Burt's contributions was to lecture on his experiences with Frank Worsley on the Arctic expedition.

His diary ends on 13 September 1944. Soon after, Burt himself contracted both malaria and beri-beri. He clung to life long enough to see the liberation of Sumatra by allied troops, but tragically he died soon after, on 28 January 1945. He is buried at the camp's cemetery where he helped to bury so many of his comrades.

Roderick Carr and the Antarctic Baby aircraft

Roderick Carr became associated with several enterprises involving Frank Worsley, notably the *Quest* expedition during which Sir Ernest Shackleton died in 1922.
Scott Polar Research Institute, No. 1529/9/15

Roderick Carr, the 'Roddy' of Frank Worsley's accounts of battling the Bolsheviks in North Russia soon after World War 1, and on the voyage of the *Quest* in 1921–1922, died as Air Marshal Sir Charles Roderick Carr, KBE (1945), CBE (1941), DFC, AFC; he also won several other notable awards.

He was born at Feilding, New Zealand, in 1891, and educated at Wellington College. When the war broke out in 1914, Carr enlisted and went overseas with the Wellington Mounted Rifles, seeing action in Egypt and Palestine. Aircraft were being used by both the British and the Turkish forces on the Middle East front, and Carr developed an interest in the new art of aviation.

In 1915 he transferred to the Royal Navy Air Service. He distinguished himself in action on the Western Front, in France, before joining the Royal Air Force in 1918 to start a remarkable RAF career in which he became one of the most senior officers in the service during World War 2.

In 1919 he met Worsley in North Russia, where they were both part of the shadowy Allied effort to resist the surge of support for the Bolshevik revolution and to prop up right-wing Russian provincial governments by military means. Carr won his Distinguished Flying Cross at this time, and in a bizarre sequel to that odd period he was for a time Chief of Air Staff in the new Baltic state of Lithuania.

It was his contact with Worsley that led Carr to quit the RAF for a short time, to sail on the *Quest*, under the overall command of Sir Ernest Shackleton, who had also been employed in North Russia. Shackleton died at South Georgia before the expedition's real task had begun, and Carr was present at the building of a cairn in honour of the great explorer on the South Atlantic island in early 1922.

Carr was to have flown the Avro 554 Antarctic Baby seaplane carried in the *Quest* when she left England. Hugh Robert Mill says Shackleton had been obliged by bad weather 'to change his plans and to omit the [planned] call at Cape Town, though his seaplane and the polar equipment had been sent on from Madeira to await the *Quest*'.

The troublesome engines of the *Quest* ruined the plan to fly in the Antarctic. The repairs at Rio were to take four weeks, and Shackleton decided to head straight to South Georgia and omit the call at Cape Town. This decision came after the aircraft had been unloaded.

Frank Wild wrote, 'In the belief that we would still be carrying on the full programme, the aeroplane had been sent to the Cape by mail steamer.'

The Antarctic Baby was built in 1921 specially for the expedition, and tested on Southampton Water. It was a two-seater, and was to have been used for photographic surveys. Limited space on the *Quest* meant dismantling the aircraft for stowage, and it had to be possible to re-assemble it while wearing gloves. Rigging problems had to be eliminated, so tubular steel struts replaced wires, and all the bolts were extra large.

In 1923 the Antarctic Baby was bought by a Canadian concern, Bowring Bros Ltd of St John. It was fitted with skis and shipped to Newfoundland for seal spotting. The aircraft was flown for four seasons before being replaced by a more modern aircraft in 1927.

Carr rejoined the RAF with a permanent commission in 1926, and the following year he was chosen by the RAF to officially represent Britain in an attempt to win the world non-stop flight record direct to India. Several attempts failed to set this record, but for a time he held the world record for the longest non-stop flight.

At the start of World War 2, Carr commanded a flying school and also had a senior appointment in France until the German invasion. For a time he was the top air officer in Northern Ireland, and from 1941 to 1944 he commanded a heavy bomber group in Bomber Command, based in Yorkshire. In the last year of the war, he was appointed as deputy chief of air staff at Supreme Headquarters of the Allied Expeditionary Force.

In 1945 he was posted to command the British air bases in South East Asia, and the following year he was air officer commander in chief in India. He retired from the RAF in 1947 and died in England in December 1971.

Bibliography

BOOKS: POLAR

Bickel, Lennard, 1976, *Shackleton's Forgotten Argonauts* (Macmillan, Melbourne)

Dunnett, Harding McGregor, 1996, *Shackleton's Boat: The Story of the James Caird* (Neville & Harding, London)

Fisher, Margery and James, 1957, *Shackleton* (Barrie, London)

Huntford, Roland, 1985, *Shackleton* (Hodder & Stoughton, London)

Hurley, Frank, 1925, *Argonauts of the South* (Putnams)

Hussey, L.D.A., 1949, *South with Shackleton* (Sampson Low, London)

Jones, A.G.E., 1992, *Polar Portraits: Collected Papers* (Caedmon of Whitby)

Lansing, Alfred, 1959, *Endurance: Shackleton's Incredible Voyage* (Hodder & Stoughton, London)

Marr, James, 1923, *Into the Frozen South* (Cassell, London)

Mill, H.R., 1923, *The Life of Sir Ernest Shackleton* (William Heinemann, London)

Scholes, Arthur, 1953, *Seventh Continent* (George Allen & Unwin, London)

Shackleton, Sir Ernest, 1919, *South* (Heinemann, London)

Wild, Frank, 1923, *Shackleton's Last Voyage* (Cassell, London)

Worsley, Cdr Frank, 1926, *Under Sail in the Frozen North* (Stanley Paul & Co., London)

Worsley, Cdr Frank, 1931, *Endurance* (Philip Allen, London)

Worsley, Cdr Frank, 1938, *First Voyage in a Square Rigged Ship* (Geoffrey Bles, London)

Worsley, Cdr Frank, 1974, *Shackleton's Boat Journey* (Philip Allen, London; reissued by The Folio Society)

BOOKS: OTHER

Ackland, L.G.D., 1975, *The Early Canterbury Runs* (Whitcoulls, Christchurch)

Brassington, A.C., and Maling, P.B., eds, *Butler's A First Year in Canterbury Settlement* (Blackwood & Paul)

Cowan, James, 1936, *Suwarrow Gold and Other Stories of the Great South Sea* (Jonathan Cape, London)

Crane, Jonathan, 1984, *Submarine* (British Broadcasting Corporation, London)

Haigh, J. Bryant, and Polaschek, A.J., 1993, *New Zealand and the Distinguished Service Order* (Medals Research, Christchurch)

Jackson, A.J., *Avro Aircraft since 1908* (Putnam & Paul, London)

Keegan, Pat, 1938, *The First Generation* (Hilton Press, Christchurch)

Lawlor, Pat, 1976, *Wellington* (Millward Press, Wellington)

McDougall, R.J., 1989, *New Zealand Naval Vessels* (GP Books, Wellington)

Ogilvie, Gordon, 1978, *The Port Hills of Christchurch* (A.H. & A.W. Reed, Wellington)

Taffrail, 1931, *Endless Story* (Hodder & Stoughton, London)

UNPUBLISHED

Gaby, J., *Amokura* (manuscript held by the Alexander Turnbull Library, Wellington)

INSTITUTIONS

Akaroa Museum, Canterbury, NZ

Alexander Turnbull Library, Wellington, NZ

Canterbury Museum, Christchurch, NZ

Dunedin Public Library, Dunedin, NZ

Hocken Library, University of Otago, Dunedin, NZ

Scott Polar Research Institute, Cambridge, UK

British Red Cross (London)

Dulwich College (London)

James Caird Society (London)
National Archives (Wellington)
Office of The Second Sea Lord (London)
Public Records Office (London)
Royal Naval College (London)
Registry of Shipping and Seamen (Cardiff)

DIARIES

McNeish, Harry, *Endurance Diary* (Alexander Turnbull Library, Wellington)
Orde-Lees, Thomas Hans, *Endurance Diaries* (Alexander Turnbull Library, Wellington)
Worsley, Cdr Frank, *Diaries of the Endurance Expedition, the Boat Journey, the Relief Efforts and the Quest Expedition* (Alexander Turnbull Library, Wellington)

PAPERS, PERIODICALS, PRESS CLIPPINGS

Appendices to the Journals of the House of Representatives, 1899 (National Archives, Wellington)
Frank Worsley, an Elizabethan New Zealander, 1943, a National Broadcasting Service tribute (Canterbury Museum, Christchurch)
Geographical Magazine, vol. X1V1, 1974
NZ Geographic, vol. 28
NZ Marine News, vol.16, no. 1
New Zealand Railways Magazine, October, 1933
Otago Witness (Hocken Library, Dunedin)
Reported Destruction of Submarines, 1914–1919 (British Public Records Office, London)
Saunders, Edward, papers (Alexander Turnbull Library, Wellington)
Shipping Wonders of the World (Amalgamated Press Ltd, London, 1936)
The Dominion (Wellington)
The Press (Christchurch)
Tripp, Leonard, papers (Alexander Turnbull Library, Wellington)
Worsley, Frank, papers held by the Bamford family, Claygate, Surrey, Canterbury Museum (Christchurch) and the Bamford Papers (Scott Polar Research Institute, Cambridge).

Index

AGMV MARQUIS

Québec, Canada
1999